• HALSGROVE DISCOVER SERIES ➤

The Lakeland DALES

TERRY MARSH

HALSGROVE

First published in Great Britain in 2004

British Library Cataloguing-in-Publication Data
A CIP record for this title is available from the British Library

ISBN 1 84114 357 X

HALSGROVE
Halsgrove House
Lower Moor Way
Tiverton, Devon EX16 6SS
Tel: 01884 243242
Fax: 01884 243325
email: sales@halsgrove.com
website: www.halsgrove.com

Printed and bound by D'Auria Industrie Grafiche Spa, Italy

Contents

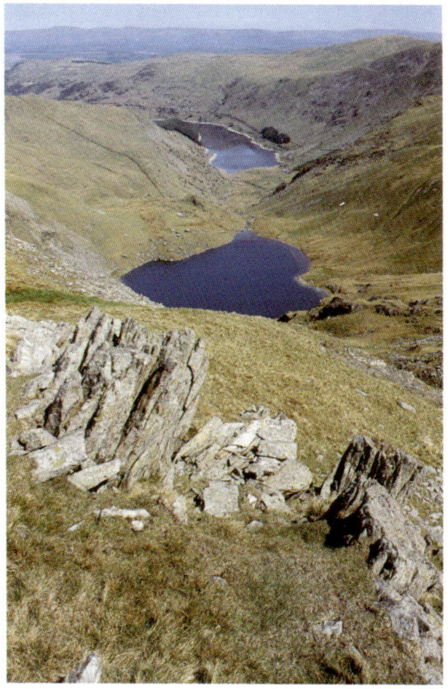

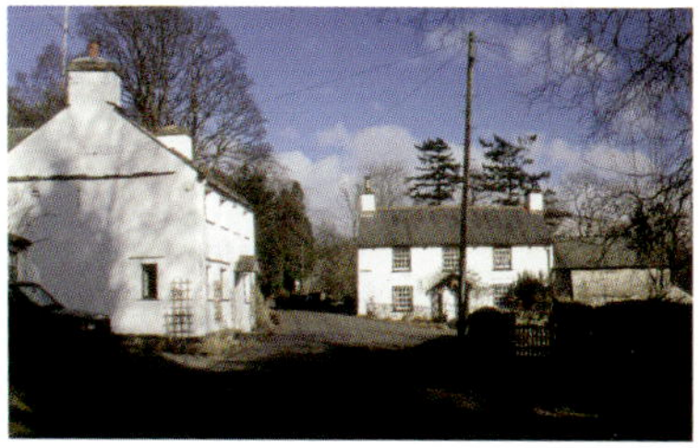

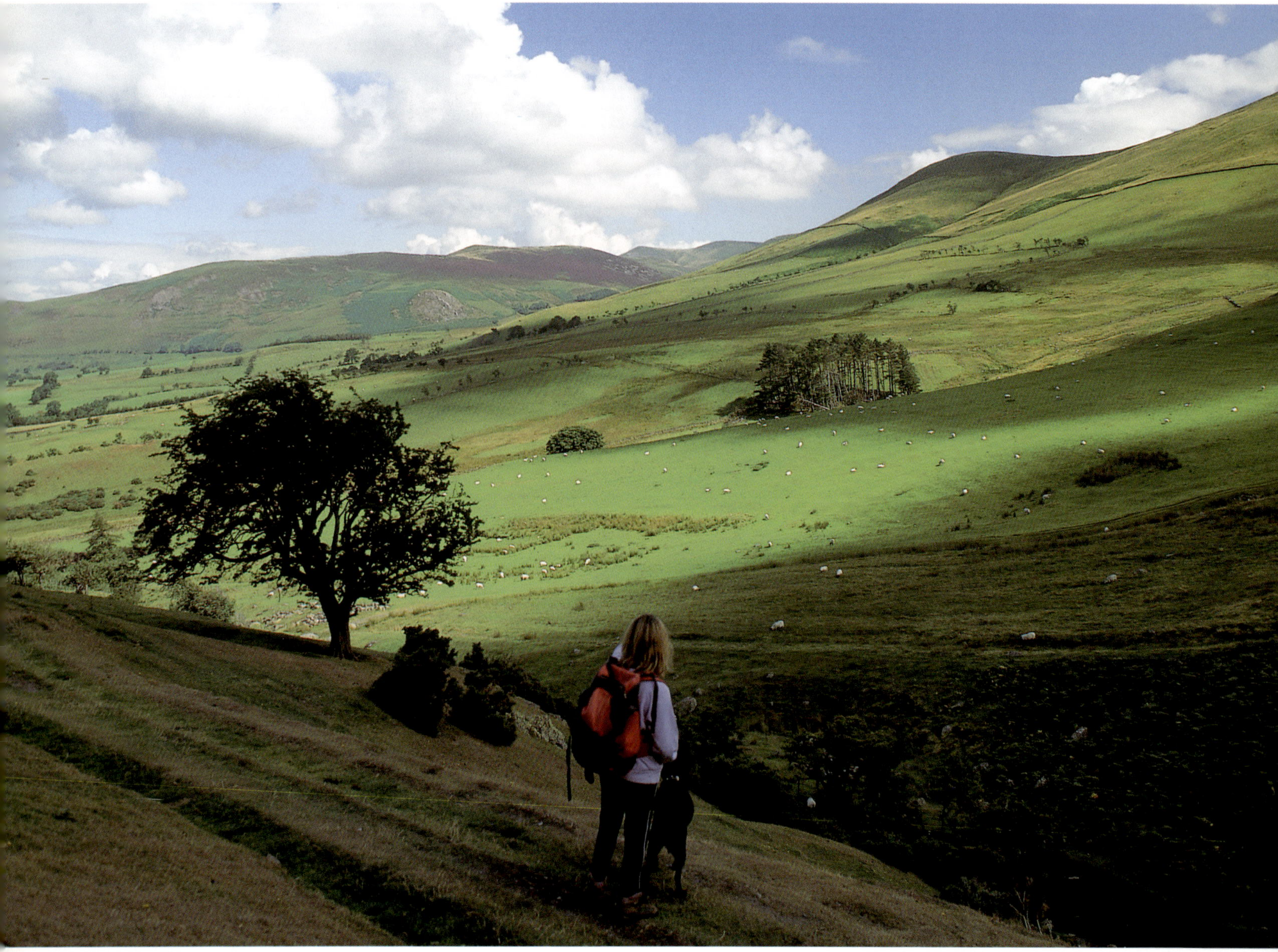

Introduction

Yorkshire, renowned throughout Britain for its dales, has in fact only twenty-one. The Lake District, on the other hand, has more than 100.

The name 'dale' comes from the Scandinavian *dahl*, meaning a valley. One can only assume that in Yorkshire the emphasis was on dales because there were precious few lakes. Yet ironically, toying with semantics, the Lake District has only one lake – Bassenthwaite. All the other expanses of open water are called 'meres', 'tarns' or simply 'waters'.

In his *Good Guide to the Lakes*, Hunter Davies expresses the opinion that only eight of the Lakeland dales are worth seeing: Langdale, Borrowdale, Dunnerdale, Wasdale, Eskdale, Ennerdale, Swindale and the Vale of Lorton. Oddly, that selection omits Patterdale and the huge dales which contain Windermere and Coniston Water. But it is, after all, only a subjective opinion, and folk will find in the host of other dales detailed in this book, many of them small and remote and, in the scale of things, quite insignificant, tranquil retreats and secret places that few people visit. Who with certainty could put their finger on Blengdale or the River Keekle, Lindale, Woundale or Heltondale?

On a stage where the major parts are taken by stunning lakes and lofty heights it is easy to overlook the chorus. Ticking your way through a list of summits is easy; they stick up and are fairly noticeable. Less so the numerous dales.

So in this book I seek to champion the cause of all the dales, great and small. To an extent, I confine myself within the boundaries of the National Park, except that many dales outside the park boundary have their sources within the park. It seems pettifogging to exclude these totally: an elastic boundary encompasses a greater girth, and while elements of what follow may seem like an academic exercise, the fundamental purpose is to bring to greater attention the many and varied dales of the supporting cast.

Opposite page: *The lush pastures of Barkbethdale.*

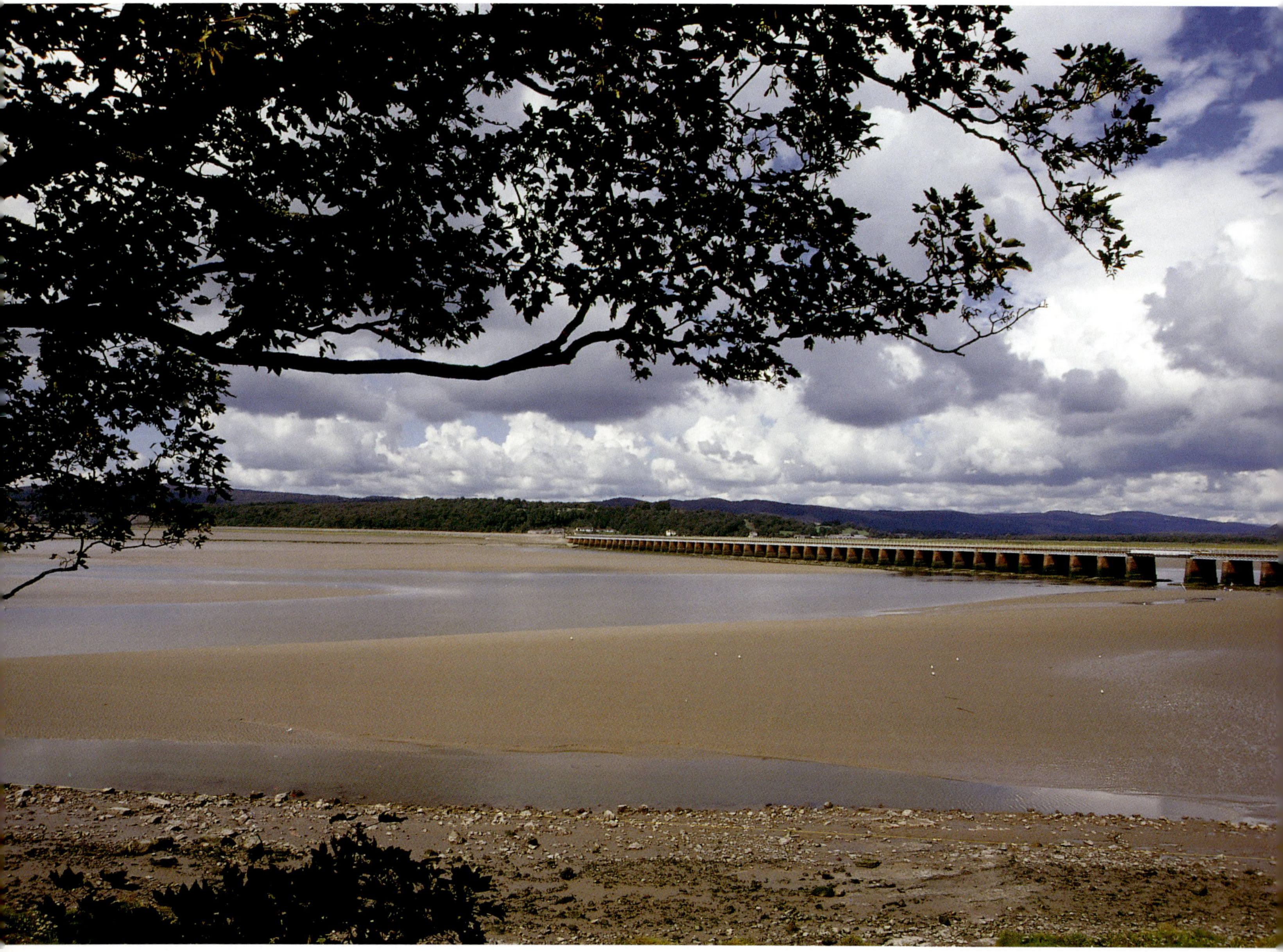

A bit of Kendal Mint Cake

Six rivers flow into the Kent Estuary near Milnthorpe: the Kent gathers the Gowan, the Sprint and the Mint, while the rivers Gilpin and Pool, which drain the Lyth Valley, combine a couple of miles north of the Gilpin's confluence with the Kent. Collectively, the countryside they drain is one of the least well-known areas of Lakeland, though it is traversed by virtually everyone heading into the Lakes from the south or east.

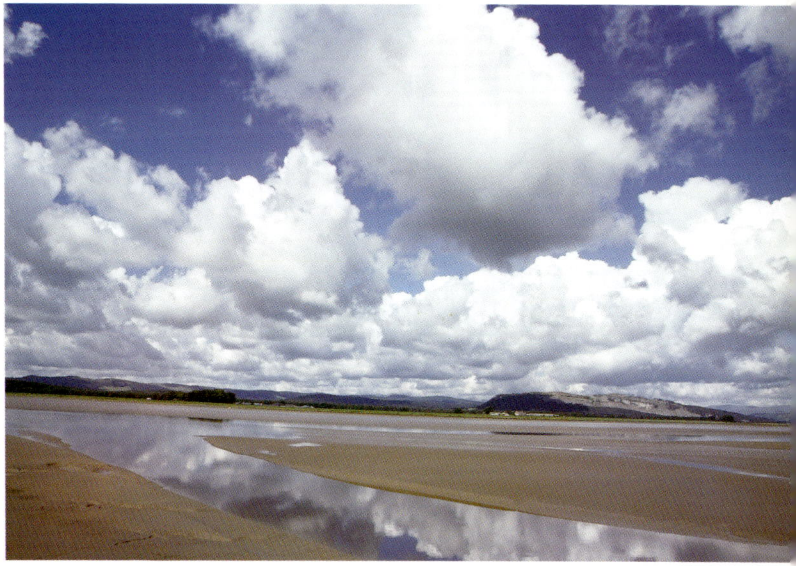

Above: *Whitbarrow, and the wide expanse of Morecambe Bay.*

Opposite: *At Arnside, the River Kent flows beneath the railway viaduct into Morecambe Bay.*

The vast expanse of Morecambe Bay, across which the River Kent fashions a variable course, also collects the waters from that part of former Lancashire known as Furness. Windermere gathers in the drainage from Trout Beck, Fairfield, Easedale, Grasmere, Rydal and Ambleside as well as Langdale and the River Brathay, which rises on the slopes of Wetherlam above Greenburndale. From the southern tip of Windermere, the River Leven flows south-west to meet the River Crake, which emerges from Coniston Water, the two meeting at Greenodd before spilling into the Bay at Greenodd Sands.

Only along its northern catchment boundary does this vast area reach any notable height; Fairfield (873m/2864ft) and High Street (828m/2716ft) forming its highest ground. Elsewhere, this is a region of softer, undulating landscapes, well-wooded with myriad villages and hamlets tucked neatly into its folds.

Geologically, it is a region of Silurian rocks, notably Kirkby Moor Flags, Coniston Flags and Coniston Grits. The result is a more gentle landscape with once-extensive woodlands, great ornaments in the countryside that cloaked such hills as there are, and which were later coppiced to provide charcoal. This

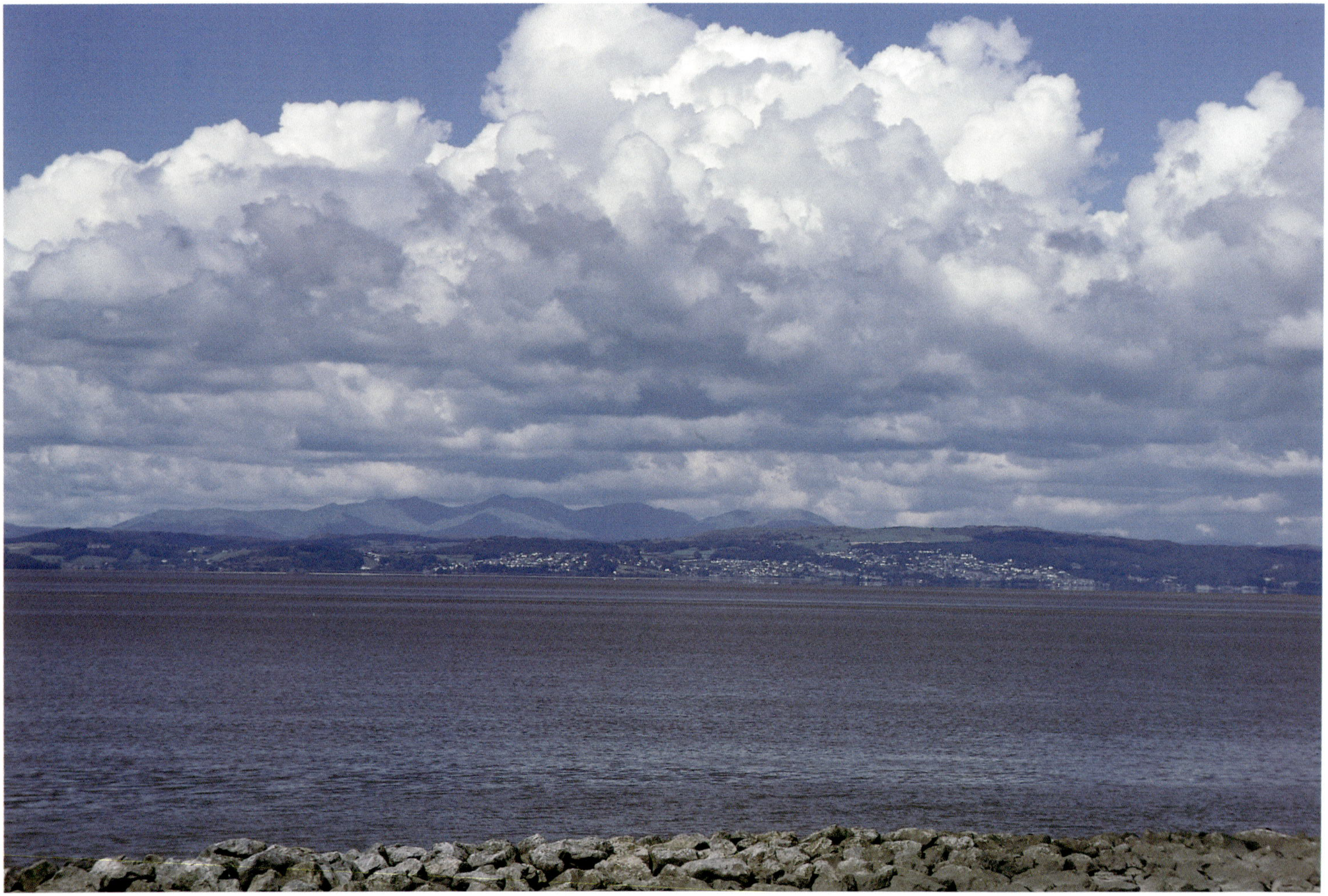

On the southern edge of Lakeland, Grange-over-Sands is where the River Winster meets the seas at Morecambe Bay.

in turn led to an unexpected by-product – gunpowder – an industry initiated in 1764 by a local Quaker, John Wakefield of Kendal, who built the first gunpowder mills along the River Kent near Sedgwick, to take advantage of a ten-foot drop in the water to produce the necessary power for the mill.

Along the River Kent

The pastoral nature of the countryside around Kendal, was commented upon as long ago as the seventeenth century, when Celia Fiennes recorded in the pages of *The Journeys of Celia Fiennes* the quality of the '...very rich good land enclosed, little round greens hills flourishing with corn and grass as green and fresh...not much woods but only the hedge rows round the grounds which looks very fine.' She goes on to tell us that the name of Kendal comes from the 'River Can', which was '...pretty large but full of rocks and stones that makes shelves and falls in the water...stor'd with plenty of good fish.'

The Kent, rising on the southern slopes of High Street between Thornthwaite Crag and Mardale Ill Bell, is reputedly the swiftest river in Lakeland, following a fairly brief course (40km/25 miles) and dropping 740m (2430 feet) in the

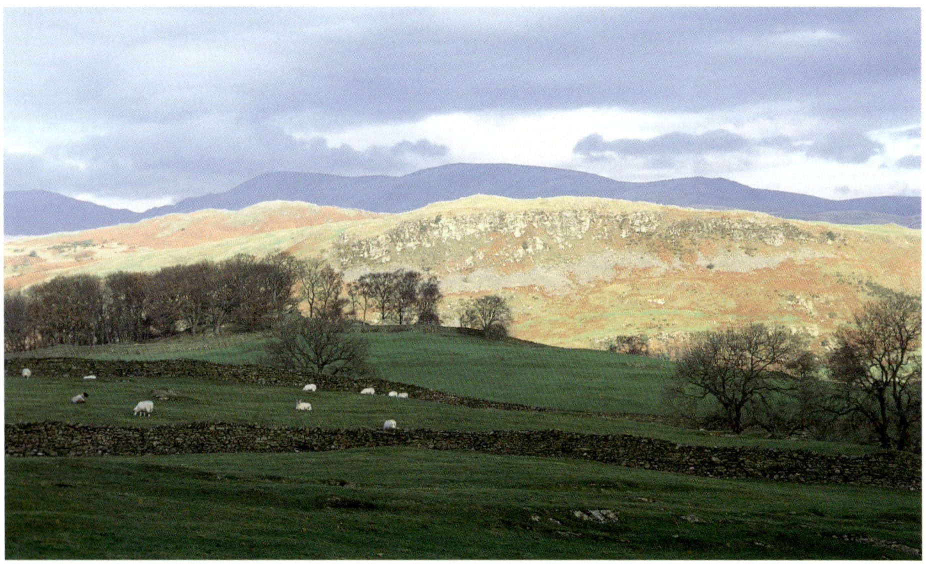

The distant Kentmere Fells from the hills above Kendal.

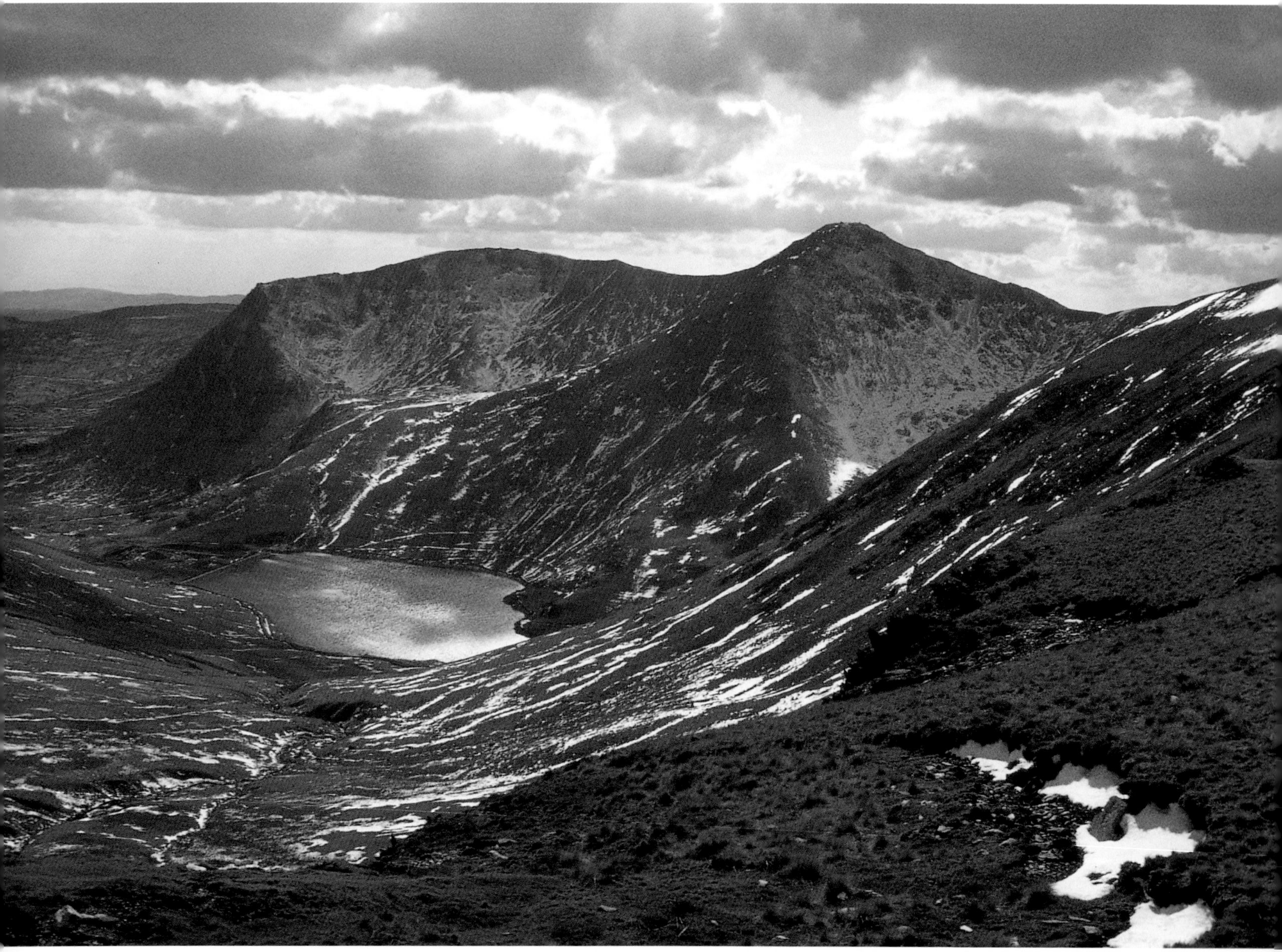

process. A marked variation in river flow, however, led to the construction of the Kentmere Reservoir, primarily to benefit the owners of the ninety mills that sprang up in the hundred years between the mid-eighteenth and nineteenth centuries. So loathe to switch to steam power following its introduction post-1850 were the mill owners of Kentdale, that the new form of power had less impact here than elsewhere.

This was a time when the Kent and its tributaries were more important in terms of the number of mills and horsepower generated than many Midland areas. At its peak, Kentdale had one mill for every 315 people, compared with 1 to 1350 in Birmingham. The mills were engaged in all manner of production, some grinding corn, other making woollen, linen and cotton, or shaping bobbins, making paper, snuff, carpets, rope, and, of course, gunpowder.

Upper Kentdale is extravagantly wild and rugged. The valley is hemmed in to the west by the long ridge that embraces Yoke, Ill Bell, Froswick and Thornthwaite Crag, and to the east by a rather more gentle ridge that culminates in Kentmere Pike. Passage northwards into Mardale involves crossing a high and narrow pass, Nan Bield, a dramatic spot with its tiny shelter and fabulous views north and south.

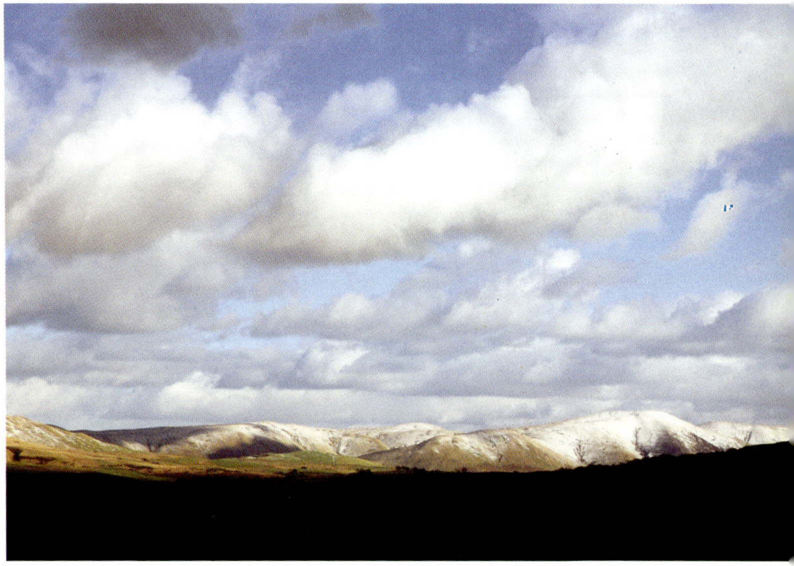

The snow-topped Kentmere Fells from Cunswick Fell.

South of Kentmere's reservoir, the valley broadens into a landscape typically associated with extensive marshlands, before the river has to negotiate the narrow neck created by the rocky upthrust on which the village of Kentmere has developed.

There used to be a lake, or 'mere', just to the south of the church, where now there is nothing more than a swelling in the river with the grandiose title of Kentmere Tarn, but the lake was only a shallow affair, and was drained in about 1840 to provide land for agriculture. Before then the vicar of Kirkby Thore, near Appleby-in-Westmorland, a renowned traveller always with notebook in hand, had observed that the lake was about half a mile long and had a boat. It was apparently good for two kinds of trout, and hosted a large number of wild swans and duck.

Opposite page: *Moody skies above Yoke, Ill Bell and the Kentmere Reservoir.*

Kentmere Hall, to the west of the village, attracted the artist Turner, who visited and sketched it in 1816; it is the oldest remaining structure, built around a fourteenth-century, tunnel-vaulted pele tower. The adjacent farmhouse is a later addition, either fifteenth or sixteenth century.

The hall was the home of a giant, Hugh Herd, the so-called 'Cork Lad of Kentmere', son of a nun from Furness who was cast out following the Dissolution of the Monasteries. The giant, not surprisingly, was a champion wrestler, and served Edward VI during the time of the Border troubles. The hall was also the home of Richard Gilpin, who has the notorious distinction of having killed the last wild boar in England, and of Bernard Gilpin (1517-83), a church reformer known as 'The Apostle of the North'.

At Staveley, the River Kent finally emerges from the long shadow of Kentdale, and sets off for Cowan Head, Burneside and Kendal. Staveley is a large, mainly residential village of grey slate cottages and houses, between the River Gowan – effectively the southern boundary of the uplands – and the River Kent. The area around Staveley has been inhabited since about 4000BC, at a time when trees grew extensively on the fellsides. The first permanent settlers were Celtic-speaking British farmers, and they were followed in AD90 by the Romans, who built a road to the south of the village linking Kendal and Ambleside.

During the Dark Ages and later medieval times, the village and its neighbours grew and were plundered like many villages throughout Cumbria. But by the time of the Industrial Revolution, Staveley was quick to expand as transport improved. So it was that the village became the bobbin-turning capital of Westmorland, so much so that by 1851 there were more families working at the manufacture of bobbins than there were engaged in farming.

Staveley was granted a market charter in the thirteenth century, and also held a three-day fair each year. In 1338 the lord of the manor, Sir William Thweng, agreed to build a chapel in honour of St Margaret. The church, of which only the tower now remains, was founded in 1388. A plaque on the tower commemorates Staveley men of F Company, Second V B Border Regiment, who served in the South Africa Campaign 1900-01 under Major John Thompson. In 1864 it was decided to build a new church, dedicated to St James. This later church has some beautiful stained glass designed by Burne-Jones and made by the William Morris company.

Down river the dale-like nature of the countryside is replaced by undulating farmland, and the focus here is very much the town of Kendal.

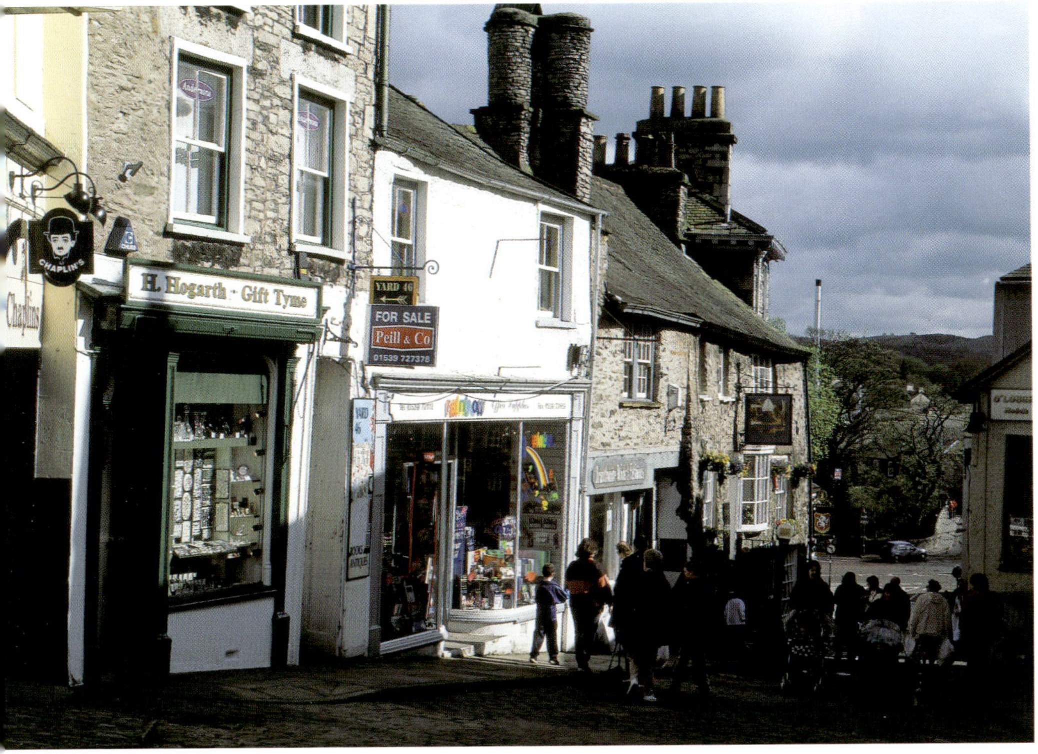

Circular chimney pots grace the buildings in the centre of Kendal.

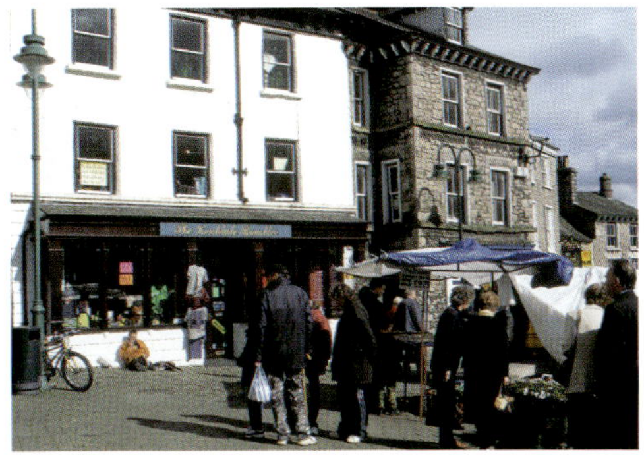

The Market Place, Kendal.

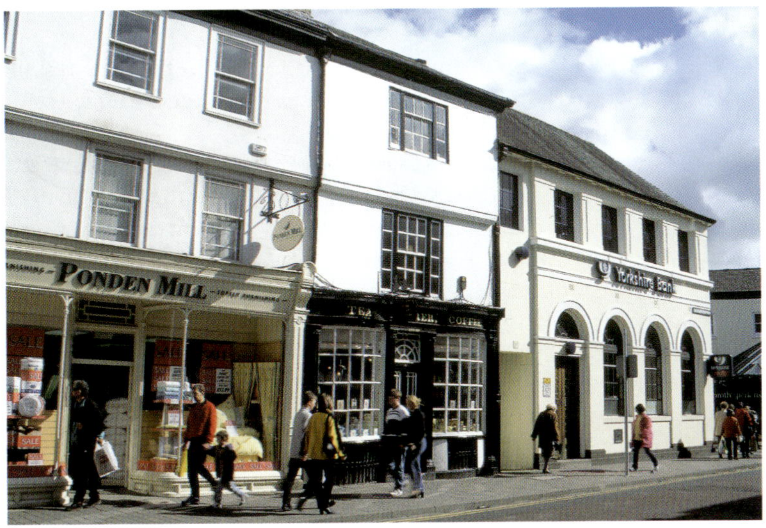

Street scene, Stricklandgate, Kendal.

Kendal Church from the grounds of Abbot Hall.

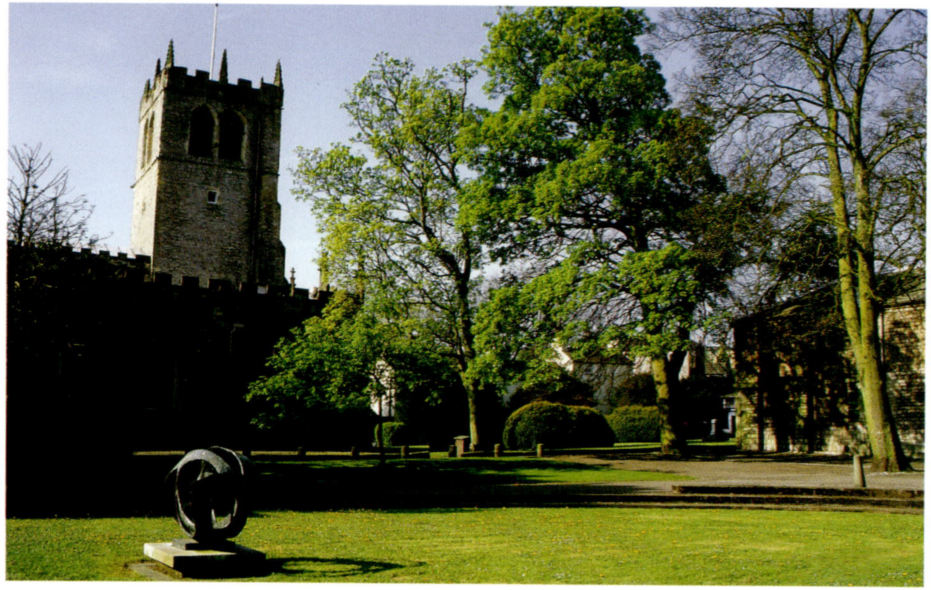

The largest town in the defunct county of Westmorland, Kendal was formerly an important woollen textile centre, an industry that was founded by John Kemp, a Flemish weaver, in 1331. The grey limestone town, built from the local rock, is always bustling, and it remains an important Cumbrian settlement.

When she visited it on her tour in 1698, Celia Fiennes wrote:

> *Kendall is a town built all of stone, one very broad streete in which is the Market Crosse, its a goode tradeing town mostly famed for the cottons; Kendal Cotton is used for blanckets and the Scotts use them for their plodds and there is much made here and also linsiwoolseys and a great deale of leather tann'd here and all sorts of commodityes twice a weeke is the market furnished with all sorts of things.*

The main artery is Highgate, from which flows a series of wynds or courtyards, now less obvious than of old, linking the main street with the River Kent. It has been suggested that these many named and numbered yards and alleyways were part of the town's defensive system, and characteristic of settlements that were constantly under threat from raiders. But many of them were built long after the Scottish raids ended, and may reflect no more than a pattern of development that had evolved by the eighteenth century.

Opposite page: *A lovely view of Kendal from the castle grounds.*

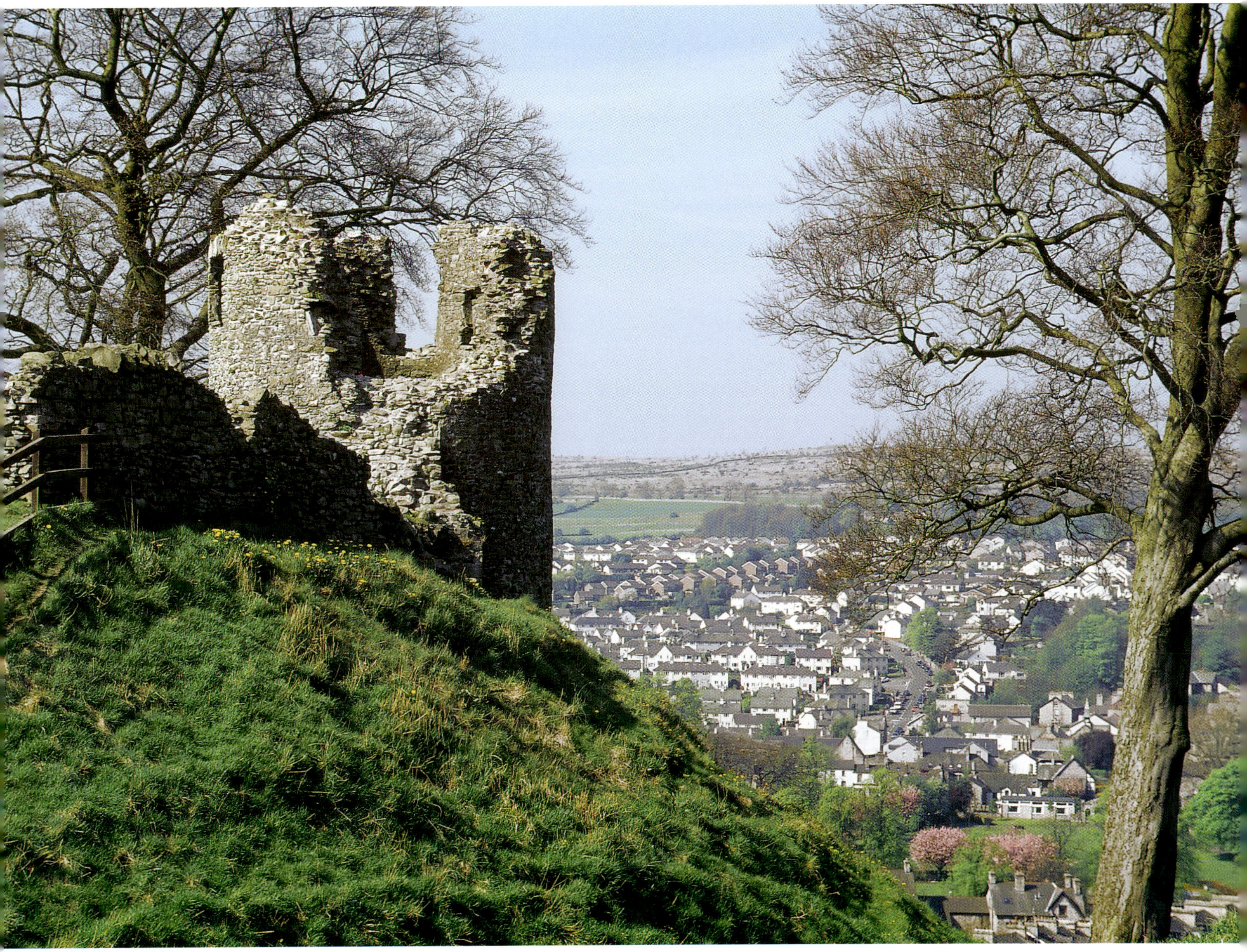

The River Kent, near the centre of Kendal.

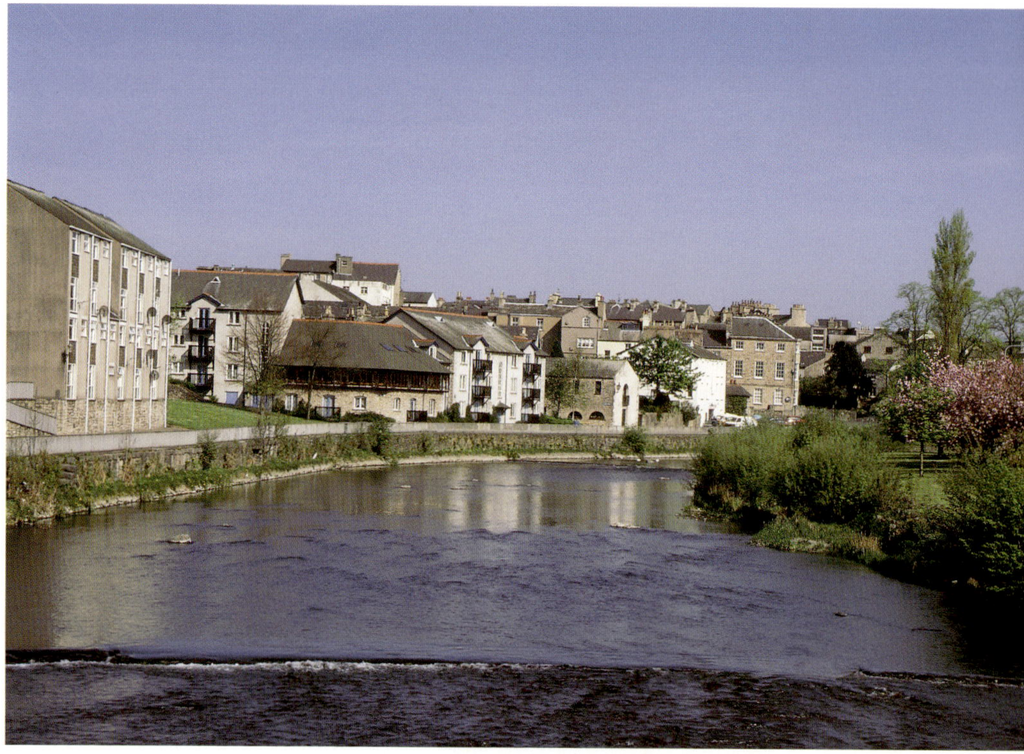

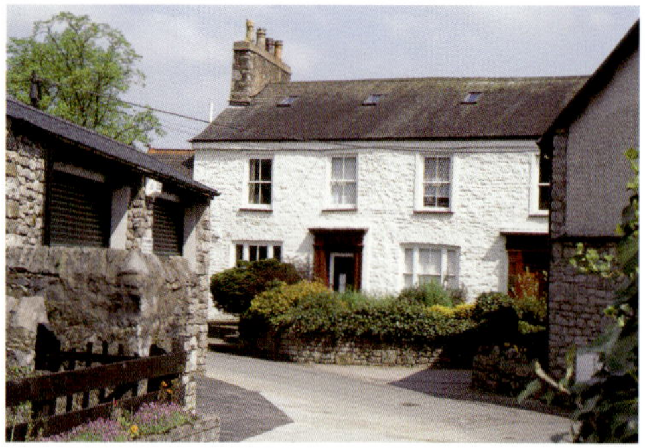

A white-washed cottage in a quiet corner of Kendal.

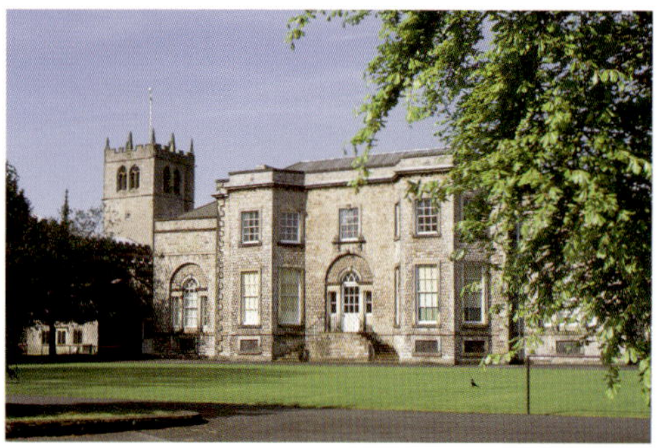

The Abbot Hall Art Gallery and Museum Kendal.

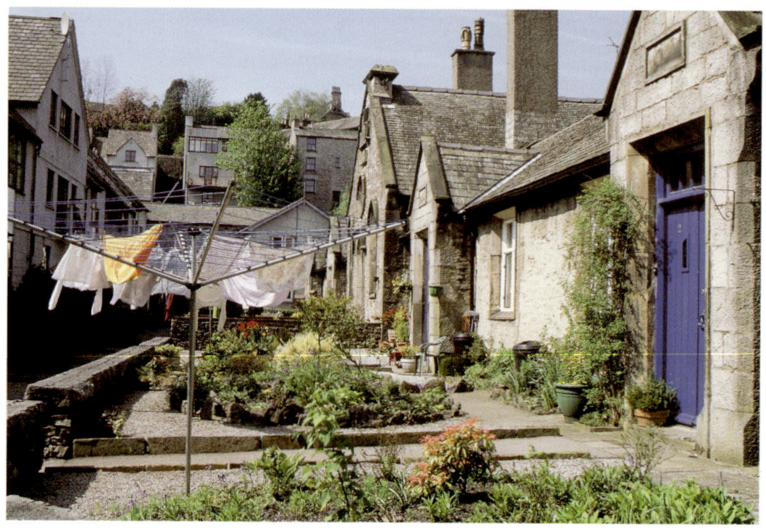

These almshouses are set in a quiet courtyard just off Stricklandgate in Kendal.

The town stands on the banks of the River Kent, and has been of strategic importance since the Romans built a fort to the south of the town. The fort, *Alauna*, was occupied from AD80 to the fourth century, and built to command the roads to Lancaster, Ambleside, Low Borrow Bridge in the Lune Valley, and Brougham.

Kendal is also famous for its bowmen, skilled archers clad in Kendal Green cloth who fought against the Scots at the Battle of Flodden Field in 1513. Not only were the bowmen renowned, but the Kendal Green was too, for Falstaff speaks of 'three misbegotten knaves in Kendal green' in Shakespeare's *Henry IV*.

And it wasn't only Kendal Green for which the town was known. Joseph Budworth, on his *Fortnight's Ramble to the Lakes*, describes how 'men and women, were knitting stockings as they drove their peat-carts into the town'. In the nineteenth century, 'Kendal Black Drop' was a popular mixture of opium and spices, and in the twentieth century, pipe smokers were able to get the very strong 'Black Kendal Twist', much favoured by *Swallows and Amazons* author, Arthur Ransome.

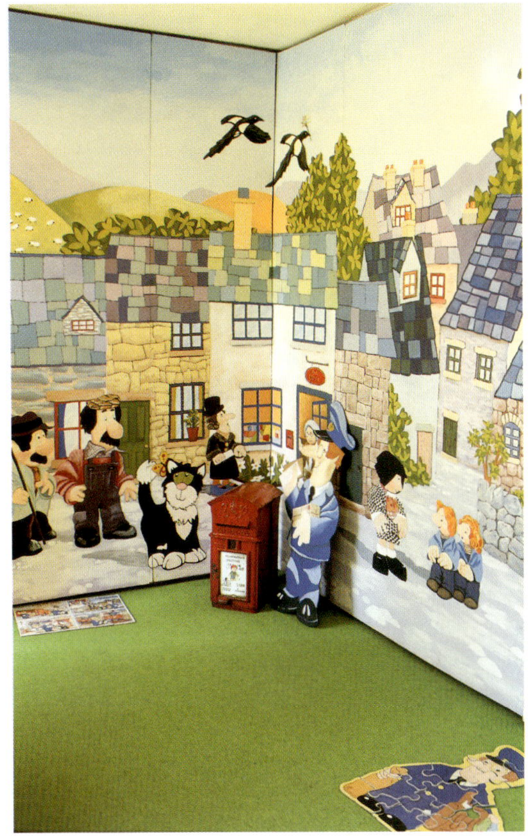

Housed in the Museum of Lakeland Life and Industry is a fine collection of Postman Pat memorabilia.

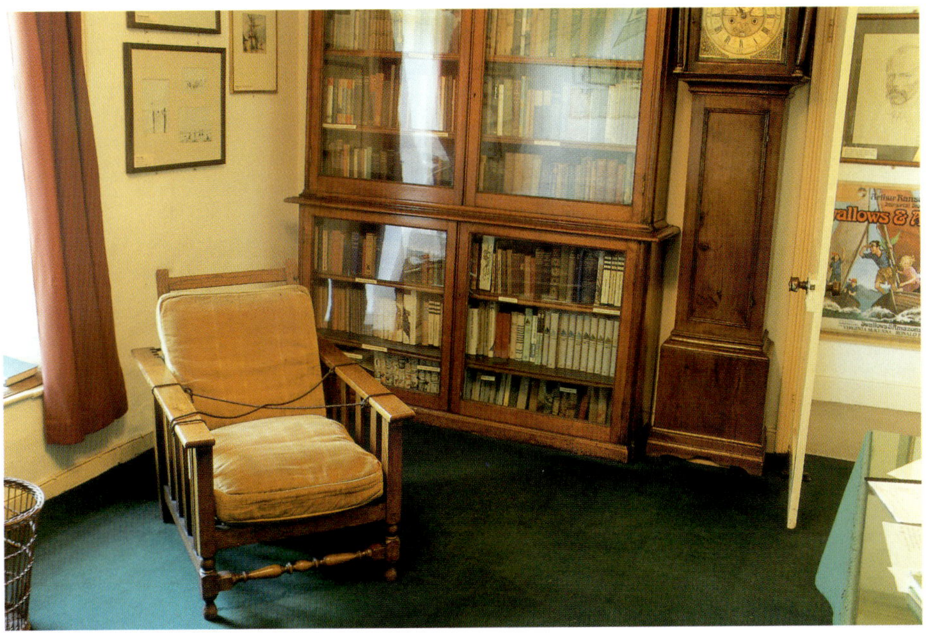

For lovers of Swallows and Amazons, *the collection of Arthur Ransome memorabilia in the Museum of Lakeland Life and Industry is fascinating.*

An aerial view of Kendal from the castle grounds, looking across to Scout Scar.

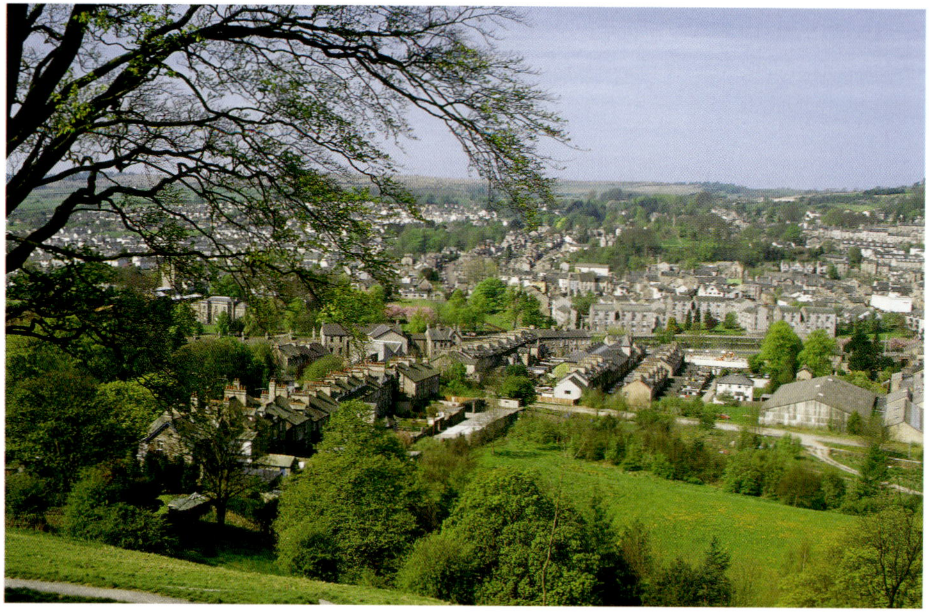

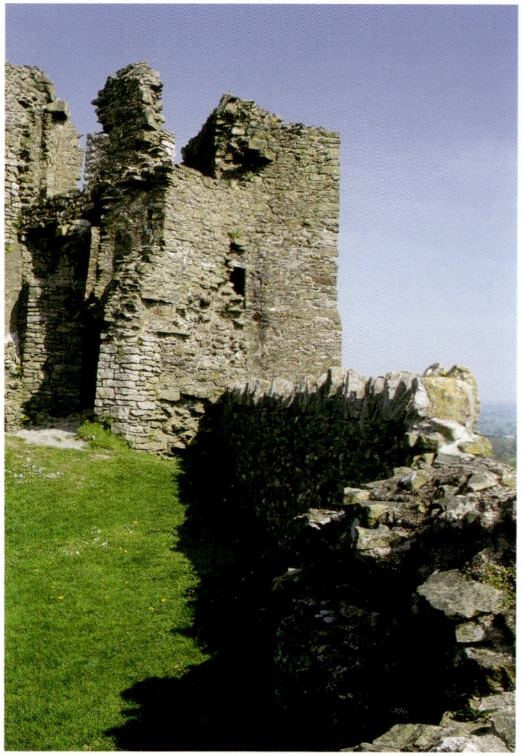

Kendal Castle, the birthplace of Katherine Parr, stands high above the town.

Kendal Castle, a roughly circular earthwork surrounded by a ditch, stands on a hill just outside the town, and probably dates from the twelfth century. In the sixteenth century, the castle was owned by Sir Thomas Parr, father of Katherine Parr (1512-48), the last wife of Henry VIII, who was born in the castle during that century.

By the late sixteenth century, the castle was in an advanced state of decay, and has remained so ever since. Even so, most of the castle wall survives along with one of its towers. The manor hall was by far the most important building in the castle, and parts of this also remain.

Above Gillingate and All Hallows Lane stands the motte and bailey of Castle Howe, since 1788 crowned by a limestone obelisk to 'The Glorious Revolution of 1688'. It failed, however, to impress Joseph Budworth who said it was, 'too small…both for the subject, and the noble rise it stands upon…it looked like a tall chimney; one could imagine, from its scantiness, there had been a want of money.'

Each year on Spring Bank Holiday Monday, Kendal commemorates the granting of its market charter – the earliest in the Lake District – by Richard I in 1189. Part of the proceedings centre on the legend of Dickie Doodle, and tells how this page of King Richard was sent north to deliver the charter to the people of Kendal.

Arriving in the town, Dickie first called at an inn, the Cock and Dolphin, where he drank excessively, made a medieval nuisance of himself, and was put in the stocks to cool off. The next day he was chased across the river to the east bank, where he was saved from his pursuers because of local rivalry between the two communities, east and west. Dickie received a warm welcome on the east bank, and its people, too, sought a charter from the king to claim their own independence. Not only did the king agree – he had quite a soft spot for Dickie Doodle, less so his eye for the ladies, which got him into trouble in the first place – but he also suggested that this part of the town should be called 'Doodleshire', with Dickie as its first mayor.

The River Kent is the boundary between the main town (left) and 'Dickie Doodleshire'.

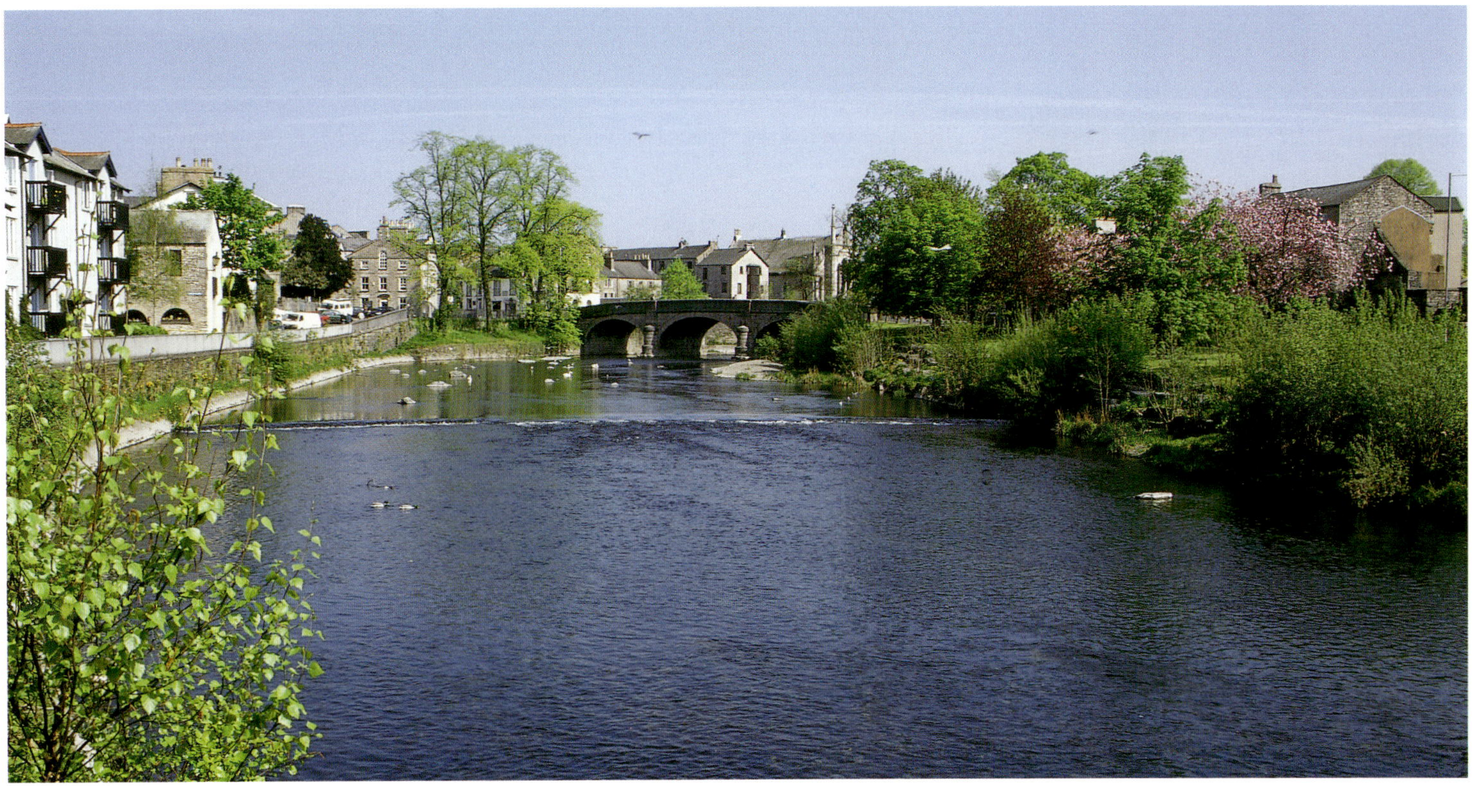

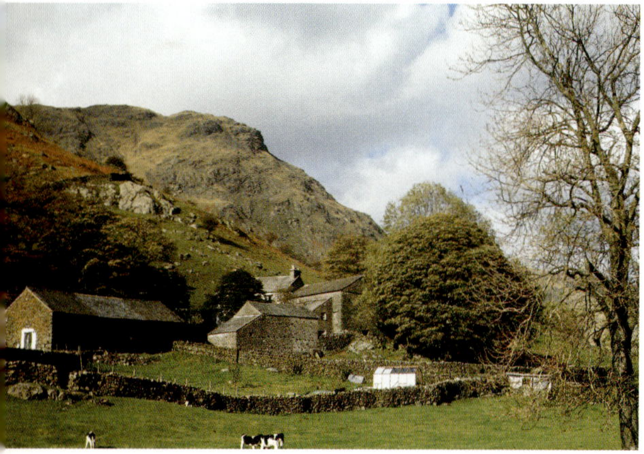

Sadgill, the last farm in Longsleddale.

The Spring, the Mint and a bit of the Lune

At Burneside, the River Kent acquires the River Sprint and, less than a mile further on, the River Mint. The Sprint rises in one of the least-visited but most accessible of the eastern dales, Longsleddale. Like Kentdale, Longsleddale is a dead end, and so is saved the attentions of through traffic; only pedestrians venture here. This is a narrow, enchanting dale, rarely-visited, dotted with seemingly random stands of trees like groups of people waiting to be called to some great event; only here and there a farm punctuates the otherwise craggy landscape. As a source of inspiration, Longsleddale may not feature high on authors' lists, but it became 'Greendale' in the *Postman Pat* books of John Cunliffe, and 'Long Whindale' in the nineteenth-century novel, *Robert Elsmere*, by Mrs Humphrey Ward.

The river's source lies high on the slopes of Harter Fell, in the guise of Wren Gill. The path that continues through the top of Longsleddale and over Harter Fell is mentioned a few times in *Robert Elsmere*, where it is described as being haunted by the ghost of a woman who travels the path at midnight on Midsummer Eve. A silent encounter produces only the shock of seeing a ghost, but if she speaks to you, you are entering the final year of your life.

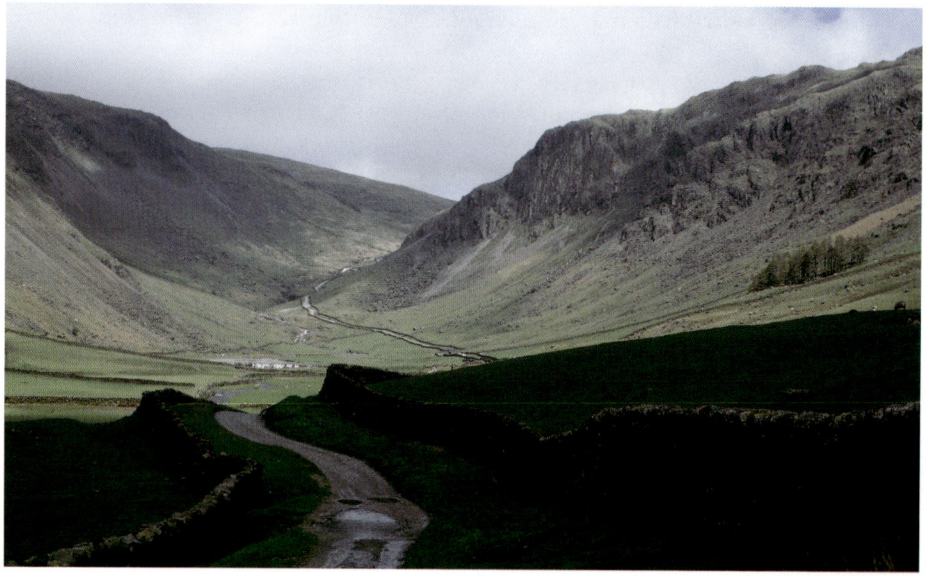

Remote and beautifully wild, Longsleddale offers superb walking.

With dramatic effect, Wren Gill plunges almost 300m (950 feet) in less than a mile, before changing direction and heading southwards between Kentmere Pike to the west and Sleddale Fell. There was a time when plans existed to drive the main west coast railway line to Scotland through Longsleddale, but thankfully that never happened, and the upper reaches of the dale remain as rugged and wild as ever.

Around Sadgill, there is a noticeable change in the landscape due to the underlying rocks. North of the hamlet, the rocks are from the Borrowdale Volcanic series, marked by gnarled outcrops and craggy fellsides. To the south, the softer Silurian slates which hallmark the south-eastern part of Lakeland, recur, though the dale loses none of its steep-sided nature. The River Sprint meanwhile dashes through a series of basins that may once have held small lakes. Stockdale is the tiniest of side dales, and between here and Middale at Wadshowe Bridge there is every likelihood that a shallow lake once existed. More openness follows, with rich farmland spread across the valley floor, at least until Bridge End, where the dale becomes narrow again.

At Yewbarrow (Ubarrow) stands the oldest building in Longsleddale, the remains of a tunnel-vaulted pele tower, probably built in the fourteenth century, and now part of Yewbarrow Hall. Downstream, the Sprint crosses the National Park boundary at Garnett Bridge, beyond which it moulds a true gorge before relaxing and threading an easy course across the glacial lowlands towards Kendal.

The Mint, by comparison, leaves the National Park at Bannisdale Low Bridge, having spent but a short time in the embrace of Bannisdale. Little more than a track runs into this remote dale rising on Bannisdale Fell, a place of steep fell-slopes, its own brand of Silurian slates and a few scattered farms. Just a short way to the north, lonely Crookdale, draining the boggy uplands of Harrop Pike, High House Fell and Great Yarlside, joins Borrow Beck to produce a second 'Borrowdale', this one far less known than its counterpart south of Keswick, but is seen by everyone who drives through the Lune Gap on the M6 motorway. A lush, green dale, Borrowdale lies beyond the National Park boundary, and sends its waters to the Lune.

The names Whatshaw Common, Gargill and Great Yarlside will be known to very few. This tiny ring of moorland fells swing clockwise from the A6, Kendal-Shap road to an insignificant Wasdale Pike. Beneath them lies Wasdale, nothing quite so dramatic as its western namesake, a miniature farming enclave that flows into Wasdale Beck and so eventually into the Lune.

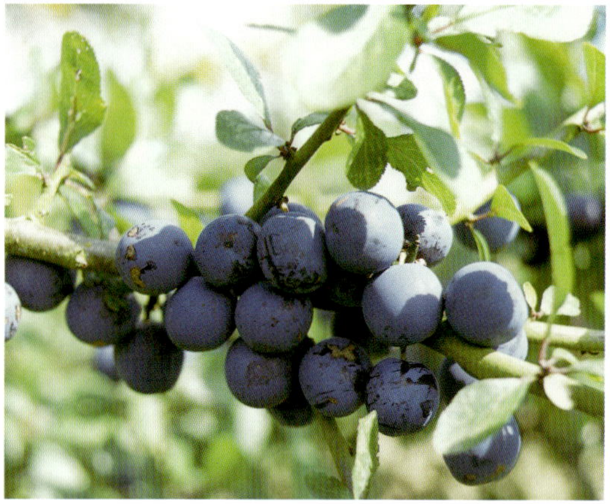

Sloes are the fruit of the blackthorn, a common shrub of Lakeland hedgerows and scrub.

Lyth and Winster valleys

The Lyth and Winster valleys lie between the limestone scarps of Whitbarrow and Scout Scar to the west of Kendal, amid undulating agricultural land with small areas of mosslands and birch woodlands on peat. The valley sides hold significant stands of woodland, punctuated by small rocky outcrops and framed by hedgerows of blackthorn and damson.

Fashioned by the rivers Gilpin and Pool, the Lyth Valley is prehistoric estuarine marshland where Man has imposed his will in the form of embankments and drainage channels, converting the land into pasture. The marshy Gilpin valley is largely treeless, its rectangular fields divided by hedges and drainage ditches, with remnants of raised mire broken only by a few limestone knolls. The dale has a fenland character untypical of Lakeland, yet it is only a few miles from the highest mountain in England.

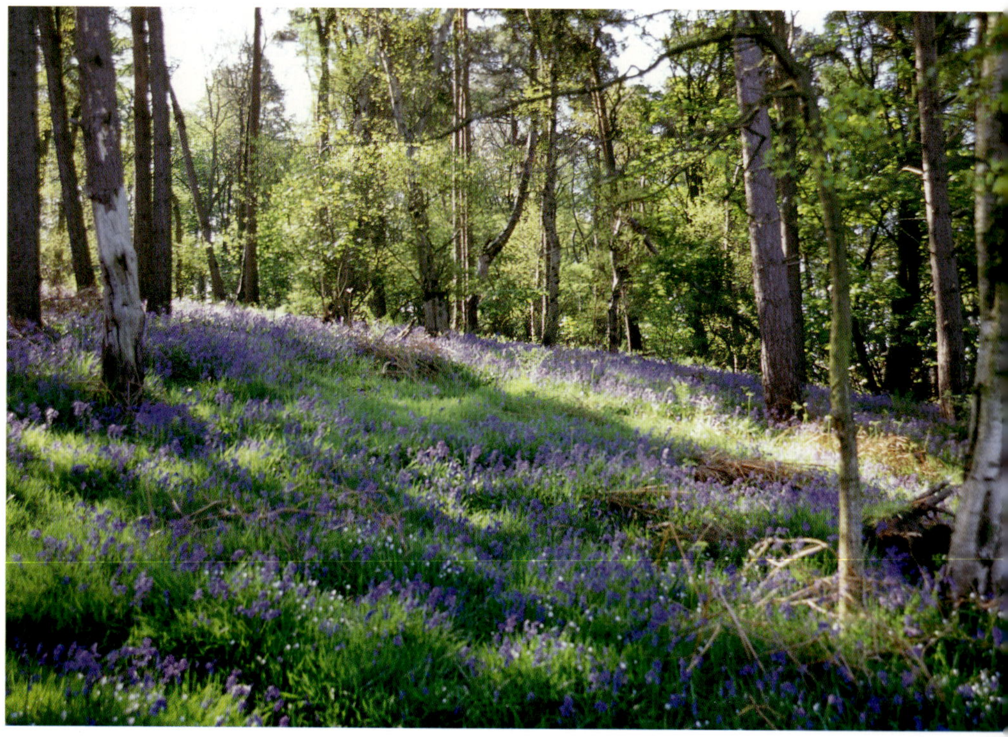

A bright touch of springtime comes to Lakeland.

The broad expanse of the Lyth Valley is especially renowned for its damsons. Westmorland damsons, as they are still known (a fond reminder of a now-defunct county), are unique, surrounding each small farmstead and growing along every hedgerow in the valley. The fruit is highly regarded for its flavour, but the market collapsed many years ago and many orchards fell into decline. But a few years ago a number of enthusiasts set up the Westmorland Damson Association to promote the use of damsons. Now, each year, just before Easter, they hold a Damson Day, a celebration of damsons with damson products such as bread, chocolates, wine, gin, beer, syrup, ice cream, bottled damsons and jam. It was like this in the old days, when every spring would see cars and charabancs heading for the valley to enjoy the splendid site of the valley in bloom.

The splendour of the valley in springtime was described by Mrs Humphrey Ward in her novel *Helbeck of Bannisdale*,

> *...the damson trees were all out, patterning the valleys; marking the bounds of orchard and field, of stream and road. Each with its larch clump, the grey and white farms lay scattered on the pale green of the pastures; on either side of the valley the limestone pushed upward, through the grassy slopes of the fells, and made long edges and 'scars' against the sky...*

The River Winster, which has much in common with the Lyth Valley, has the distinction of having its own entry into Morecambe Bay at Lindale, near Grange-over-Sands. It also marks the boundary between the former county of Westmorland and the isolated part of Lancashire known as Furness, or Lancashire-beyond-the-Sands.

From Windermere to Coniston

West of the Winster there are only two main dales; both filled with water. One holds the huge lake of Windermere from which issues the River Leven, and the other Coniston Water, which outflows as the River Crake. Both rivers join at Greenodd, bound for an entry into Morecambe Bay north of Ulverston.

Windermere, at 17km (10½ miles) long, 1.6km (one mile) wide and more than 60m (220ft) deep, is the largest natural lake in England, and is fed by numerous dales. It is renowned for its char, a fish which in its potted form was a prized delicacy among wealthy families of the seventeenth and eighteenth centuries.

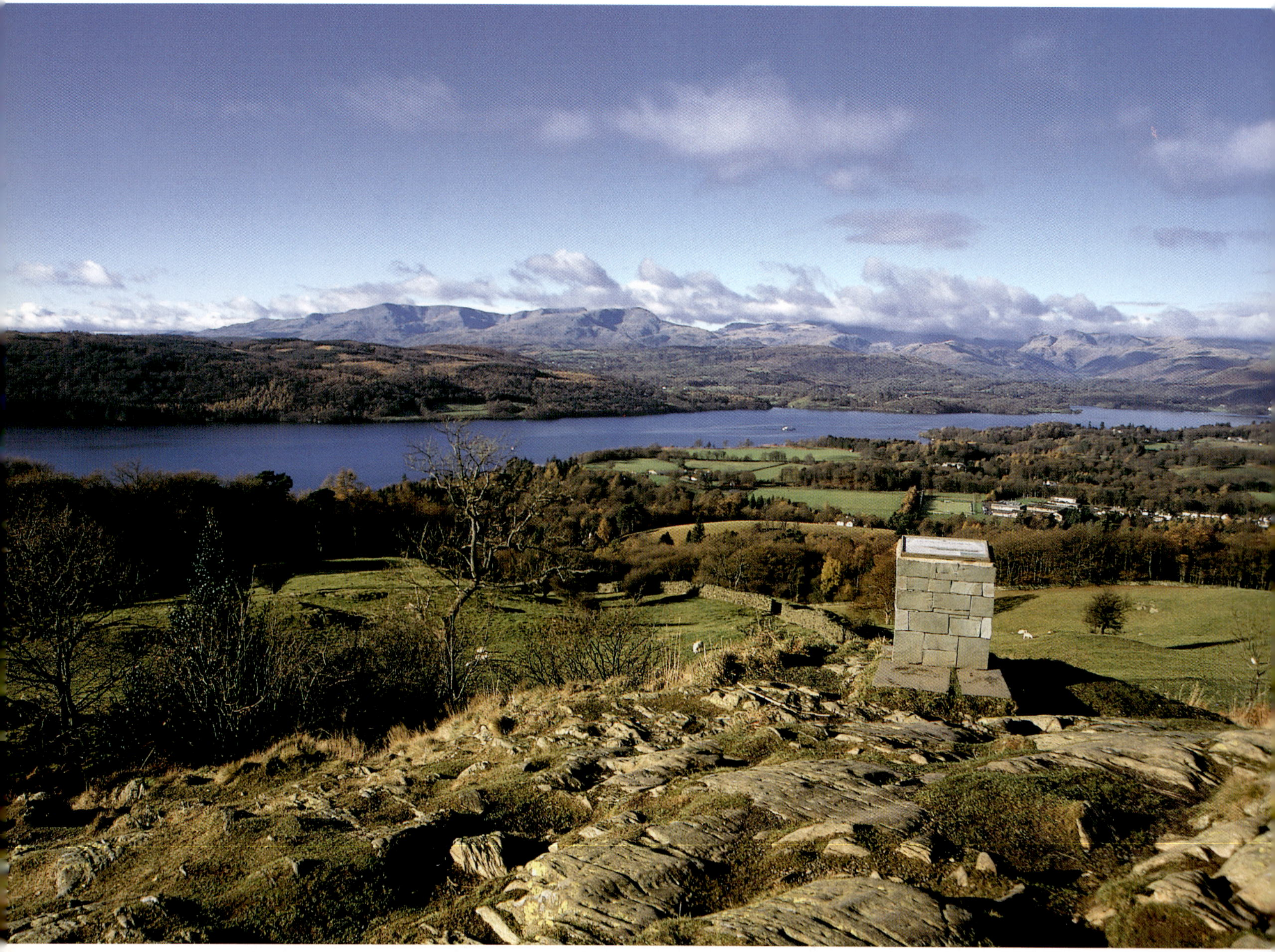

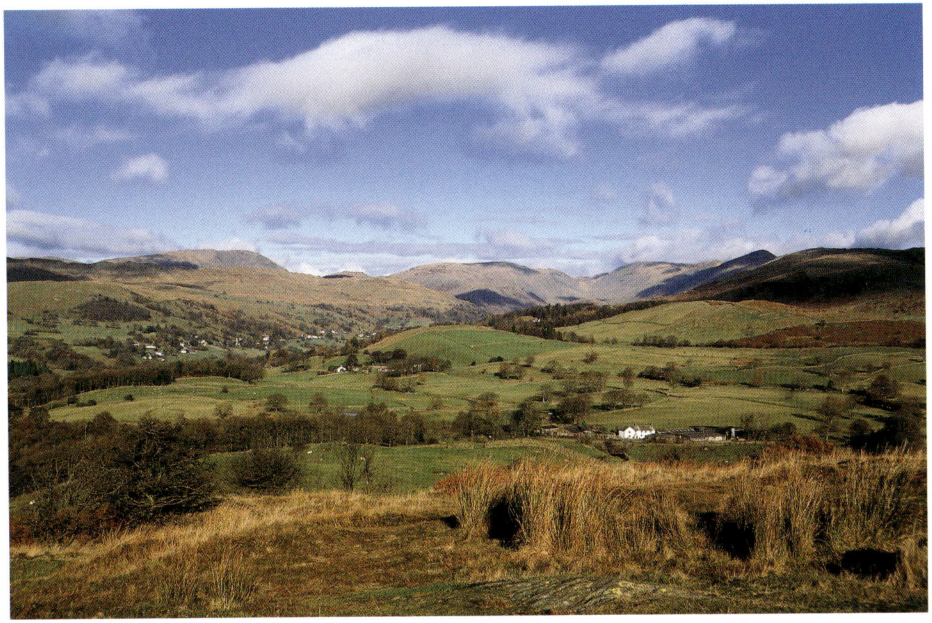

The village and dale of Trout Beck from Orrest Head. Yoke, Ill Bell and Froswick are on the right, and Stony Cove Pike is to the left of Threshthwaite Mouth. On the far left is Red Screes, directly above the Kirkstone Pass.

For many years the lake was a natural highway, used by Romans to import stone for their fort at Ambleside (*Galava*), and later to take iron ore to the smelting furnaces that developed along its shore.

North-east of the lake, the dale of Trout Beck gathers water from the high ground east of the Kirkstone Pass that drains south from Stony Cove Pike. The head of the dale, where the fell slopes crowd together, is wild and rugged country threaded with through-routes that give the walking an exaggerated sense of isolation. Separated from the main thrust of Trout Beck by the knobbly finger of High Green Knott, tiny Woundale is rarely explored in spite of spreading along the main road up onto the Kirkstone Pass.

Troutbeck is alone among the dales of the south-east in not being blind, though the way across into Patterdale can be hazardous enough in winter conditions to prevent access. The Romans certainly came this way, and the find of a Langdale axe near the village of Troutbeck and the enclosure at Allen Knott above Troutbeck Bridge both suggest that the dale was used in prehistoric times to link with the Neolithic and Bronze Age settlements among the limestone hills of Westmorland.

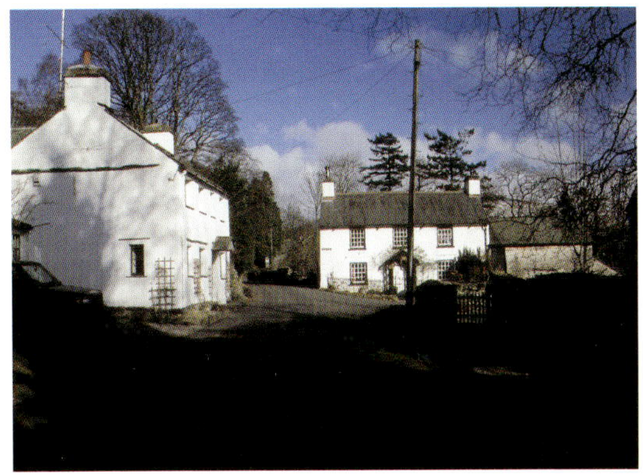

Troutbeck village.

Opposite page: *Windermere and the Coniston and Langdale Fells from Orrest Head.*

Passed by everyone heading up the Kirkstone Pass, tiny Woundale is one of Lakeland's least-known dales.

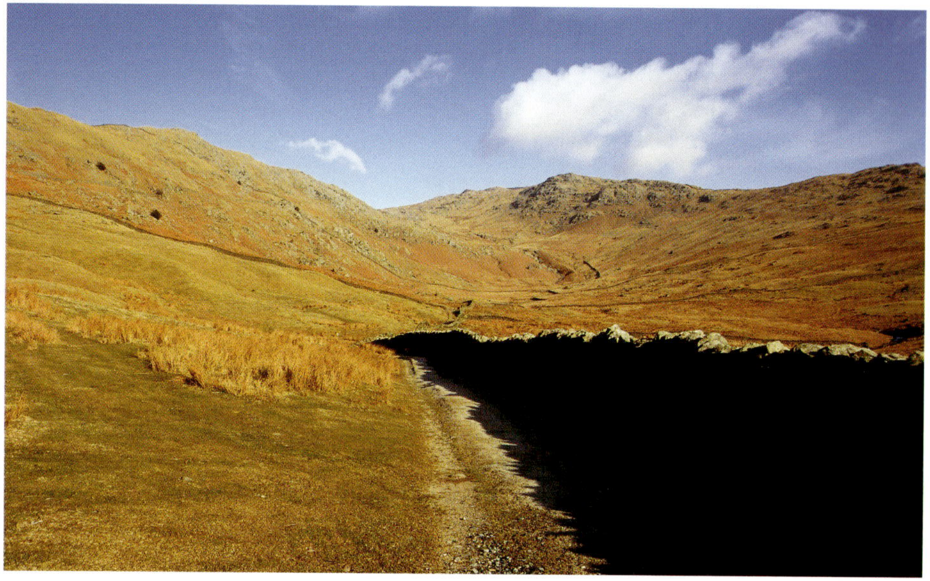

Troutbeck village appears as an elongated, attractive and relatively old-fashioned settlement along the long-established, narrow and hilly coach route from Windermere to Penrith, now bypassed by a modern highway. The main part of the village stands above the modern road, and the buildings, on closer inspection, are gathered together in groups, an arrangement that stems from the days when the villagers drew their water from wells, and so built their houses in this convenient way.

Beatrix Potter, who was keenly concerned about the protection of the Lakeland scenery and the way of life in the fell farms, used to live in the village, at Troutbeck Park Farm, where she bred the native Herdwick sheep. The area around Troutbeck Park was once a massive deer estate, hunted by the lords of Kendal.

Along the approach road to the village are a number of drinking troughs bearing saints' names, and provided for horses as they tackled the long climb over the Kirkstone Pass to Patterdale and beyond. Many of the houses are seventeenth century, and some still have spinning galleries and mullioned windows.

At one time many of the farms in Troutbeck were owned by 'statesmen', farmers who owned a small area of land from which they struggled to eke an existence. Such a farm is Townend, a fine building with whitewashed walls and stone-mullioned windows, originally a yeoman's house built around 1626, and now in the care of the National Trust. The house has a tall, tapering chimney, typical of Lakeland vernacular architecture of that era. The original seventeenth-century house is divided into two sections: the part where the work of the farm was done, known as the 'down house', and the living quarters, called the 'fire house'.

At the northern end of the village stands the Mortal Man Inn, a seventeenth-century coaching inn, formerly a small cottage called the White House. It gained its present name about the beginning of the nineteenth century, when a customer, the painter Julius Caesar Ibbetson, who lived in Ambleside and then Troutbeck, painted a new sign for it. On one side he depicted a thin-lipped person, obviously a teetotaller, and on the other someone quite the opposite, both said to be well-known people who lived nearby. From their mouths came in true cartoon-fashion 'balloons' containing the couplets:

Thou mortal man who liv'st by bread,
What is it makes thy nose so red?
Thou silly fool that look'st so pale,
Tis drinking Sally Birkett's ale!

From then on the inn was called the Mortal Man.

Troutbeck also has the distinction of being the home of one of the earliest Cumbrian poets, Thomas Hoggart (c1640-1709), a farmer known as 'Old Hoggart', and said to be an uncle of the painter William Hogarth.

Stock Ghyll, which affords a shortcut from the Kirkstone Pass down to Ambleside, can be eerie in misty conditions but is otherwise unpretentious until its waters tumble over Stockghyll Force near Ambleside. A visit to the falls and the ascent of Wansfell were firm favourites with Victorian visitors to Lakeland. The secluded nature of the falls 'buried in trees, in the bottom of the valley' gave Keats, one of a great many poets to visit Stockghyll, 'a pleasant twinge.' For hundreds of years, the falls provided the force to power a wide range of mills – carding and fulling, linen, paper, corn and saw.

Ambleside is a popular tourist centre passed through by anyone travelling from south Lakeland to Keswick. It is almost entirely composed of slate houses, cottages and hotels built in traditional Lakeland style. Even the new development in the centre of the town continues this characteristic, and the whole impression is one of a pleasing and attractive town that copes well with modern

A quiet and secluded valley, Scandale is rarely visited, yet it is easily accessible from Ambleside.

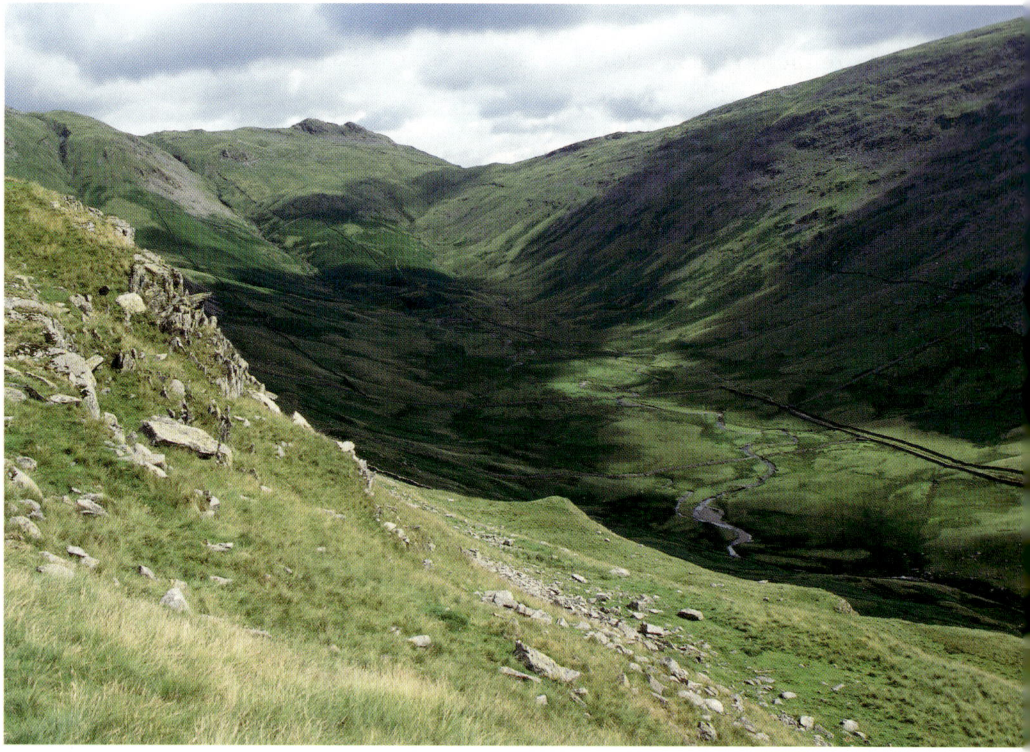

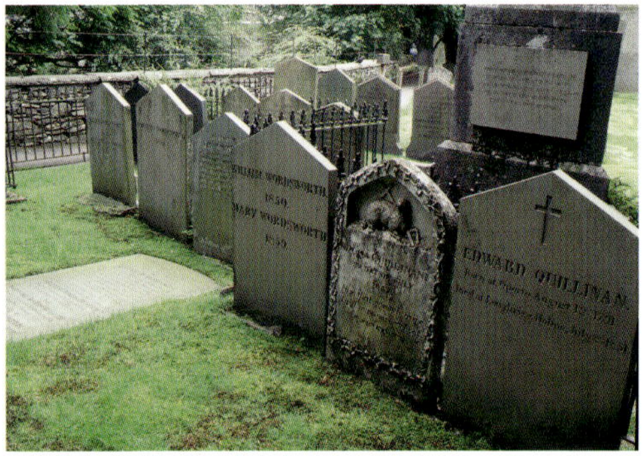

The graves of the Wordsworth family in the churchyard in Grasmere.

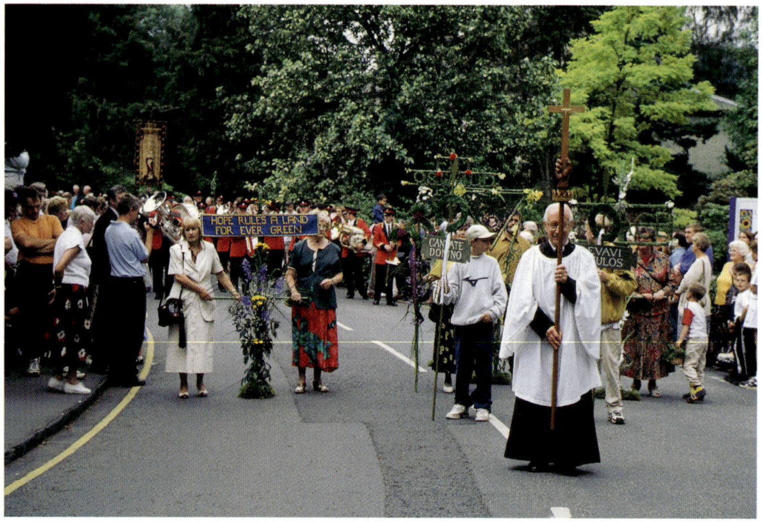

The start of the annual rush-bearing ceremony in Grasmere.

tourist attentions. Ambleside is really a large village, though it received a market charter in 1650.

The town's great inn is the Salutation, clearly, in spite of modifications, an old coaching inn. Whether it was at the Salutation or some other hotel that Thomas Gray 'on looking into the best bed-chamber, dark and damp as a cellar, grew delicate', is not clear. But Ambleside has certainly improved, and brought many noted travellers and writers to its shelter – Keats, Joseph Budworth, John Stuart Mill, Tennyson (who was working on his *Morte d'Arthur*) and Edward Fitzgerald.

The Bridge House, standing on what was probably an old packhorse bridge spanning Stock Ghyll in the middle of Ambleside, is now used as a National Trust information centre. It was built in the eighteenth century, and is said to have housed a family with six children. Originally, it was built as a summer house, part of the demolished Ambleside Hall, and in its time has been used as a cobbler's shop and an antique shop.

At Ambleside two of Lakeland's most important rivers meet: the Brathay, which harnesses the water from Greenburndale and Langdale, and the Rothay, which drains the fell uplands south of the east-west watershed, notably from Scandale, Fairfield by way of Rydal Beck, and Easedale via the small lakes of Grasmere and Rydal Water.

This is Wordsworth country, and how. This small central core of Lakeland is given over intensely to the memory of the man, his family and his works, with his homes at Rydal Mount and Dove Cottage, and the poet himself being buried in the churchyard at Grasmere. Visitors arrive in their thousands each year in search of man and myth, yet few will venture onto the fells to the north or into the sheltered Scandale much beyond High Sweden Bridge (bound for the Fairfield Horseshoe, a magnificent felltop round). This is despite the fact that a good path runs its length before squeezing past the tiny Scandale Tarn and over Scandale Pass into Caiston Glen beyond. Scandale is for connoisseurs, and for those who can arrange transport at both ends; failing that you can climb Little Hart Crag and up onto Dove Crag before returning down one of the most pleasant ridges in Lakeland, over High Pike and Low Pike.

West of the pikes, the dale of Rydal Beck contains no convenient pathways, and shares its wide, green, sunlit solitudes with hardy Herdwick and Rough Fell sheep.

Wordsworth country

There is little to the scattered grey-stone village of Rydal, strung out along the main road running north from Ambleside. The nearby lake, Rydal Water, was a favourite spot of the Wordsworths, who would often have picnics on the island. It lies sandwiched between the beetling slopes of Nab Scar and those of Loughrigg Fell, and would frequently freeze over, providing the Wordsworth household with the opportunity for skating.

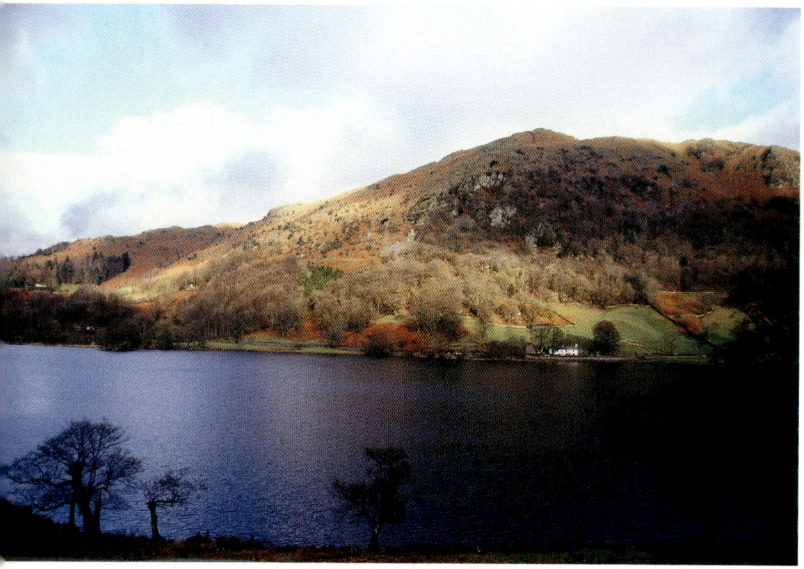

Not far from the Rydal Mount home of the Wordsworths, Rydal Water lies below Nab Scar.

Rydal Mount was home to William Wordsworth and his family from 1813 to his death in 1850. He was at the peak of his fame at this time, though his best work had all been accomplished, mostly at Dove Cottage. Socially, the house was a significant step up for Wordsworth, and put him on calling terms with the local gentry.

Not far away is Nab Cottage, a fine farmhouse dated 1702, also with poetic associations. Thomas de Quincey (1785-1859) followed the Wordsworths into Dove Cottage, but spent much time at Nab Cottage courting Margaret (Peggy) Simpson, whom he later married. The Wordsworths did not approve of the match, and Dorothy, when Peggy had a child, had this to say: 'At the up-rouzing of the Bats and Owls he regularly went thither – and the consequence was that Peggy Simpson, the eldest daughter of the house presented him with a son…' De Quincey, alas, inherited considerable debts, and was forced to sell Nab Cottage in 1833 to William Richardson and his wife, and their lodger, Hartley Coleridge.

So it was that Hartley Coleridge (1796-1849), eldest son of Samuel Taylor Coleridge, spent his last 11 years at Nab Cottage. He was another noted writer, albeit of a less high profile (in more ways than one, for he was of small stature) than the mainstream 'Lake Poets', and gravely addicted to drink, often disappearing into the fells on drinking sprees. Nevertheless, he was a popular man among the local farmers and shepherds, possessing a childlike manner and an irrepressible sense of fun. Wordsworth came to regard him as an adopted son.

The young John Ruskin attended Rydal Chapel in 1830, while on a tour with his parents, and observed: 'We were lucky in procuring a seat very near that of

Mr Wordsworth.' He was not impressed, however:

We were rather disappointed in this gentleman's appearance especially as he appeared asleep the greatest part of the time. He seemed about 60. This gentleman possesses a long face and a large nose with a moderate assortment of grey hairs and 2 small eyes grey not filled with fury wrapt inspired with a mouth of moderate dimensions that is quite large enough to let in a sufficient quantity of beef or mutton & to let out a sufficient quantity of poetry.

Nearby Grasmere is a delightful place where cottages, houses, shops and inns, most made of grey-green or purple-hazed local stone, gather in a vast natural hollow at the foot of the steady rise to Dunmail Raise. All around, fells of varying heights and steepness enfold the village, and provide by far the best view of it, while the nearby lake of Grasmere adds a sparkle that is missing from less-blessed Lakeland villages.

The London-born poet Thomas Gray (1716-71) visited the Lake District in 1769, and wrote of Grasmere that:

The bosom of the mountains, spreading here into a broad bason (sic), discover in the midst Grasmere-water; its margin is hollowed into small bays with iminences; some of rock, some of soft turf, that half conceal and vary the figure of the little lake they command...a little unsuspected Paradise.

Beyond Grasmere the dale divides; one branch climbing steadily northwards to Dunmail Raise and then onwards to Thirlmere. The other veers north-west, first into the broad, farmland expanse of Easedale, and then into the narrower, more rugged Far Easedale. Lording above the two dales is Helm Crag, a notable feature and a popular ascent from the village. Rock formations on its summit have prompted the names 'The Lion and the Lamb', when viewed from the south, and 'The Howitzer' when seen from the pass – you can see why.

The two Easedales, not surprisingly, were favoured haunts of the Wordsworths being on their doorstep at Dove Cottage: they knew them as 'The Black Quarter', a reference to the way they fall into shade early in the day. This is a hugely-popular dale in summertime, with or without the Wordsworthian associations, but it is a lovely place reached from Grasmere via Goody Bridge. Here the dale divides; to the right the continuation leads along an old

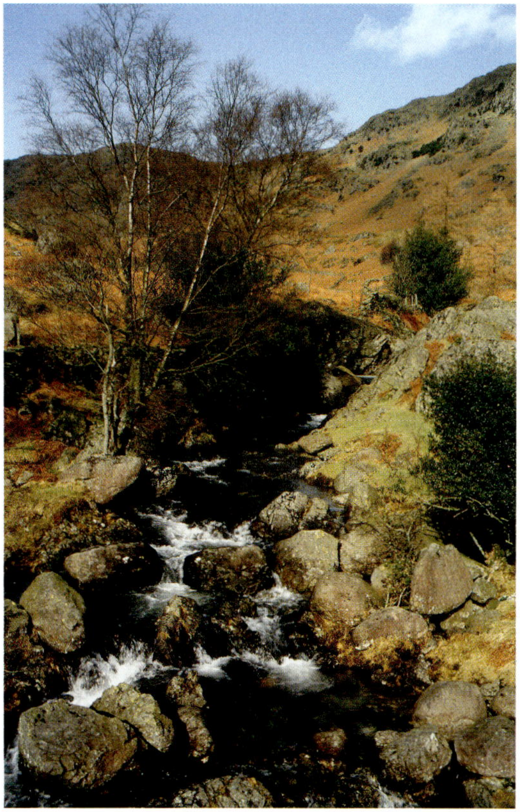

Ascending into Far Easedale.

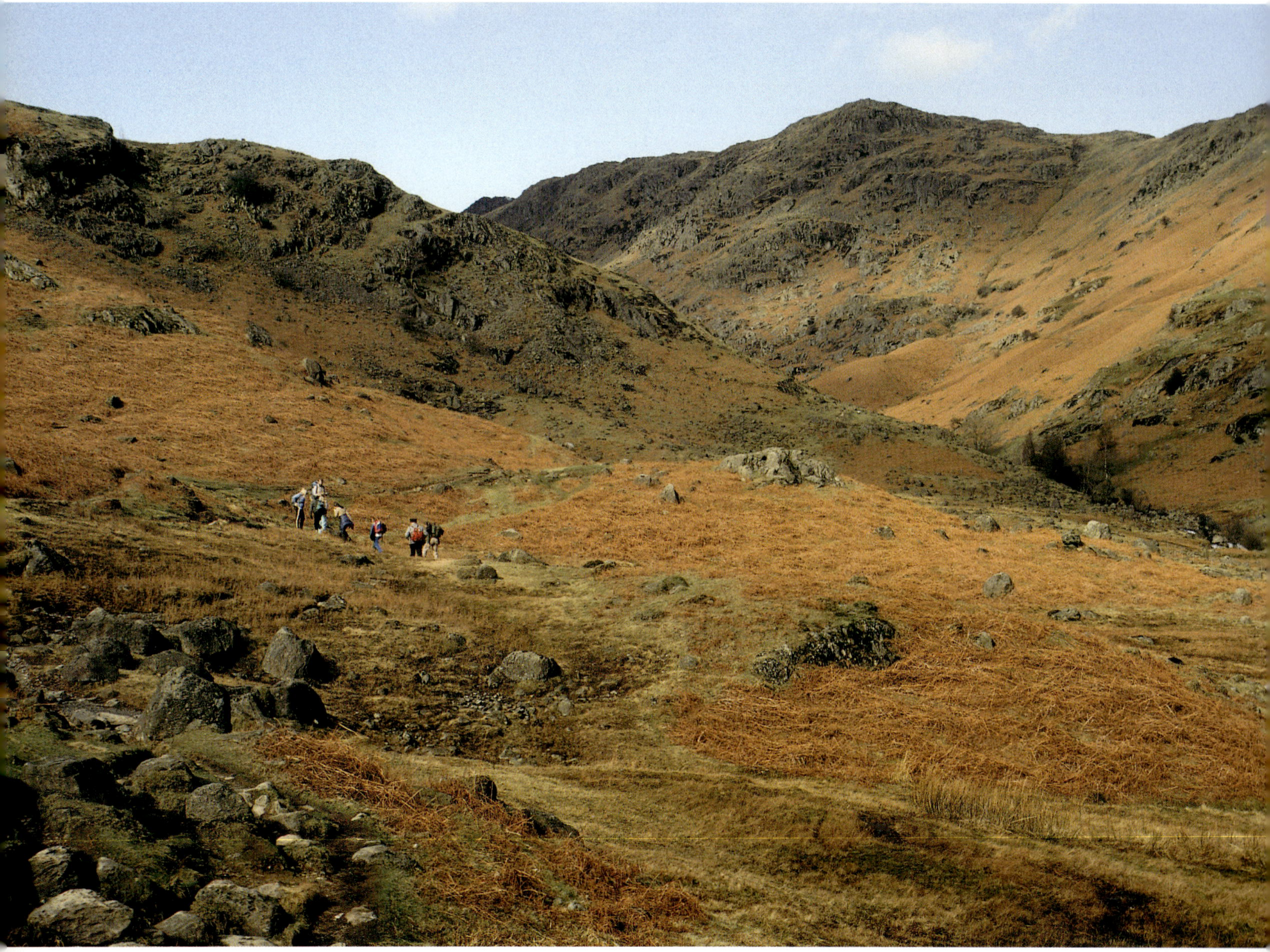

packhorse road into the beautifully-desolate Far Easedale and so over Greenup into Borrowdale; long, lonely miles that will attract strong walkers.

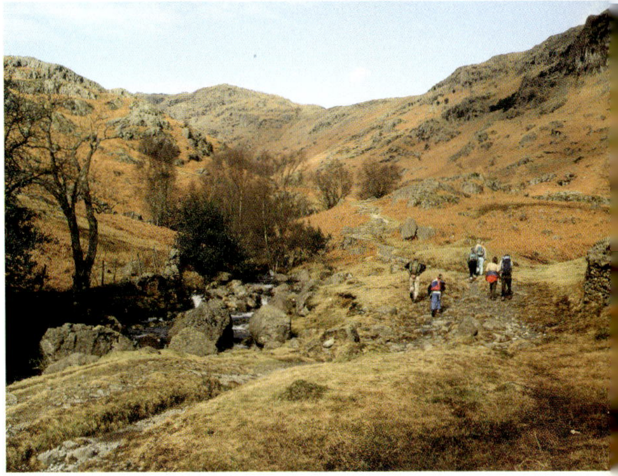

Heading into Far Easedale.

At Stythwaite Steps (Stythwaite being the old name for the lower part of Far Easedale), the two dales are separated by a knob of fell. Easedale lies west of here, from Goody Bridge reached along an old packhorse trail that crosses the foot of Blindtarn Gill. The farm buildings tucked into the base of the fell were once the home of the Greene family, far from affluent statesmen farmers who died in a snowstorm while returning from a sale in Langdale. Unable to find their way home, the two parents lived out their final moments in the storm's icy embrace.

Meanwhile, their eldest daughter, Sally, no more than a child herself, took charge of her siblings, tended the fire, milked the cows and pressed on with the work of their farm until the storm abated. Once the alarm was raised, their dead parents were soon found on the ridge above Blindtarn Moss – so near, and yet so far. Dorothy Wordsworth was instrumental in setting up a group of Grasmere women to help the orphans; she and William gave employment to Sally, and the other children all found good homes nearby.

North of Helm Crag, the hidden charms of Greenburndale are rarely explored. A good path runs through from Ghyll Foot into the dale, and climbs onto the western end of Helm Crag at Rough Crag, but few venture this way. Most walkers also ignore Steel Fell, which sits on the watershed and overlooks Dunmail Raise; those seeking peace and quiet might bear this in mind.

Into Langdale

There are two Langdales, one Great the other Little, and they are so wonderfully different.

Great Langdale is unique, the only 'twisted' dale in Lakeland in contrast to the straight-line trough associated with Ennerdale or Wasdale. In its upper reaches it is split by The Band (a gentle way onto the dalehead fells) into Mickleden and Oxendale before the valley terminates at the huge wall of rock presented by Crinkle Crags and Bowfell. From the moment you enter Great Langdale by leaving the Coniston road at Skelwith Bridge, it is clear you are heading for dramatic country. As you reach Elter Water, the Langdale Pikes are already announcing themselves, peering over the intervening woodland and

Opposite page: *Far Easedale Gill.*

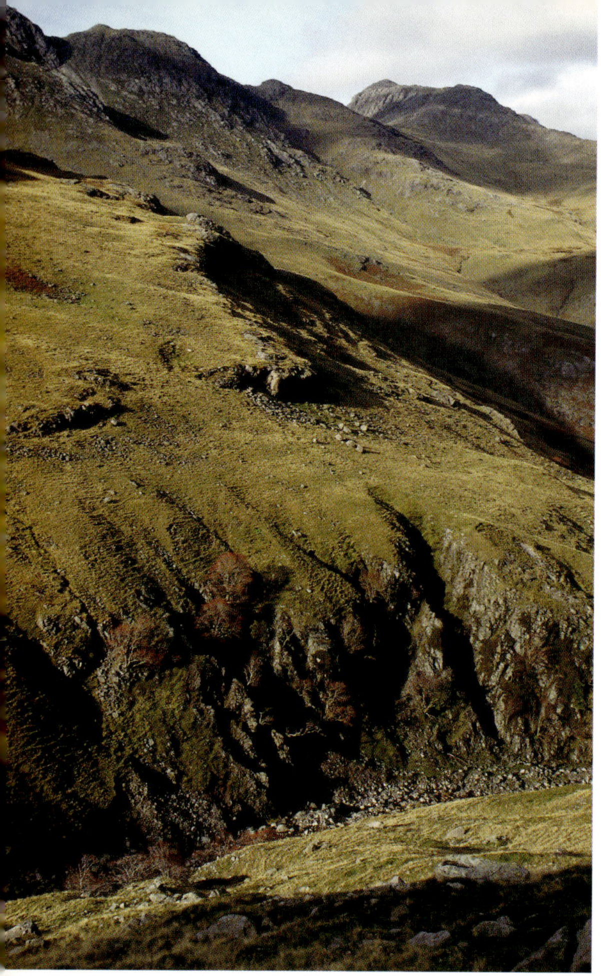

Bowfell and Crinkle Crags from the head of Oxendale.

hummocky interlude of Lingmoor Fell. Chapel Stile delays the moment, but then the great cirque of fells that border Langdale burst into view.

Anyone with a mind for geology will see in the dale abundant evidence of the ways in which glaciation can affect the landscape. As you wander up Stake Pass at the head of Mickleden, so you tread the course of an ice-fall of a small glacier that had its birth above in the hummocks of Langdale Combe – not an ice-fall of Himalayan proportions, but an ice-fall no less. The flat floor of Mickleden and its steep rocky sides exhibit a classic U-shaped glacial profile.

Stickle Tarn is cradled in a hanging valley beneath the cliffs of Pavey Ark and issues into the valley in the form of foaming Mill Gill. Nearby Dungeon Ghyll flows from another, wider hanging valley between the two main Langdale Pikes.

Many years later, this whole landscape was covered with trees, though it takes a leap of imagination to visualise that today. But the roots of Scots pine and broadleaved trees have been found more than 600m (2000ft) up above the Langdale valley, revealed only when torrential rain, as in 1966, sweeps away

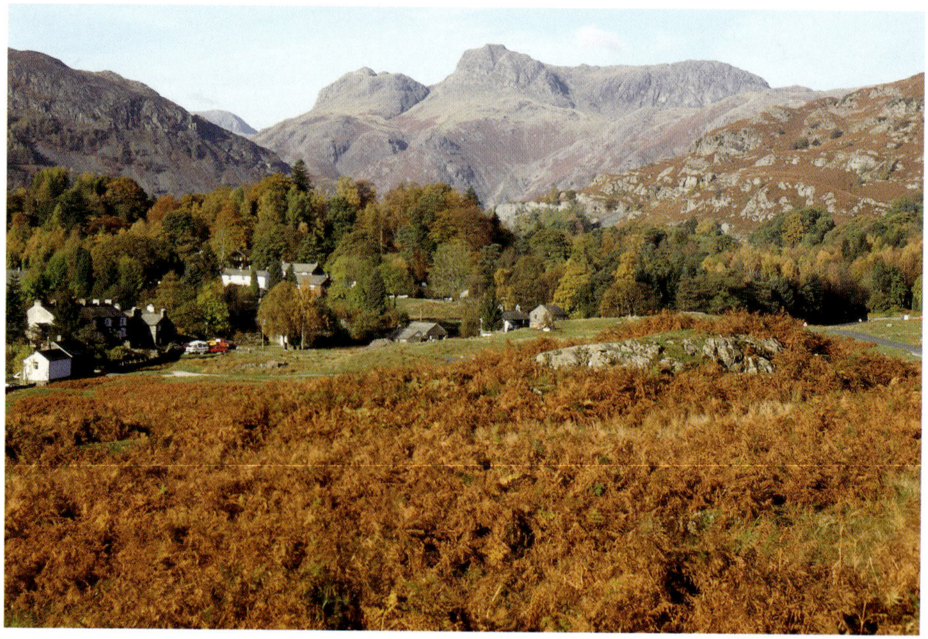

An autumnal view over bracken to the Langdale Pikes from Elterwater Common.

much of the ground cover. Certainly vast areas of the dale would have presented a woodland view to prehistoric man as he worked to find suitable fragments of tuff from which he fashioned stone axes. On a calm day it is tempting to believe for one moment that the ringing sound echoing around the valley is the aural shadow of prehistoric man chipping away rocks; in reality, it is far more likely to be the sound of the paraphernalia carried by rock climbers.

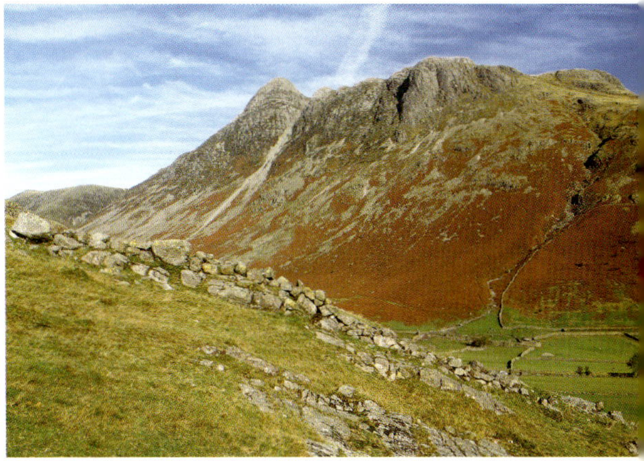

Pike of Stickle, Loft Crag and Harrison Stickle from the foot of The Band at the head of Langdale.

The dale bottom, which in the case of Mickleden shows evidence of extensive settlement in the past, was once filled with alder and willow woods, with birch and oak where the land was drier. Much of the dale was cleared during the third millennium BC to provide pastureland for the men who worked the axe factories. But where the woodland remained in Langdale, as elsewhere, pine martens roamed freely over the open fells, though they are scarce here today.

John Stuart Mill described Great Langdale, as 'wholly unlike any we had yet beheld.' Wordsworth simply thought it was a dale 'which should on no account be missed' Above the dale, the shapely 'Pikes' are craggy and forbidding, but in reality easily ascended, unless you decide on the slanting Jack's Rake across the

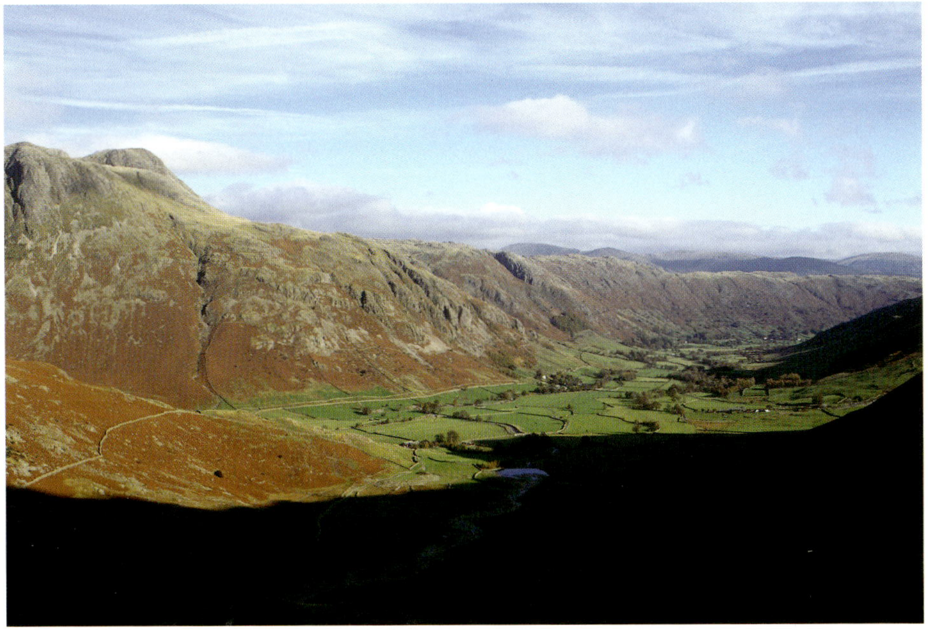

Upper Langdale from the path through Oxendale.

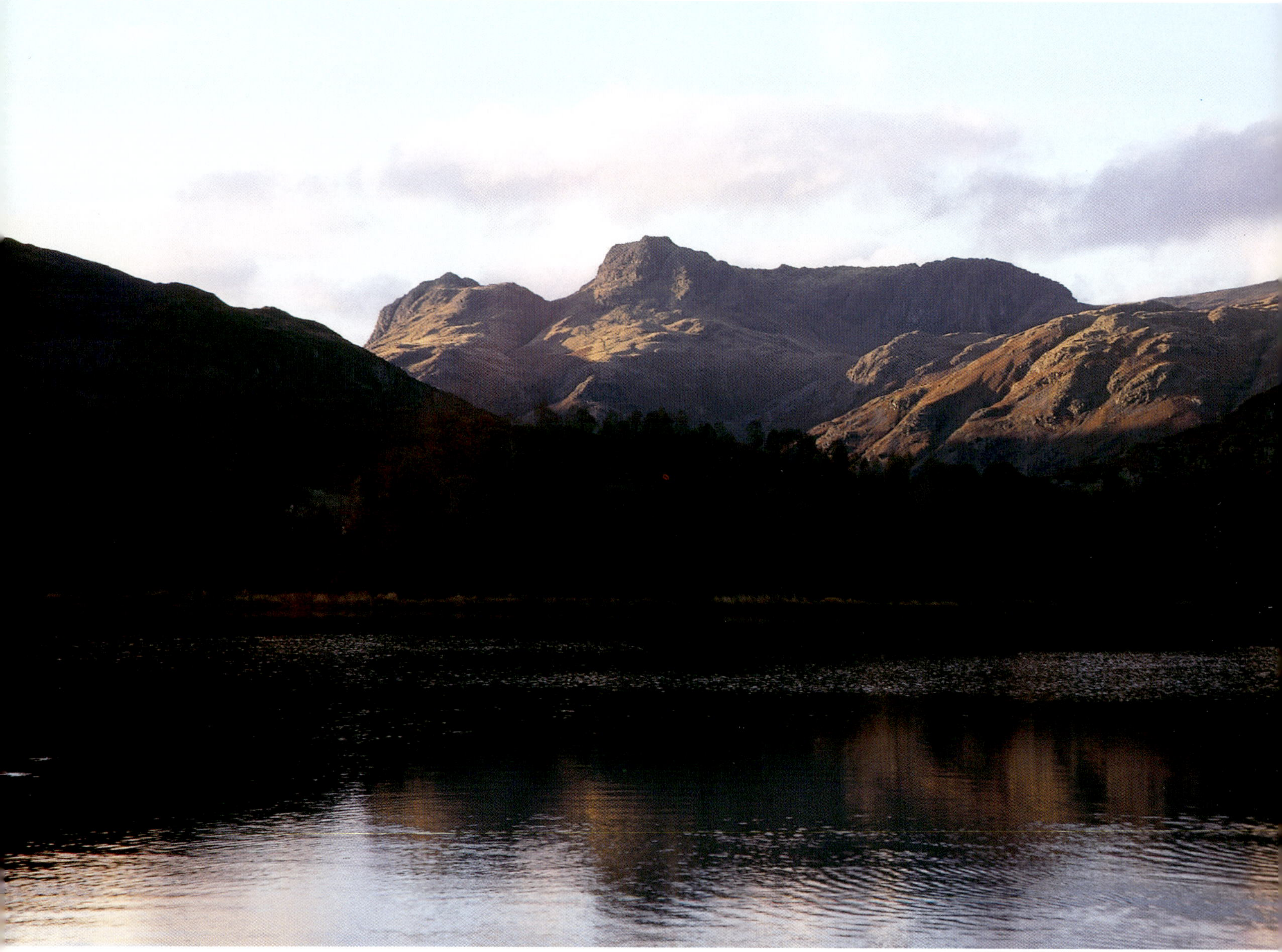

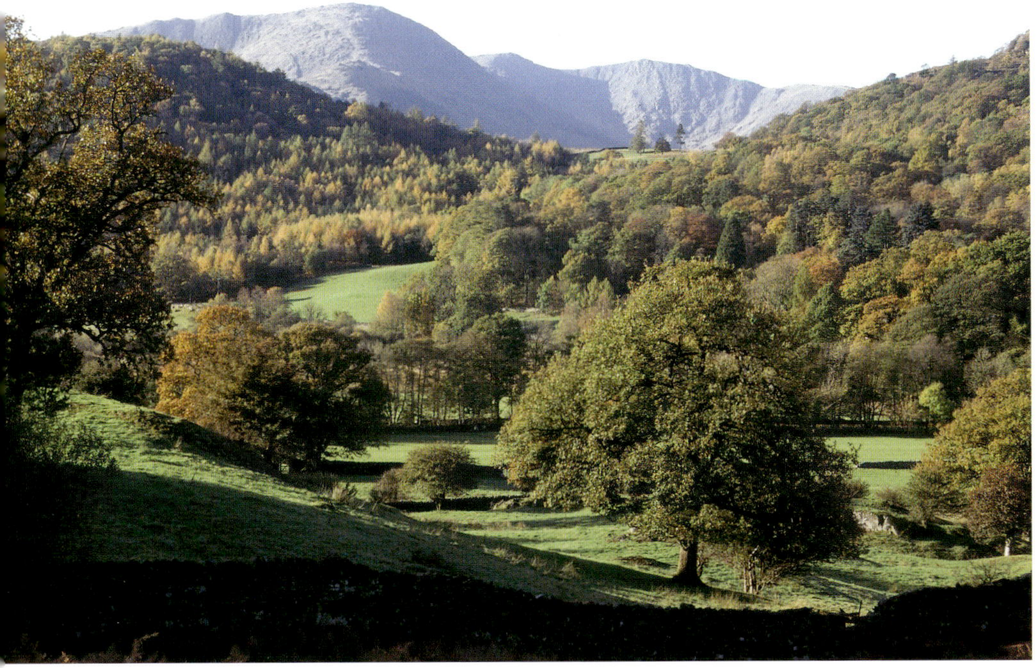

Wetherlam and Greater Langdale.

Opposite page: *Evening light on the Langdale Pikes seen over Elter Water*

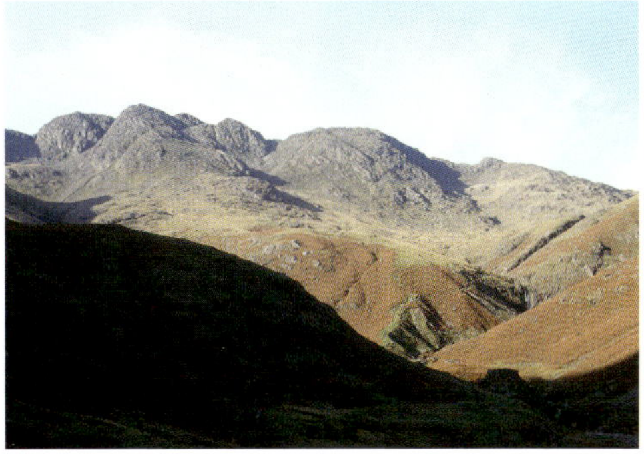

Crinkle Crags and the head of Oxendale.

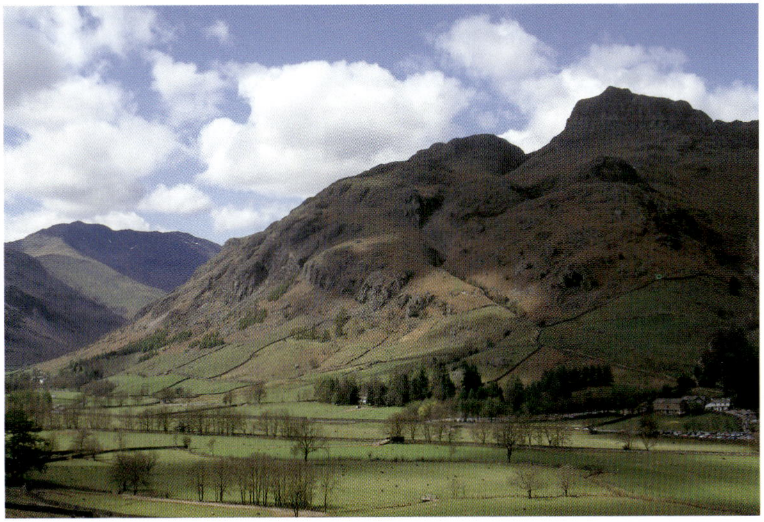

Upper Langdale and the edge of Mickleden, with Bowfell on the left.

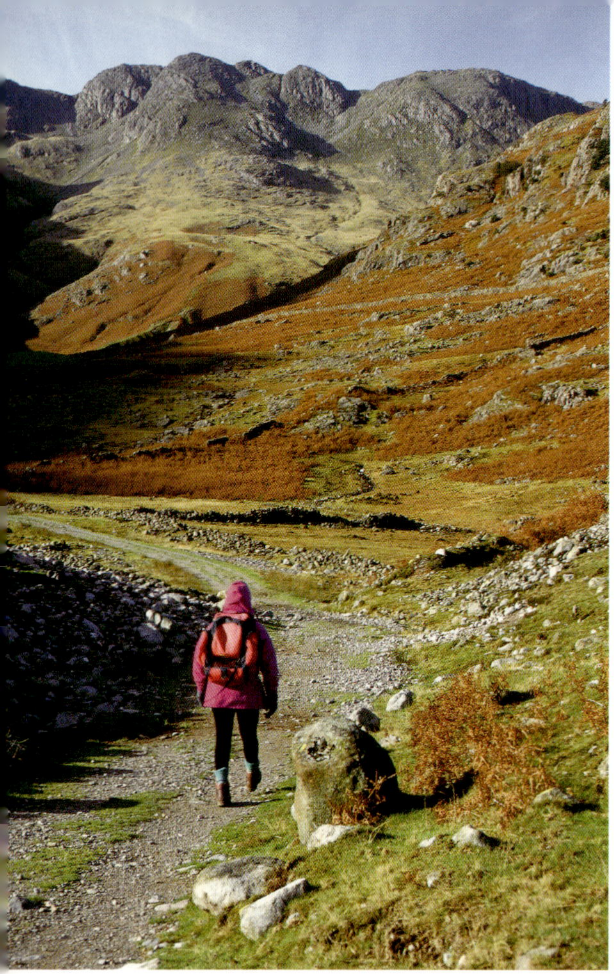

Heading into Oxendale.

vertical wall of Pavey Ark. Joseph Budworth climbed Pike of Stickle in 1792, but found the slopes so steep that he 'tied up [his] right eye, which could not have borne the vast precipice almost perpendicularly under [him].' In those days, and indeed until less than a hundred years ago, it was generally considered ill-advised to venture among the fells without a guide; the days of the fell rambler were yet to come.

Oxendale is a rough-and-rugged dale, but one that lacks the penetration of Mickleden. But it does have a dramatic headwall in the form of Crinkle Crags, which is splendidly (if energetically) ascended through the dale and so up a constructed track towards Red Tarn, nestling in a shallow hollow below Pike of Blisco. A return down The Band makes an excellent circuit, which strong walkers can extend to include an ascent of Bowfell. Between the two fells lies the shallow cluster of Three Tarns from where you gaze across the wide, wild abyss of Upper Eskdale to the Scafells.

Great Langdale is linked to Little Langdale by a small hanging valley which today houses Blea Tarn, an evocative setting below the crags of Wrynose Fell and Pike of Blisco. Once across this neck of land, the entry into Little Langdale

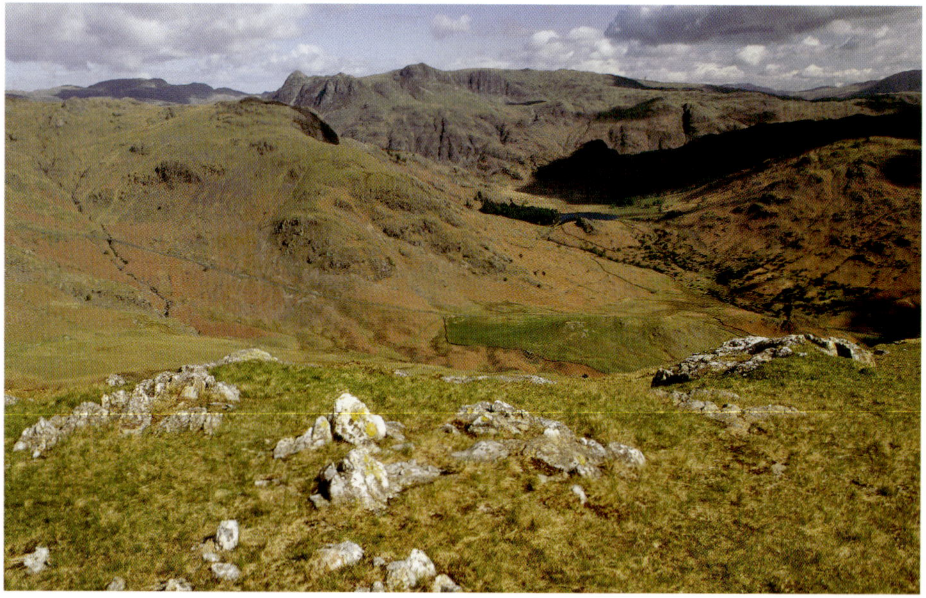

Blea Tarn lies in a shallow basin in a linking dale between the two Langdales.

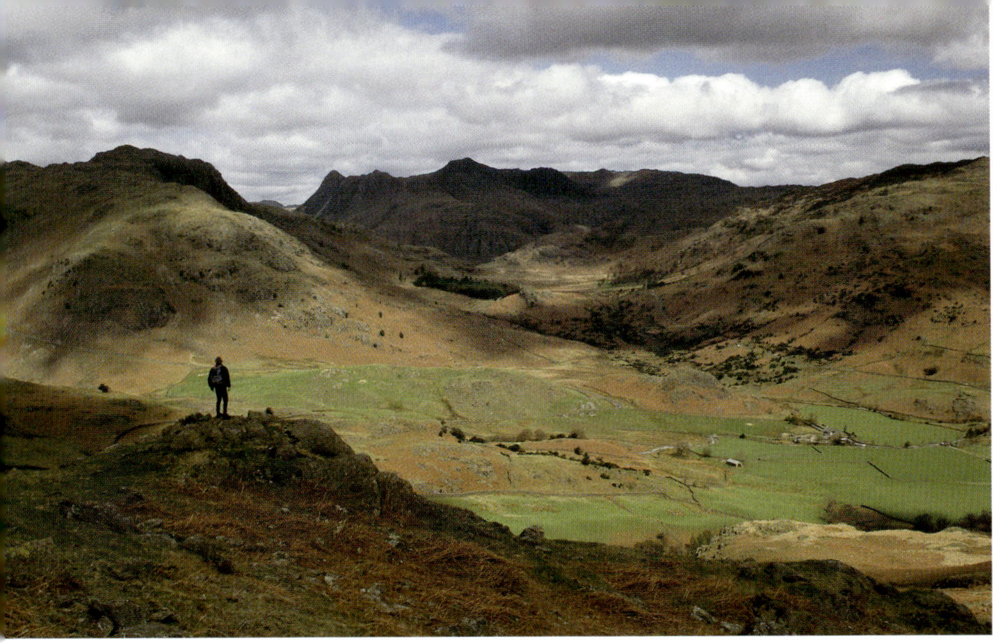

Looking across to the Langdale Pikes from above Greenburndale.

is breathtaking – it may also take parts of your car, too, if the dreamy beauty of the dale detracts from a driver's attention, for the roads here are narrow, twisting and not at all suited to motor vehicles.

On foot is the best way to explore, for in this manner you can pursue a delightful circuit from the village of Elterwater, along the course of the River Brathay as far as frothy Skelwith Force and its bridge, and by the Cumbria Way to woody Colwith Force. Beyond, the wide expanse of Greenburndale opens up, and with it the mirror-spread of Little Langdale Tarn. Here, Slater's Bridge, which spans Greenburn Beck, is one of the finest packhorses bridges in Lakeland, a higgledy-piggledy construction of profound ingenuity. The short rise above gives a grandstand view of the tarn and the way over Wrynose into the Duddon Valley. A brief skirmish with the road, and then a fine stony track leads down from Dale End Farm back to Elterwater.

Greenburndale has its own tarn, a tiny reservoir tucked in among the Tilberthwaite Fells, sheltered by the craggy heights of Wetherlam, Swirl How, Wet Side Edge and Rough Crags.

Elterwater was once the focus of a thriving charcoal-burning industry, using juniper wood from the surrounding fells to produce gunpowder, an industry that survived into the twentieth century. The name of the village is thought to be Old Norse for 'Swan Lake', a reference to the visits in winter months of Whooper swans.

The head of Tilberthwaite.

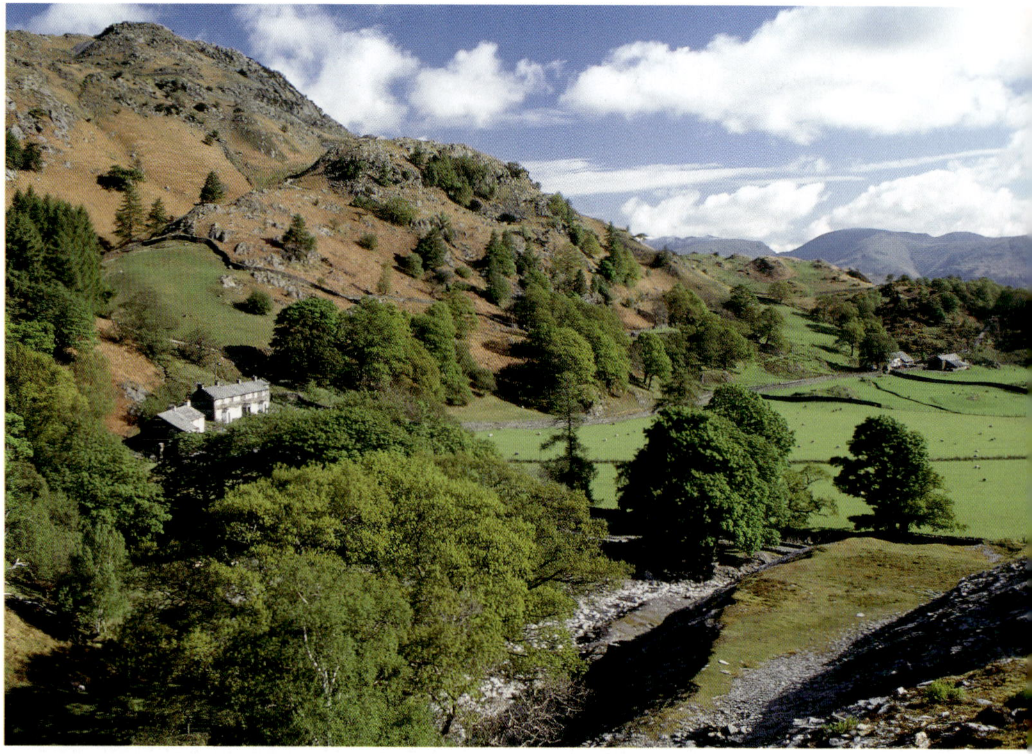

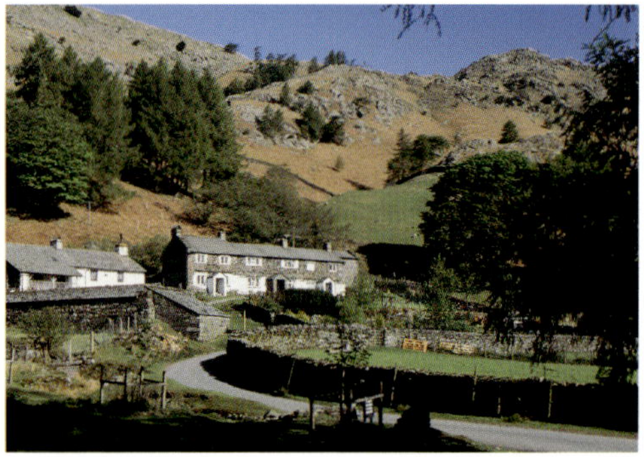

A neat row of cottages in Tilberthwaite.

The Eastern Fells from above Tilberthwaite.

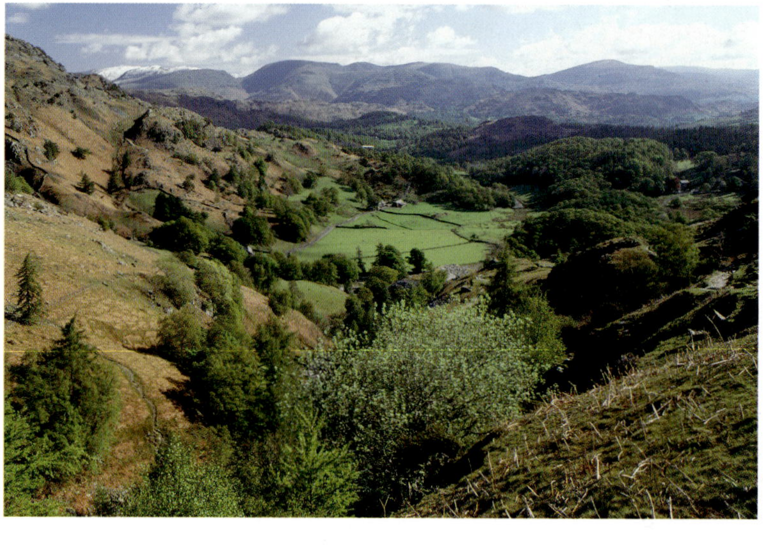

The landscapes of Beatrix Potter

Childrens' story-teller Beatrix Potter lived at Near Sawrey, and looked out on a green and wooded landscape close by the expanse of Esthwaite Water. The dale here is less pronounced, extending southwards as a broad, water-filled basin from the village of Hawkshead to which tourists turn in their droves.

Esthwaite Water, bounded by green fields, woods and reeds, is low-lying and nutrient-rich with a diverse flora, and is generally rated among anglers as one of the finest waters in the Lake District, excellent not only for trout (rainbow and wild brown), but for pike and coarse fishing (roach, rudd, perch, tench and even the occasional eel). It was here that the great crested grebe first began nesting in Lakeland, in 1908. Wordsworth, who went to school in Hawkshead, especially liked the lake, writing in *The Prelude*:

...oft before the hours of school
I travelled round our little lake, five miles
Of pleasant wandering. Happy time!

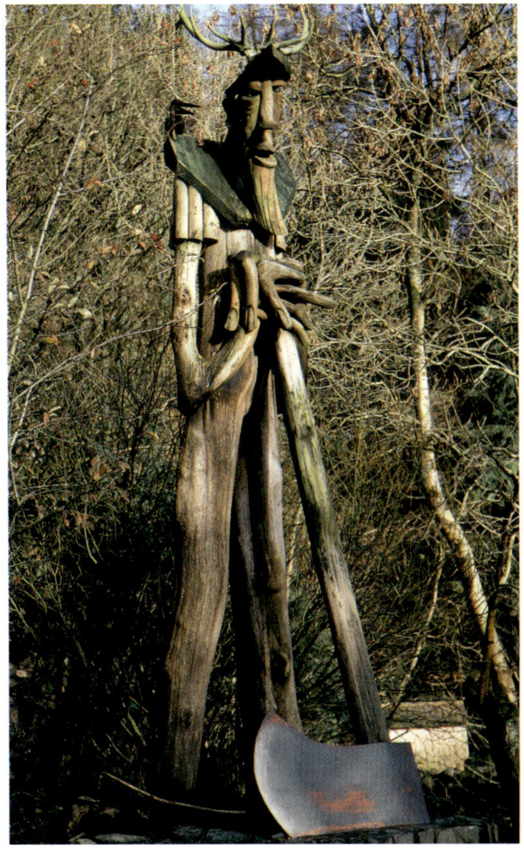

'The Guardian of the Forest': wood sculpture in Grizedale Forest.

Esthwaite Hall was the birthplace of Edwin Sandys (1516 or 19 to 1588), founder of Hawkshead Grammar School, a keen ecclesiastical politician and translator of the 'Bishops' Bible', produced under the authority of the established Church of England in 1568. Sandys was sometime bishop of Worcester and then of London before becoming Archbishop of York. His father was Lord William Sandys who was an officer in the English army, knighted and made lord, becoming Lord Chamberlain under Henry VIII, and involved in the downfall of Cardinal Wolsey.

Beatrix Potter was born in 1866 in South Kensington, London and lived a lonely life, having little contact with other people. She was sixteen when her family first visited the Lake District, staying at Wray Castle. During this time, one of the people she met was Hardwicke Rawnsley, vicar of Wray Church, who was to become one of the founders of the National Trust. His views on preserving the natural beauty of Lakeland made a great impression on the young Beatrix, who loved the unspoilt beauty around the family's holiday homes. Beatrix often watched squirrels in the woods and rabbits in the vegetable gardens, and would turn her hand to making drawings of them. Rawnsley encouraged her in this, and back in London, Beatrix made

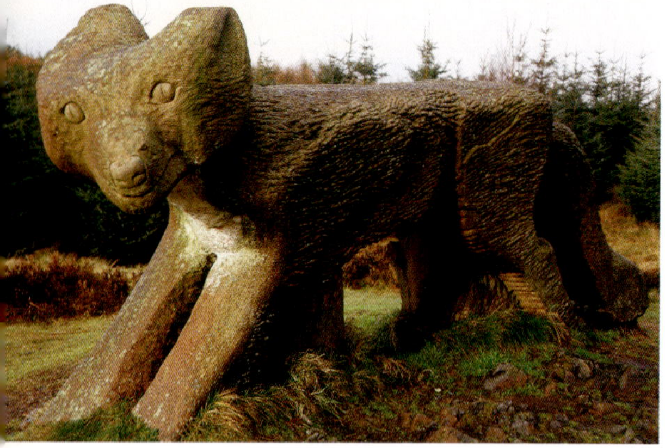

One of a series of 'ornaments' which decorate the pathways of Grizedale Forest.

greetings cards from her pictures, and started the book that was to become *The Tale of Peter Rabbit.*

In 1903, Beatrix bought a field in Near Sawrey, and then in 1905 acquired Hill Top, a little farm in Sawrey, where for the next eight years she busied herself writing more books. In 1909, she bought Castle Farm, opposite Hill Top, which became her main Lakeland base. Now in the hands of the National Trust, Hill Top is still as it was then, and now the most-visited literary shrine in the Lake District.

In 1913, Beatrix married William Heelis, a solicitor in Hawkshead. Then started the next stage in her life, being a Lakeland farmer, which lasted for thirty years. Years later, she purchased Troutbeck Park Farm, and became an expert in breeding Herdwick sheep, winning many prizes at country shows with them. When she died in 1943, Beatrix Potter left fourteen farms and 4000 acres of land to the National Trust, together with her flocks of Herdwick sheep.

Coniston's Water

The River Crake, which flows from its birthplace high on the Coniston fells, continues southwards through the dale now filled with Coniston Water to reach Morecambe Bay at Greenodd Sands.

The village of Coniston is one of the most popular places in the Lake District, its name deriving from the Anglo-Saxon for the 'king's village'. The fells that surround it have the characteristic ruggedness of Borrowdale Volcanics, although the village is built on slates and shales.

In spite of the development nearby of slate quarries and copper mines that in the nineteenth century brought the village much of its prosperity, the character of the village, which gathers about its fine church of St Andrew, remains largely unaffected. A number of the terraced cottages date from the mid-eighteenth century.

The copper mines, for which the area is renowned, probably date from Norman times, but were mainly worked from the sixteenth century, when, as at Newlands, German miners were employed. The main valley rising along Church Beck into the fells is still known as Coppermines Valley, and was the scene of extensive mining activity until the end of the First World War. The ore

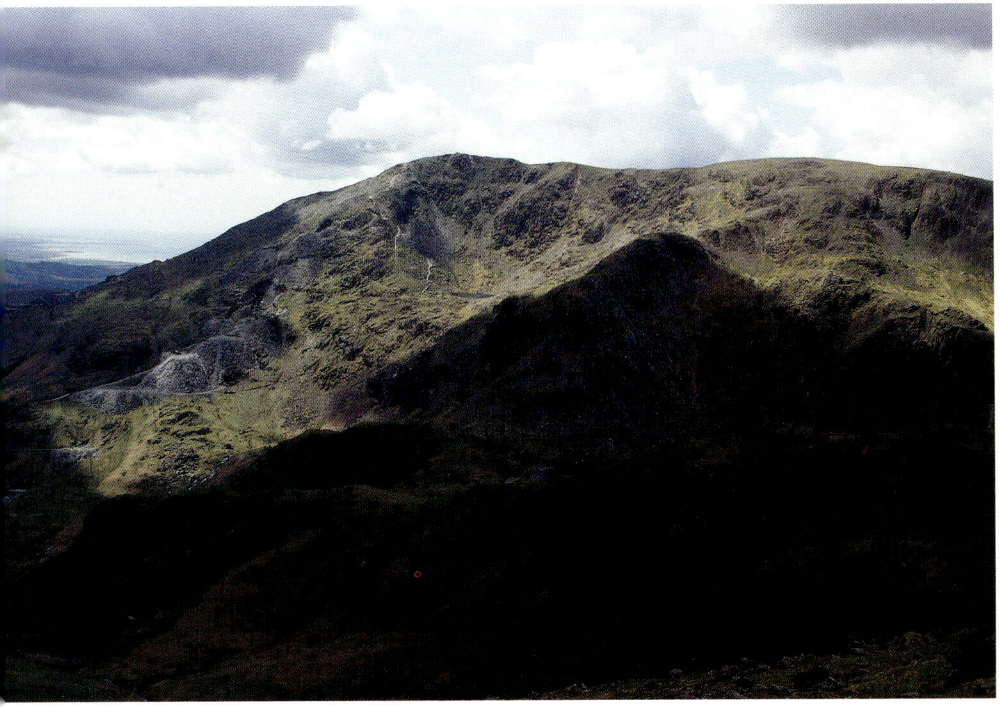

The upper reaches of the Coppermines Valley and the Old Man of Coniston, seen from Wetherlam.

was taken out of Coniston on a railway opened in 1859, which linked with the Furness Railway near Broughton-in-Furness; now only the trackbed remains.

The beauty of both the village and the valley of Coniston has attracted countless visitors since the days of the first Viking invaders. Tennyson (1809-92) spent part of his honeymoon in Coniston; William Gershom Collingwood (1854-1932), the English artist and archaeologist, moved to Coniston to be private secretary and collaborator to John Ruskin, and Arthur Ransome (1884-1967), the journalist and writer of children's books, made Coniston the setting for *Swallows and Amazons*, and used Peel Island at the southern end of Coniston Water as his 'Wild Cat Island'.

The Victorian poet, art critic and social reformer John Ruskin is closely associated with Coniston. He lived at Brantwood, on the eastern shores of Coniston Water, from 1871 until his death in 1900, and brought a profound and enduring influence to bear on the world of art of his time. Spending the last years of his life at Brantwood, Ruskin declined the prospect of burial in Westminster Abbey and lies buried under a Celtic cross in the churchyard in Coniston.

Coniston Water viewed from the slopes of Wetherlam.

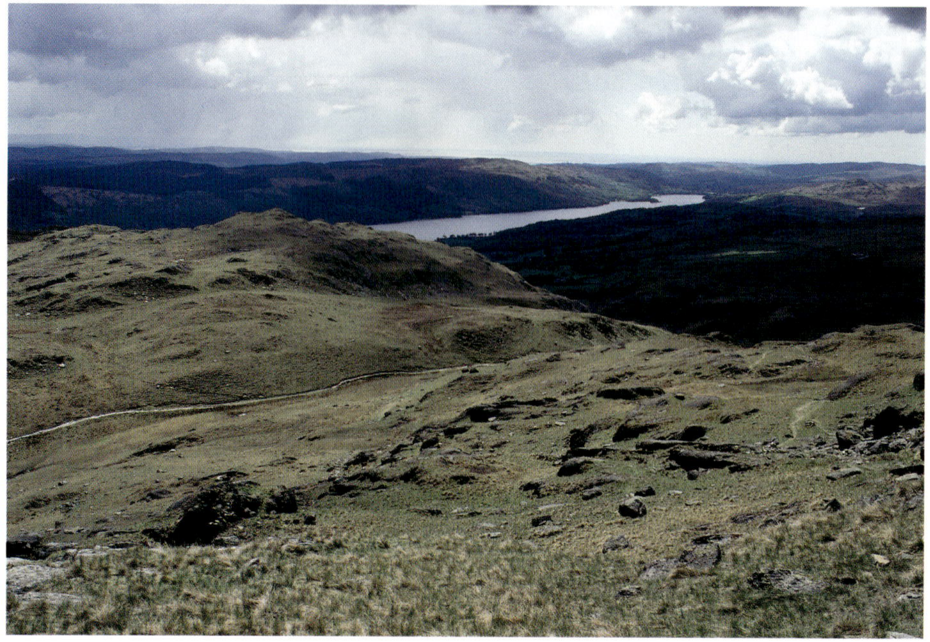

Brantwood is one of the most beautifully situated houses in the Lake District, with fine views both of Coniston Water and the Coniston Fells. During Ruskin's time there – he bought it in 1871 for £1,500 – Brantwood became one of the greatest literary and artistic centres in Europe. Ruskin himself was one of the most respected figures of the Victorian age, a social revolutionary, as well as a poet, artist, prophet, critic, and first Slade Professor of Fine Art at Oxford, who counted among his disciples such notables as Tolstoy, Marcel Proust and Mahatma Gandhi. A keen conservationist, Ruskin foresaw the 'greenhouse effect' more than 100 years ago, and many people have been as inspired by him, as he was by the landscape around his home.

Coniston Water is one of the longest straight stretches of placid water in the Lake District, 8km (5 miles) long, and was used during Donald Campbell's ill-fated attempt at the world water-speed record in 1967. His jet-powered boat, *Bluebird*, went out of control as he attempted to become the first man to break 300mph on water, and Campbell was killed; the remains of *Bluebird* were finally recovered from the lake in 2001.

Before the arrival of cars, Coniston Water was an immensely popular lake with visitors who came on the Furness Railway, an especially agreeable outing as the railway company also operated a steamer service on the lake using *The Gondola*. First launched in 1859, *The Gondola* stood unused for a long time at the southern end of the lake, but it was restored and brought back into service in 1980. Arthur Ransome, as a child, was allowed to steer the boat, and the experience was turned into Captain Flint's houseboat in his *Swallows and Amazons* and *Winter Holiday*.

There is evidence of human settlement around Coniston since Bronze Age times, with a considerable expansion of human presence in Norse times. Indeed, the lake was formerly known as Thurston's Mere, 'the mere of the lord Thurston'. Following the Norman Conquest, much of the land where Coniston now stands came under the control of Furness Abbey, which heralded a period of much exploitation of woodland, for charcoal, and the fells themselves, for minerals.

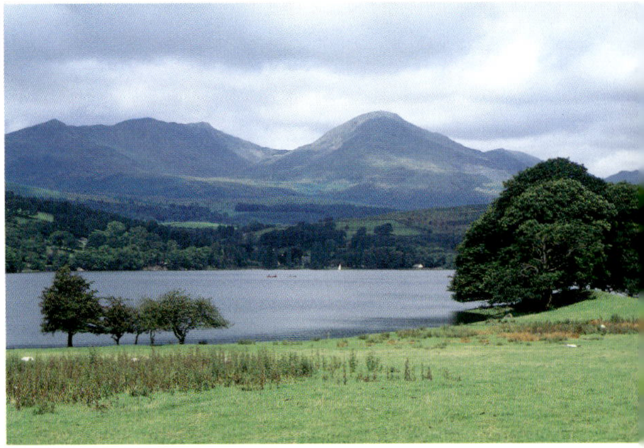

The Coniston Fells, seen across the lake from near Selside.

Charcoal, needed for iron-smelting, was a major industry in these parts, so vital that iron ore was often carried to the woodlands, rather than the other way round, and as a result a number of small smelting sites, or bloomeries, were established, traces of which can still be found along the lakeside. This industry lasted from the fifteenth to the seventeenth century, and resulted in the fell-sides, once densely wooded, being denuded of great swathes of their tree cover. Now there is no natural woodland left; what trees are seen were planted during the nineteenth century and later.

The moors above the hamlet of Torver have been settled since prehistoric times. W G Collingwood, in *The Lake Counties* writes, 'All these fells must once have been the happy hunting-grounds of primitive races, children of the mist, perhaps surviving long after the outskirts were settled by civilized folk.'

Long involved with the many traditional industries of Lakeland – stone and slate quarrying, iron smelting, charcoal production, bobbin manufacture, farming and milling – Torver, overlooking Coniston Water, developed significantly when the Furness Railway came here in 1859.

It was the home of a renowned Icelandic scholar, Thomas Ellwood, rector of Torver chapel, who wrote a small, but rather uninteresting, history of the village, *Leaves from the Annals of a Mountain Parish*.

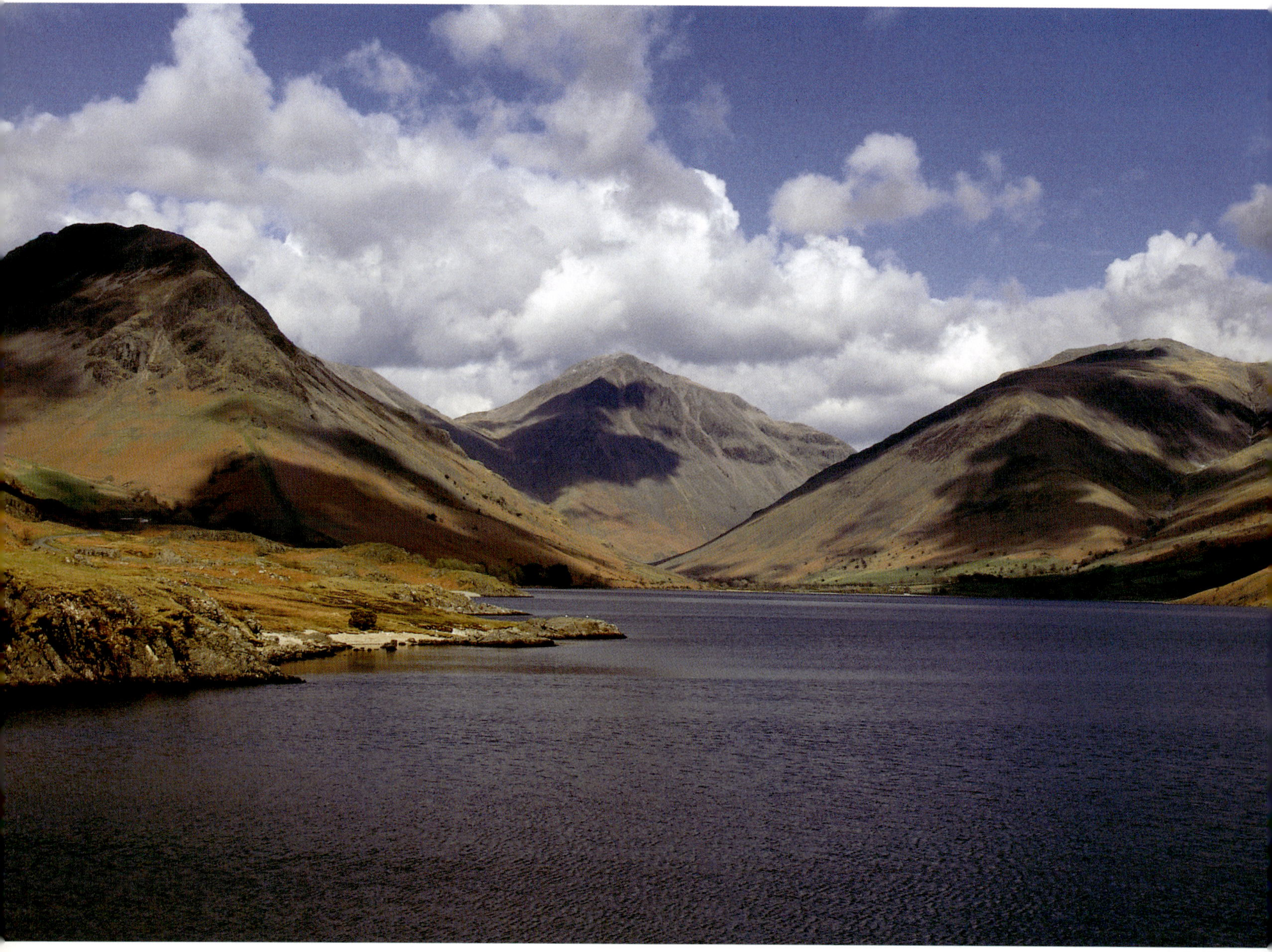

Into Furness and Copeland

There is no more remarkable a contrast of landscapes than that found within the vast sprawl of land known as Copeland Forest, which occupies the south-western edge of Lakeland. From the rugged, craggy, scree-ridden heights of the Scafells and Ennerdale to the soft, pastoral regions of the coastal plain, it is a place that embraces both the most-visited fells and the least-visited, and empty dales that will be unfamiliar to Lakeland visitors even of long-standing.

Here the delectable Duddon, haunt of dippers and grey wagtails, fashions a course through wooded Dunnerdale only a few miles from the Esk, which drains from the highest summits in England. Wasdale, too, is famed for its iconic symbol of Lakeland, that great view along the length of Wast Water to Yewbarrow, Great Gable and Lingmell. Ennerdale is also a popular place, in spite of being the only major Lakeland dale into which access is strictly on foot. But Miterdale, Blengdale, yet another Mosedale, and the dale of the Calder will find few who profess to know their intimate secrets. And the River Keekle (outside the National Park boundary) and maybe even the River Ehen, are waterways I suspect few could pinpoint with certainty. This is a region to which time and a familiarity with more populous destinations eventually bring the inquisitive; a place where isolation has preserved much of its unspoiled quality.

One of the remarkable features of the political geography of Lakeland is the attachment of these lands between the Duddon and Windermere to the repulsively bleak and industrial county of Lancashire. The anomaly came about because in 1092 the lands were granted to a powerful Norman nobleman, Roger de Poitou who already controlled much of Lancashire. The gift of Furness merely extended his reach into Lakeland. It was not until 1974 that Lancashire's hold on this part of Lakeland was prised free.

Opposite page: *The Wasdale trio: Yewbarrow, Great Gable and Lingmell.*

The Barony of Copeland, which covered all the land between the Derwent and the Esk, land subject to Forest Law until the thirteenth century, was among the most remote parts of England, a 'plus' that it still enjoys into the twenty-first century.

This is still a world apart; a place of wide, wind-swept solitudes and hidden sanctuaries.

Dunnerdale

Along Wrynose Bottom, the River Duddon threads a lazy, meandering course from its source just south of Langdale's Pike of Blisco. In its upper reaches, the dale drops from the Wrynose Pass into a profoundly attractive landscape unfolding into the haze and plummeting quickly to pursue a more gentle gradient alongside the infant Duddon to the hamlet of Cockley Beck, where, Wordsworth describes:

> *Mid sheltering pines, this Cottage rude and grey;*
> *Whose ruddy children, by the mother's eyes*
> *Carelessly watched, sport through the summer day.*

There's been a road through here for 2000 years, though it's been surfaced for less than sixty. The Romans were first: they called it the Tenth Highway, linking forts at Ambleside and Ravenglass. During the seventeenth and eighteenth centuries, it was a packhorse trail transporting copper ore from Greenburn to the coast, but it was decimated by tank training during World War II. After the war, the road was completely rebuilt, gaining a tarmac surface in the process. The dale is littered with boulders jettisoned by the retreating glacier that etched the blueprint for the scenery we see today.

At Cockley Beck, the Romans continued their eastward course, climbing to Hardknott, the steepest and highest mountain road pass in Lakeland. Here the river is joined by the marshy finger of Moasdale, a bleak dale sandwiched between Ulpha Fell and Hard Knott. A bridleway runs its length, linking up with Lingcove Beck to provide a decidedly unusual route onto Crinkle Crags.

At Cockley Beck bridge, the River Duddon, however, heads south. This is Dunnerdale, the 'Dundale' mentioned frequently but never described in Arthur Ransome's novels. The river was said by Wordsworth to be his favourite, a

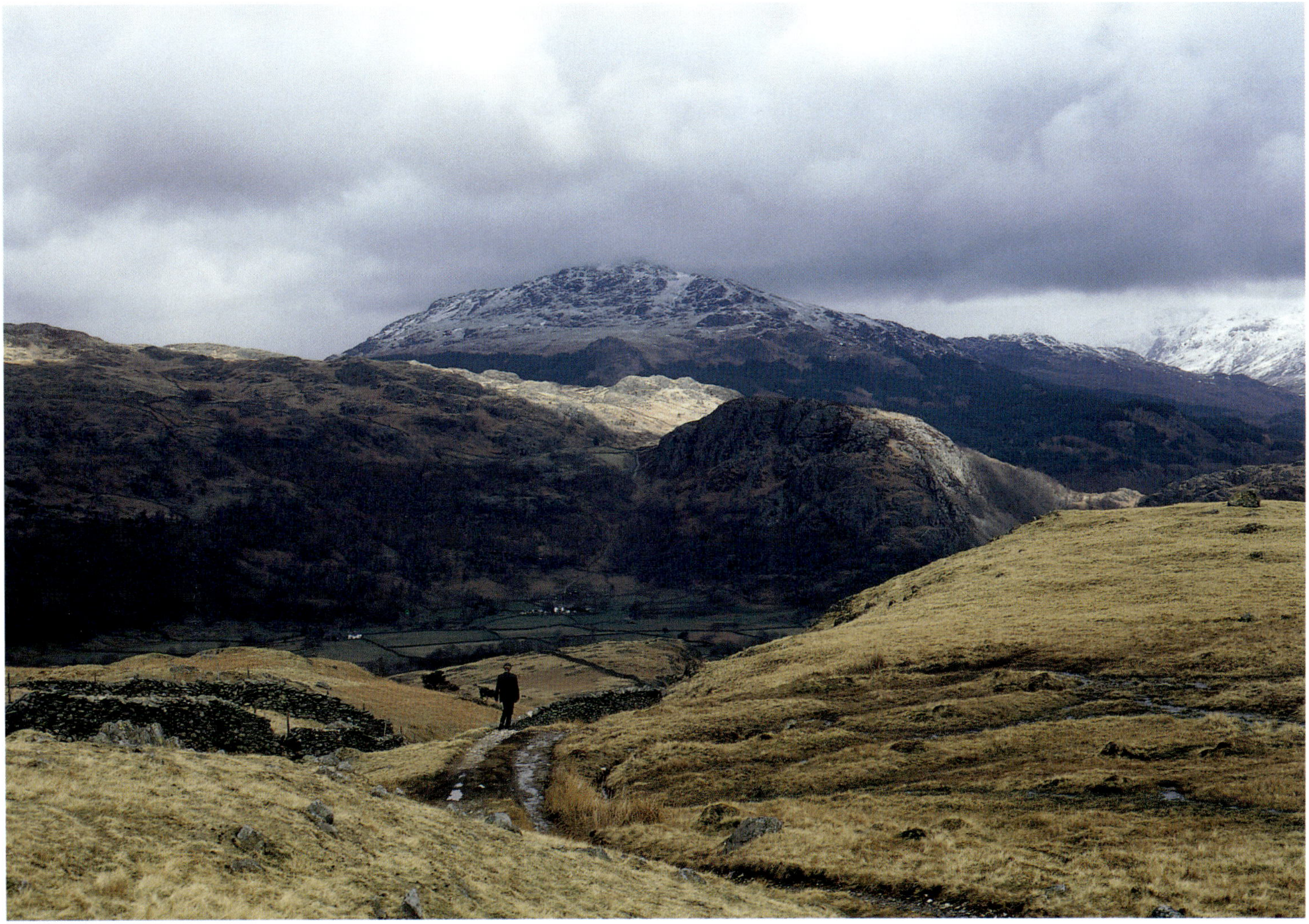

Descending into Dunnerdale: the snow-capped fell is Harter Fell.

Among the rough ground of the Dunnerdale Fells.

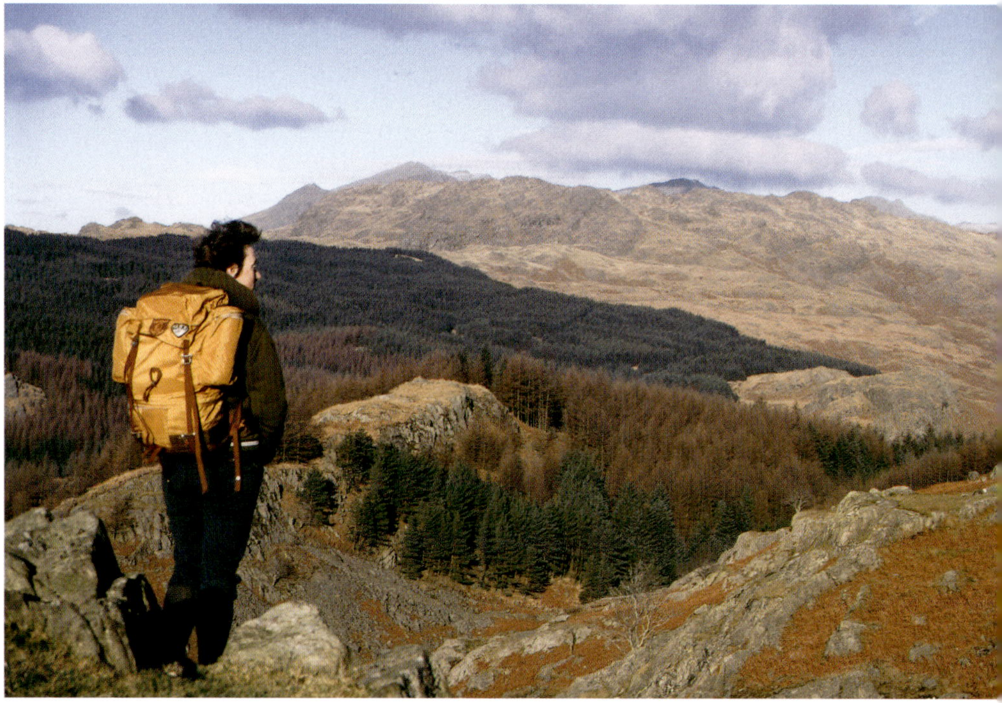

place he came to fish during his schooldays in Hawkshead, and which inspired an entire series of sonnets – *The River Duddon* – which he wrote in 1820. This is the place that lured writer and artist John Pepper to spend his winters, a place he described in his book *Cockley Beck*, where he found himself 'stricken with sanity', where there was 'so much beauty, such peace. Peaks rose into the stars like psalms.' It is a far cry from anywhere, and as beautiful a part of Lakeland as you could wish to find.

Southwards the Duddon tumbles through gorges green and lush, past Hinning House where I used to take rookie fell walkers from Wigan for a fun weekend romping over the hills from Coniston. If they wanted beer, it was nearly three miles walking each way down to Seathwaite, a small hamlet containing several houses, a parish church and an inn. The church was the domain of the Reverend Robert Walker (1709-1802), who gained some notoriety as a formidable man in more ways than one.

Known to Wordsworth as 'wonderful Walker', he was born in Seathwaite and later preached at the parish church for over 60 years in the eighteenth century, and also taught local children. He was a painfully frugal man, but remarkable for his generosity and goodness, and in spite of a very low stipend of five pounds per year managed to leave over £2000 in his will. His character and constitution enabled him to augment his stipend by ploughing fields, spinning cloth, and writing letters for those who could not read or write. He also availed himself of a number of local customs known as clog-shoes, harden-sark, whittle-gate and goose-gate, which gave a man in his position the right to claim shoes, clothing, food and lodging from the parish, as well as grazing on the common for his geese.

At Ulpha the dale road divides, one arm looping out onto the moors of Whitfell, before deciding against it and returning to the valley. The name of this small village near River Duddon means 'the enclosure where wolves are trapped', or 'Wolf's Hill', from Old Scandinavian. To the east, the Dunnerdale Fells, low in comparison with the summits further north and east, are a convoluted maze of crags and tarns; to the west, calm order returns in the guise of soft, grassy, windswept fells that undulate northwards to remote Devoke Water and south to the dome of Black Combe.

At the beginning of the fourteenth century a deer park was made at Ulpha by one of the lords of Millom, and a fragment of the park still exists among the wooded hummocks below Ulpha. Hunting took place across all the rounded fells to the west, served by Frith Hall, which was built in the fifteenth century as a hunting lodge.

Flanked by wooded fellsides for much of its length and on the boundary of the National Park, Dunnerdale finally reaches tidal water near the market town of Broughton-in-Furness, feeding out onto the Duddon Sands.

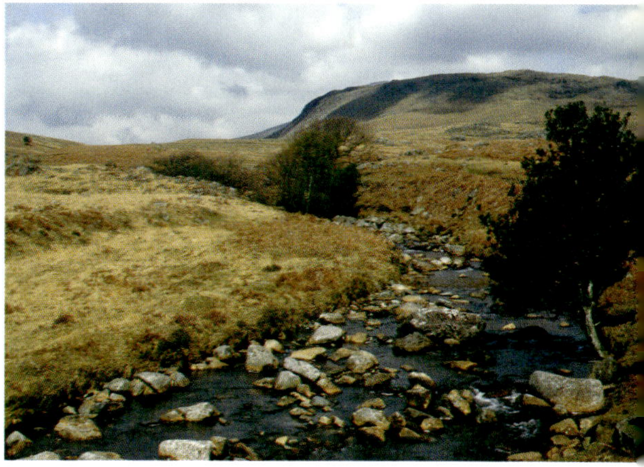

Eskdale Fell and Whillan Beck: the top of Scafell is just visible above the fell.

Eskdale

It is to the Esk that falls the responsibility of draining the highest ground in England. Its upper reaches, known as Great Moss, gather water flowing west from Crinkle Crags, Bowfell, Esk Pike, Great End and the Scafells. High on Great Moss is a remote and wondrous place to be when the mists swirl around the craggy slopes whose tops disappear into grey, and a silence, broken only by the sound of running water or the call of a lamb, clamps moodily onto the austere landscape. Here, among the highest fells, there is no clue that before

The infant River Esk near Lingcove Bridge.

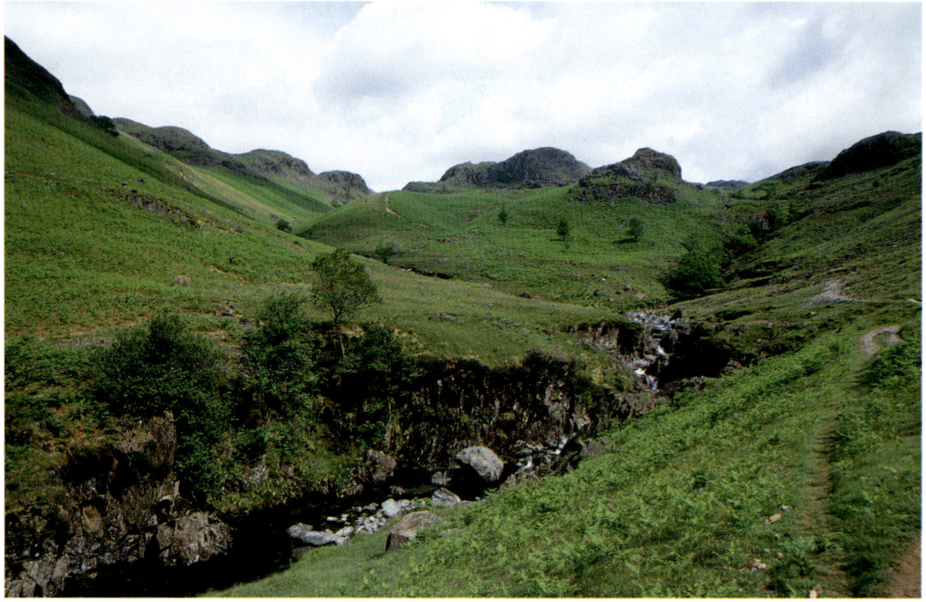

long this river, shallow, wide and pebbly, flows through a fecund dale bright in spring with wild flowers and the song of birds.

The main thrust of Eskdale is, up to a point – that point being the end of the Ravenglass and Eskdale railway line at Boot – quite well known, but it is not over-populated even at the height of summer. Dominated by rocky outcrops, it is a lush, green valley once managed by the monks of Furness Abbey, and (in pre-National Park days) threatened with almost complete afforestation.

From the foot of the Hardknott Pass, at Brotherikeld, the valley turns north-eastwards, dividing into two as it reaches the craggy circle of hills formed by Crinkle Crags, Bowfell, Esk Pike, Ill Crag and the two highest summits in England, Scafell Pike and Scafell; the rather more modest Slight Side completes the ring. This is known as the Eskdale Ring, a route from Brotherikeld to be undertaken only by strong walkers, and certainly among the toughest walks in the Lake District.

Opposite page: *The upper reaches of Eskdale are wild and remote.*

In its lower reaches, Eskdale was most likely the first of the Lakeland valleys to be accessed by the Norse people. Then as now, Upper Eskdale is largely uninhabited save for a scattering of farms and hundreds of sheep, sheep whose 'monastic' ancestors were largely responsible for denuding the landscape of trees.

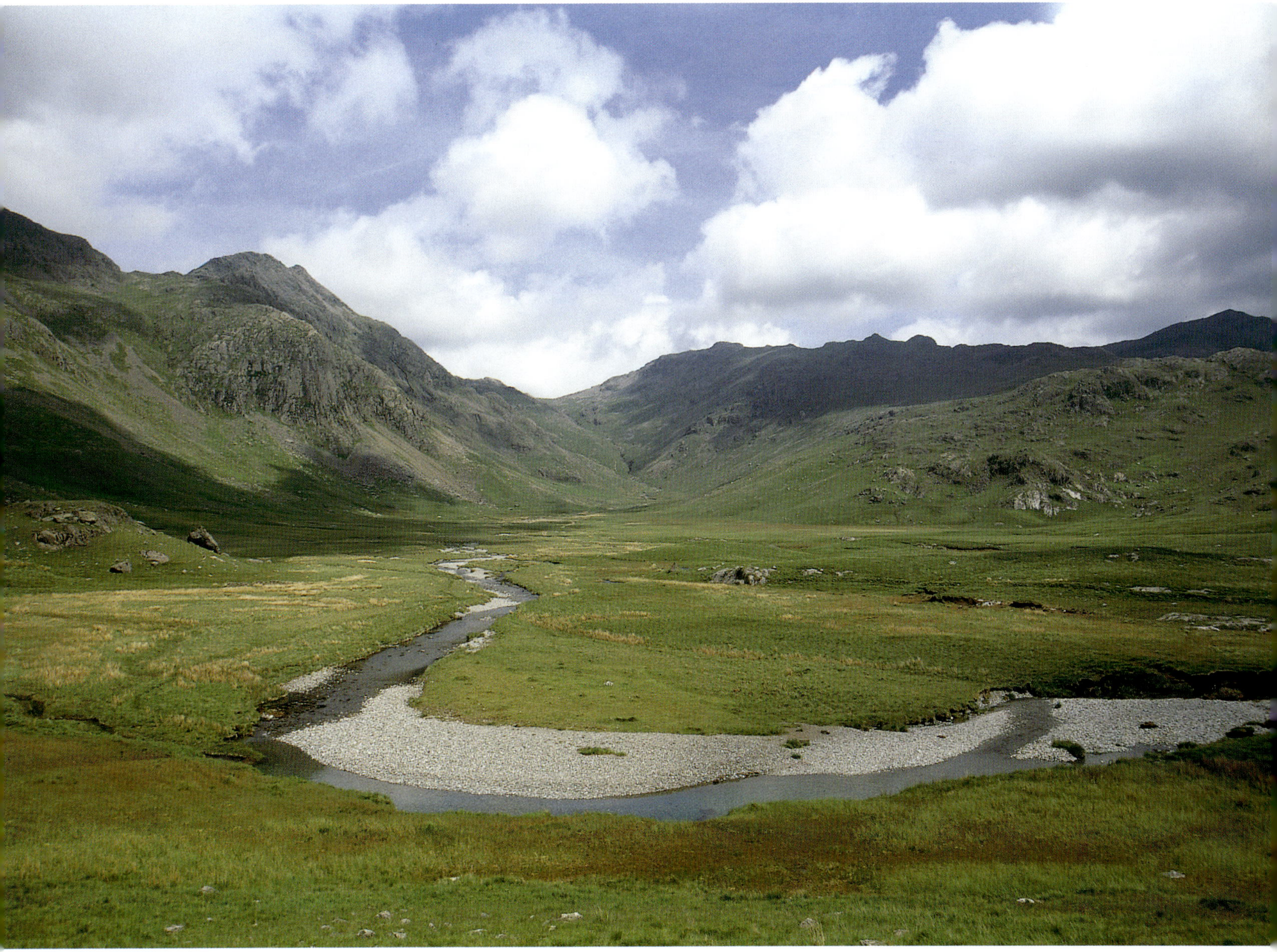

Scafell Pike, the highest summit in England, seen from the moorland arena of Great Moss.

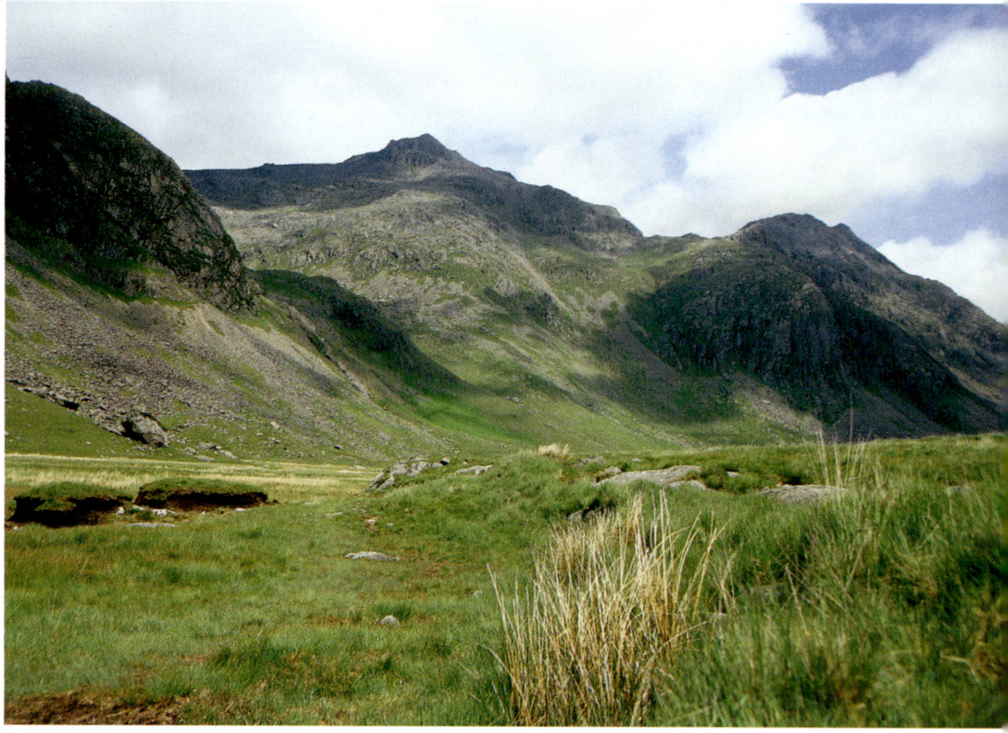

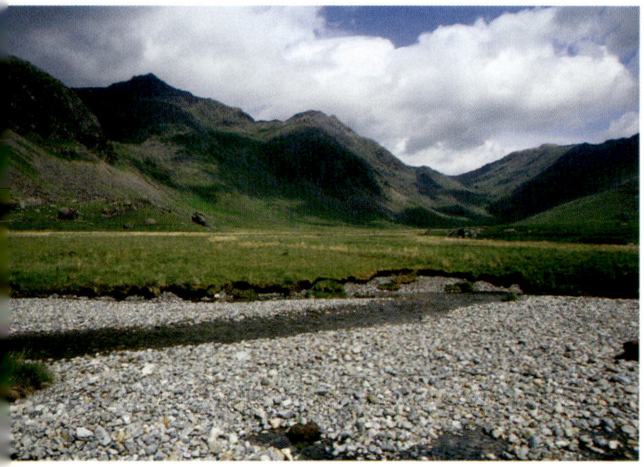

Rugged landscapes at the heart of England's highest fells.

The route into the huge amphitheatre, a glorious, atmospheric bowl below England's highest peaks known as Great Moss, regularly sees the passage of walkers' boots, but as arenas in Lakeland go, this is less well-known. Yet it is a fabulous place; ruggedly handsome, demanding and very isolated in poor weather, and incredibly beautiful. Few people, I suspect, venture here for Great Moss alone; most may well be heading across Esk Hause to more distant valleys, or trudging up towards Mickledore – Samuel Taylor Coleridge's 'hyphen' between Scafell and its 'fierce yet irresistible neighbour' – for passage onto Scafell Pike (or Doe Crag as it was known in the days before tourists), or left to Foxes Tarn to bag Scafell.

On the way in to Upper Eskdale, the route passes Taw House, an old stone farmhouse with a large barn. It was to Taw House that Samuel Coleridge headed, following his traumatic descent from Scafell on 5 August, 1802. He stayed the night, and the next morning was guided by his host, Vic Towers, back into Upper Eskdale, before ending the day by heading for Devoke Water.

Above Brotherilkeld, the Hardknott Pass, undoubtedly Lakeland's most challenging section of highway, forces a way through a mountain gap and down a formidable series of hairpins, some of them blind, to Cockley Beck at the head of Dunnerdale. But most motorists grappling with the twists, turns and gradients of the pass, are unaware of the massive Roman fort only a short distance from the road.

Hardknott Fort (*Mediobogdum*) is one of the finest Roman forts in Britain, dramatically-sited on a shelf above the pass. It was constructed in the early part of the second century to oversee the road linking other forts at Ambleside (*Galava*) and Ravenglass (*Glannaventa*), though that road and the present road are not the same, and it may well have followed a much older, prehistoric thoroughfare. The fort is almost certainly Auden's 'fortress like a motionless eagle eyeing the valley', described in *Spain 1937*. The eagle simile also features in one of Wordsworth's Duddon sonnets (XVII):

Aloft, the imperial Bird of Rome invokes
Departed ages, shedding where he flew
Loose fragments of wild wailing, that bestrew
The clouds and thrill the chambers of the rocks;
And into silence hush the timorous flocks
That, calmly couching while the nightly dew
Moistened each fleece, beneath the twinkling stars
Slept amid that lone Camp on Hardknott's height
Whose Guardians bent the knee to Jove and Mars.

Although the fort would have been surrounded by trees when it was first built, it nevertheless commanded a good view eastwards to the top of the pass, and down the length of Eskdale. It would certainly have been a wild and inhospitable place to be garrisoned. Archaeological evidence suggests that the fort was abandoned during the time of Antoninus Pius (AD138-61), coincidental with the pushing northwards of the frontier of the Roman Empire in Britain, but was later reoccupied when the Antonine Wall was abandoned. The fort itself ceased to be occupied around the turn of the second century.

Before long the main dale reaches the small village of Boot, which lies just off the main valley road, at the Eskdale end of the Ravenglass and Eskdale Railway. Its few buildings and quiet ways betray no hint of the activities that flourished here in years gone by.

Eskdale Mill dates from 1578, though there is evidence of milling having taken place here for almost 700 years. The mill today is one of the few remaining corn mills with two waterwheels. It remained for many years in the same family, handed down from father to son, and occasionally daughter to son-in-law.

The milling of corn ended in the 1920s, though the machinery continued to be used for some time afterwards to produce electricity for the mill cottage. In 1972, the mill was acquired by the then Cumberland County Council, and the restoration of one waterwheel and a pair of stones was completed in 1975.

Once a centre for pearl-fishing and smuggling brandy and tobacco and formerly a Roman supply base, the village of Ravenglass is today renowned for the narrow-gauge Ravenglass and Eskdale Railway. In 1208, King John granted the Lord of Egremont the right to hold a market here, and an annual fair, although the market was terminally affected by the coming of the railways. The village lies on an estuary where three rivers – the Esk, the Irt and the Mite – meet, and enjoys a sheltered position that in the past made it an important harbour.

Of the fort built here by the Romans, nothing now remains. The ivy-clad ruins of the Bath House however, known locally as Walls Castle, are a prominent feature in the town, and remarkable for being among the tallest and best-preserved Roman buildings in the country.

Muncaster Castle, set in beautiful gardens to the east of Ravenglass, has been the home of the Pennington family since the 1200s, though the present structure is the product of extensive alterations in 1783 and 1862-6.

The castle is the home of the Gordon Duff Pennington family, and houses a wide variety of classical furniture, some fine tapestries, and paintings by renowned artists such as Joshua Reynolds and Thomas Gainsborough. One of its greatest treasures is the 'Luck of Muncaster', an enamelled glass bowl given to a fifteenth-century member of the family, Sir John Pennington, by Henry VI, who took shelter in the castle after the Battle of Hexham in 1464. Legend has it that the king was found hiding in a hollow tree by a local shepherd and taken to Muncaster. On his departure the king left behind his drinking bowl in gratitude, and tradition decrees that so long as the bowl remains intact, the Pennington family will prosper.

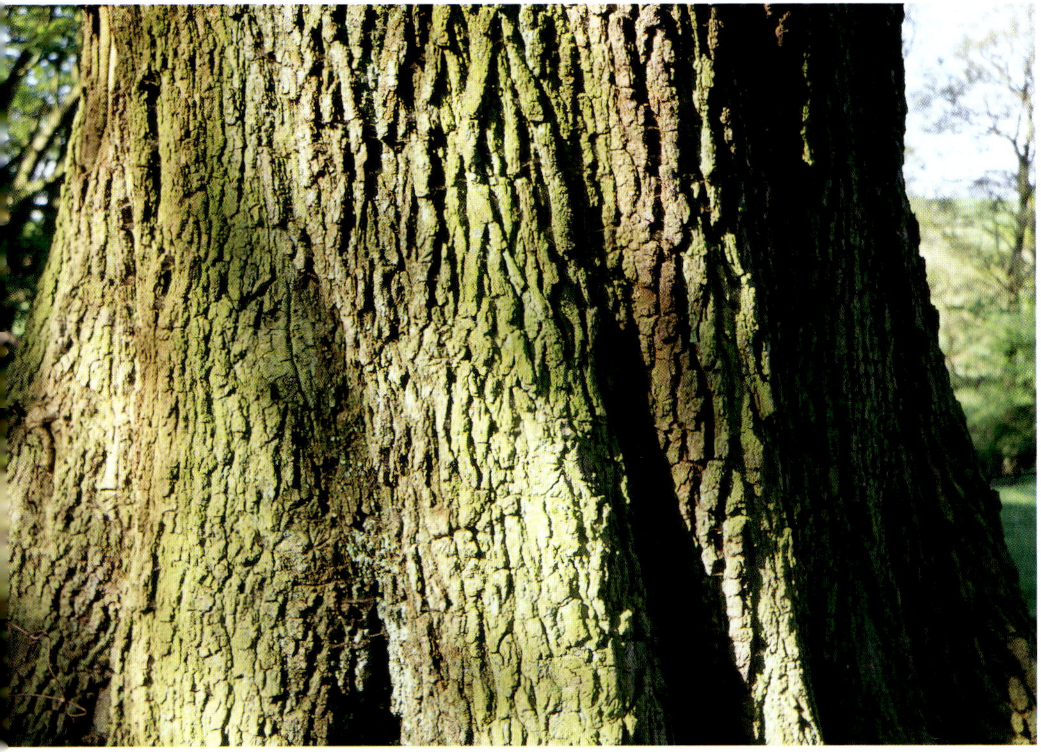

Detail of an oak tree.

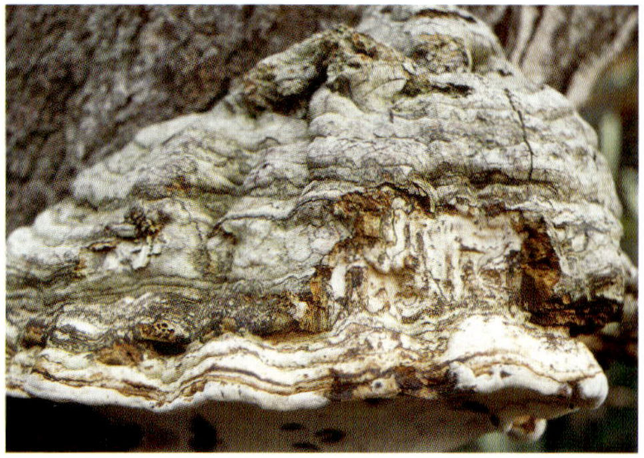

Bracket fungus.

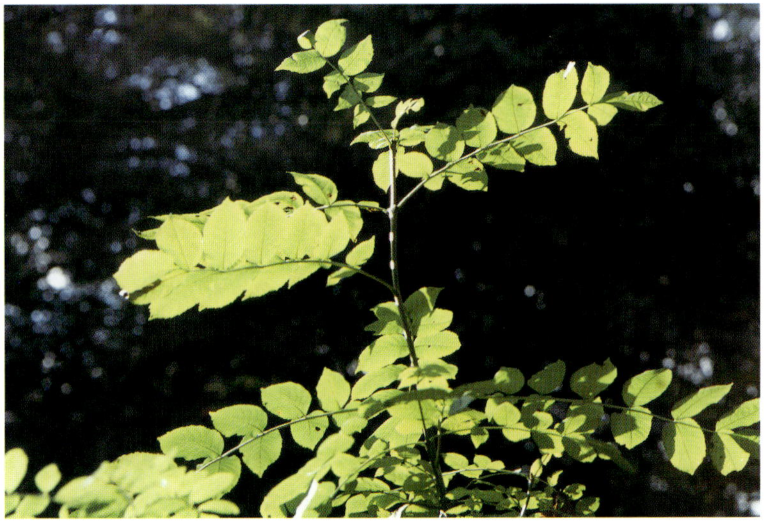

Sunlight shines through ash leaves.

Between Ravenglass and Boot in Eskdale runs the Ravenglass and Eskdale Railway, on a track that is only 38cm (15 inches) wide. The original line was much wider, and was opened in 1875 to transport iron ore from the Nab Gill mines at Boot, about 13km (8 miles) higher up the valley. It started carrying passengers a year later, but has experienced a chequered history.

In 1877, the railway company became bankrupt, but, because of the pressing need still to carry iron ore, the line continued to operate under the Official Receiver. Over a period of time, however, the demand for iron reduced, as did the remaining supplies of ore in the mines, and the line once again encountered financial difficulties. The line was closed in 1913, but was re-opened as a narrow gauge railway in 1915 by Mr Bassett-Lowke, a model-maker. The smaller trains took up the carrying of goods and passengers, aided by the opening of granite quarries and a developing tourist trade. But tourism proved insufficient to sustain the service after the granite quarries closed in 1953.

In 1960, the line was bought at auction by a group of enthusiasts, and is now run by a new company as one of the county's major tourist attractions. In Richard Adams' *Plague Dogs*, Snitter and Rowf jump on one of 'Ratty's' trains to make their escape.

The Mite

At Ravenglass, the River Esk is joined by the River Irt, which has found its way out of Wasdale. But between the two lies a little-known dale through which flows the River Mite.

Across the whole of the wild moorland area which the Mite drains and extending out to the coast there is extensive evidence of early settlement which is fascinating to explore. On Brat's Hill there are five stone circles, the largest being a single ring. There are five cairns within this ring, from which an excavation in 1827 exhumed the remains of burnt bones and the horns of a stag. There are more circles on nearby White Moss and Low Longrigg, along with a large number of cairns.

Miterdale is a secret valley with little to betray its presence at either end. It has all the qualities of every Lakeland valley but in miniature. The source of the

River Mite on Eskdale Moor is an enchanting spot – a large amphitheatre of rock concealed even from walkers a few strides away at Burnmoor Tarn.

From between the moorland summit of Boat How and the steep rise to Illgill Head and Whin Rigg - whose gentle flanks are in stark contrast to the forbidding scree slopes that face into Wasdale – the River Mite flows almost arrow-straight as far as Bowerhouse. It soon enters a steep V-shaped valley, with barely space for a footpath. After a mile or so, the dale assumes a different character as it reaches the slopes above the ruined Miterdale Head Farm, now swathed in dark forest. As the valley opens out around Low Place Farm below the flanks of Whin Rigg, the landscape becomes more gentle, but closes in again on reaching the ancient oak woods of Porterthwaite below the impressive upthrust of rock known as Great Bank.

Below Porterthwaite, passing the packhorse bridge which conveys the ancient bridleway to Wasdale, you come to an old bobbin mill with its obsolete mill pond. Close by, the Bower House Inn is a typical Lakeland hostelry. There was a time when there were thousands of country inns like Bower House, but now there are only a few left. They date from the times when travelling was fraught with danger and the roads had potholes in which you could lose a coach and four. In those times the wayside inn was a sanctuary of warmth, comfort and companionship.

Beyond this journeyman's halt, the River Mite meanders lazily below Muncaster Fell, a modest height but one which commands an impressive view of Eskdale, Miterdale and of the coastal plain.

From Muncaster Tarn, which shimmers on its lonely height, you may come to view this far-flung reach of Lakeland, emerald in spring, purple and gold in autumn. And from its shapely ridge, which offers an airy view of the old harbour and the rolling dunes of Ravenglass to the west and the Isle of Man floating like a jewel in some far ocean, you may find yourself dreaming of all that has gone to make the Lakeland of today.

The Romans tramping northward, far from home, along the windswept sea-coast; the Christian missionaries who landed with St Bega at Tomlin Head; the Vikings who filled the seaways below with their shapely ships or gathered for heathen worship in the hamlet of Gosforth; the monks of Calder building their abbey in the woodlands further north; the barons of medieval times raising

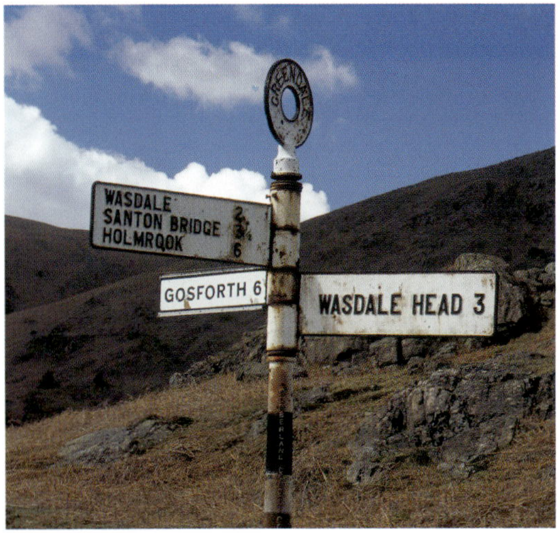

Wasdale signpost.

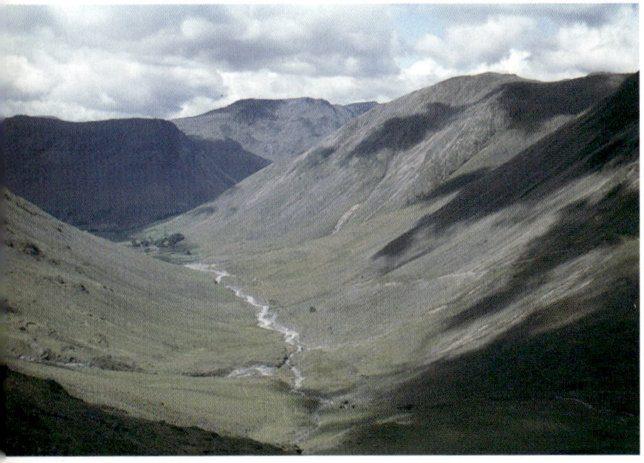

The top end of Wasdale as seen from the Styhead Pass. The fells in the background are Kirk Fell, Red Pike and Yewbarrow.

Opposite page: *Yewbarrow and Great Gable.*

their fortresses and defences; the fishermen of Tudor times following the whims of the Irt and Mite and Esk and fishing the shallows for pearl-bearing oysters, or the stranding of some proud vessel from the Spanish Armada on the shore. There is much to ponder, much on which to reflect, and this is the place to do it, far from the brouhaha of tourism.

A mile upriver from the coast, Muncaster Corn Mill stands on a site where there has been a mill since at least 1455. The present building dates from the early eighteenth century, and electricity was generated by the mill until 1958, using a waterwheel. Regular working at the mill ended in 1961, but the mill was restored to working order in 1976-7. A large waterwheel turns in the mill race, and traditional stone-ground flours are once more produced. The mill operates regularly throughout the summer.

Wasdale: a masterpiece of creation

Wasdale is wild and inescapably dramatic, a sharp contrast to the lush green ways of Eskdale. At the head of the dale, Yewbarrow, Great Gable and Lingmell pose boldly, and combine to create the most distinctive skyline in Britain.

But what characterises Wasdale, setting it apart from other dales, is its magical display of light, cloud and reflection. The backdrop of high fells is quite stunning, and the further up the valley you progress the more the landscape expands. First the shadow-filled crags and gullies of Scafell appear; then Lingmell, Great End, Great Gable and twin-topped Kirk Fell overlooking the broad, side valley of Mosedale with Pillar and the Black Sail Pass at its head; and, finally, the bilberry-clad flanks of shapely Yewbarrow.

Rather better known as a launchpad for the fabulous cirque of fells which surround it, the tiny hamlet of scattered farms and cottages at Wasdale Head, is reached by a long and winding road. Most visitors to Wasdale arrive in mid-valley, usually from Gosforth, to be greeted by a splendid view of the massive mountains of Yewbarrow, Great Gable and Lingmell.

But the most stunning spectacle on this approach is that of the Wastwater Screes, a seemingly-vertical downfall of all things rocky and perilous that appears to slip without a pause beneath the waves of the lake. The atmosphere is powerful, impressive, sometimes intimidating but always irresistible

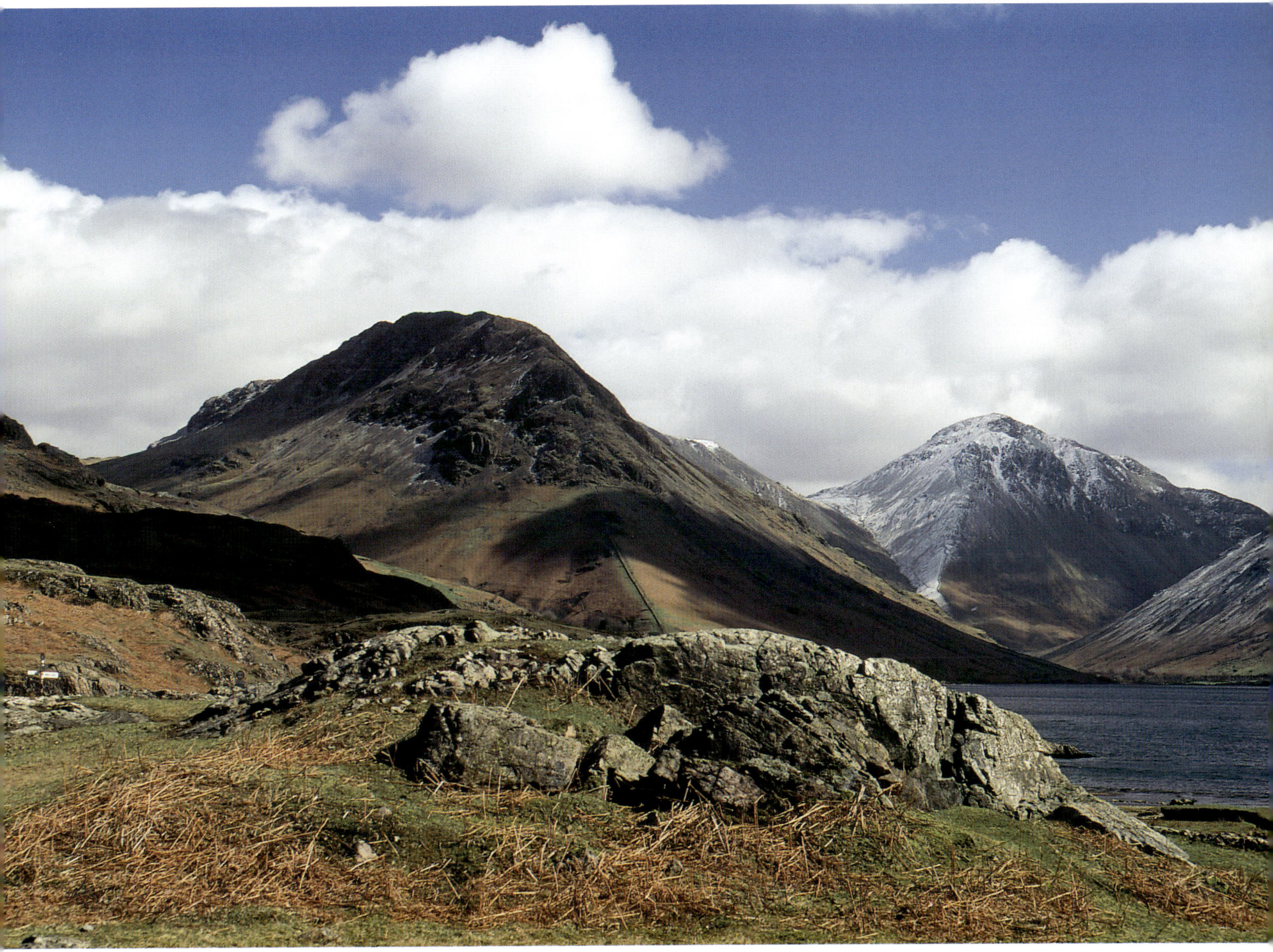

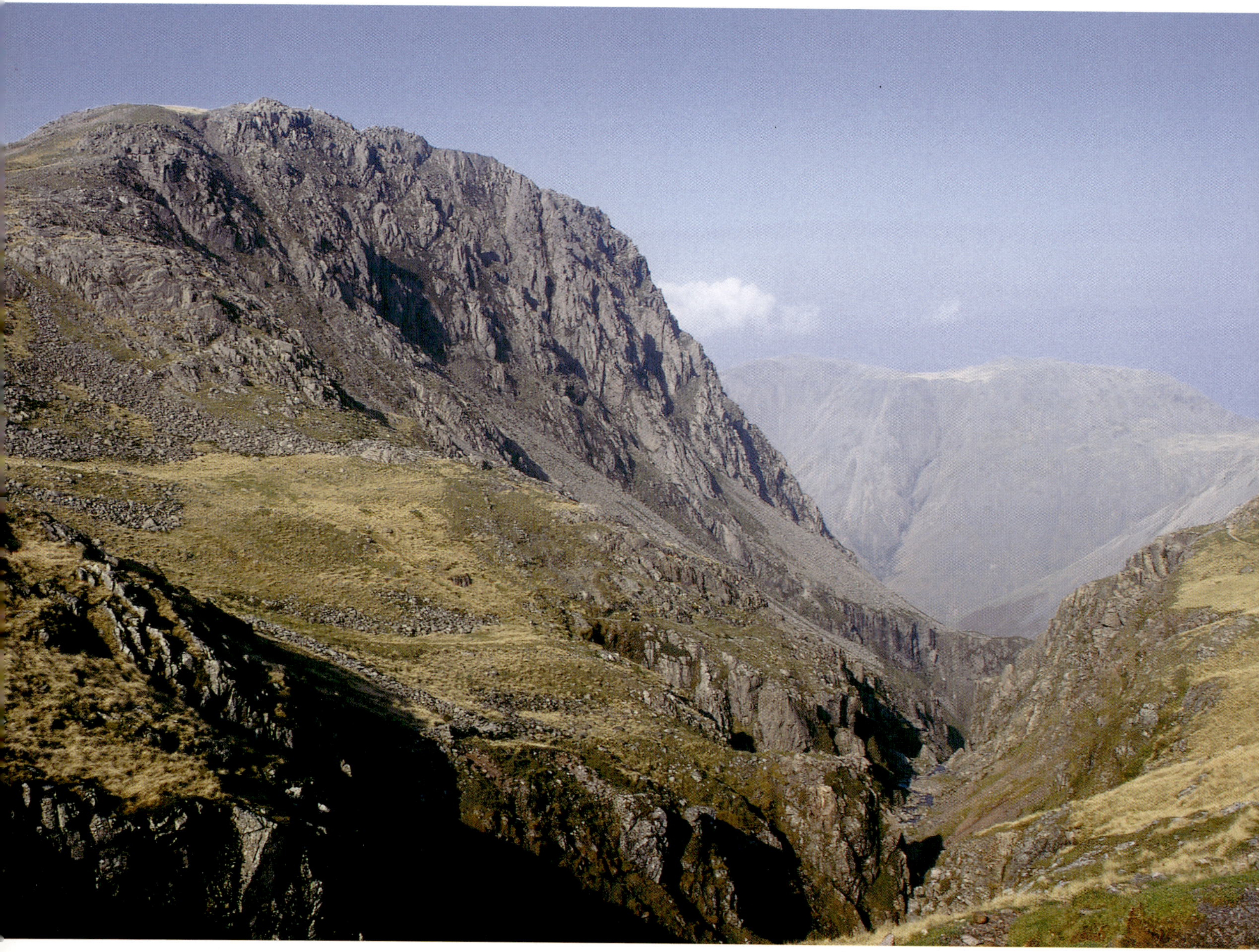

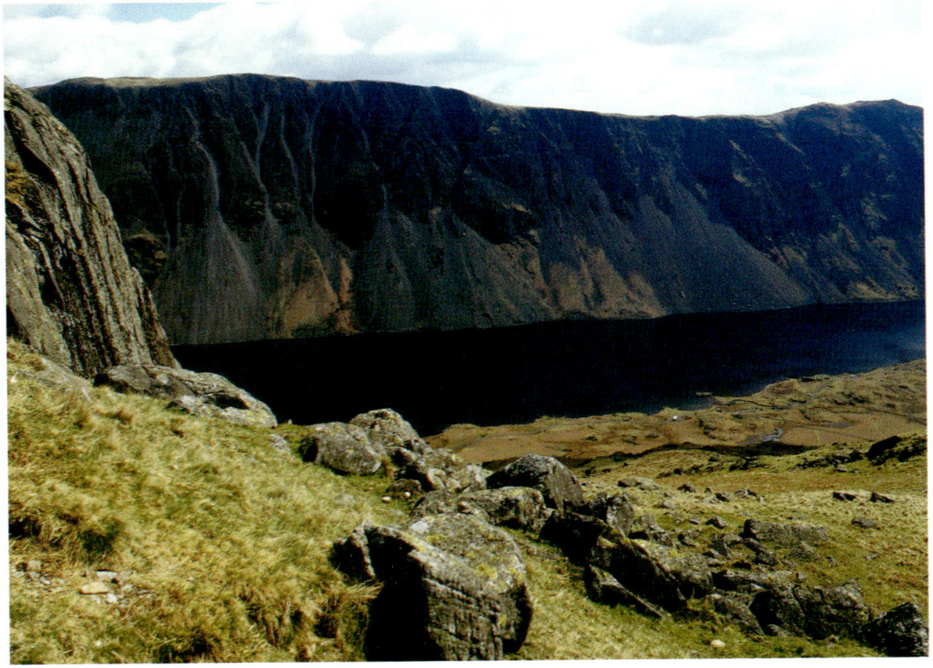

Wast Water, Illgill Head and the Screes from Middle Fell above Greendale.

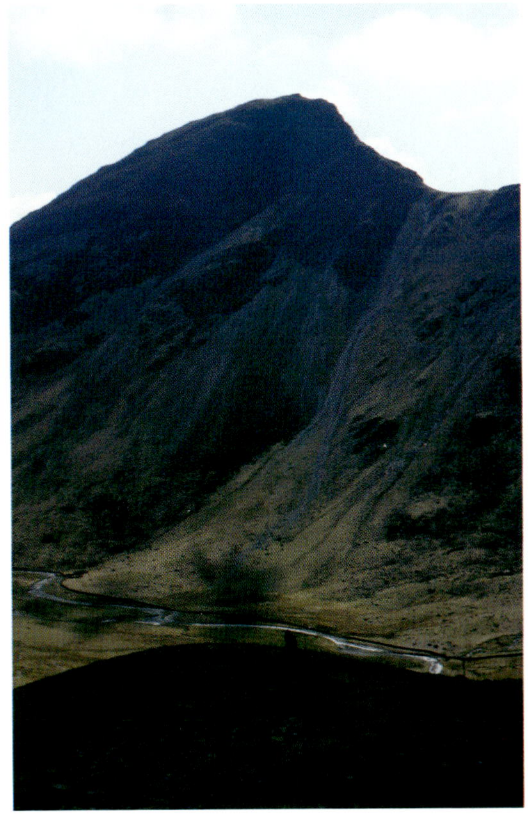

End-on view of Dore Head and Yewbarrow rising above Mosedale.

and unforgettable. It is indisputably a masterpiece of creation. Coleridge was certainly impressed, writing in 1802:

> *It is a marvellous sight/a sheet of water between three & four miles in length, the whole (or very nearly the whole of it's right Bank formed by the Screes…consisting of fine red Streaks running in broad Stripes thro' a stone colour – slanting off from the Perpendicular, as steep as the meal newly ground from the Miller's spout.*

The lake itself is the deepest in England, plunging to more than 80m (260ft), and the mountains behind it are the highest, rising to the summit of Scafell Pike 978m (3210ft). It is these two extremes that combine to make Wasdale Head one of the most outstanding natural scenes in the country.

The dale boasts the most simple and endearing church. Dedicated to St Olaf, but only in 1977, this tiny church looks like a low-lying shed, shrouded by yew trees. At the start of the twentieth century, the church still had unglazed mullioned windows and a soil floor, and was without its own churchyard. The dead of Wasdale were carried across the fells on a corpse road that can still be traced, for burial at Boot in Eskdale.

Opposite page: *No place for the unwary, Piers Gill is a steep-sided, rocky ravine below Lingmell.*

The 'symbolic' head of Wasdale.

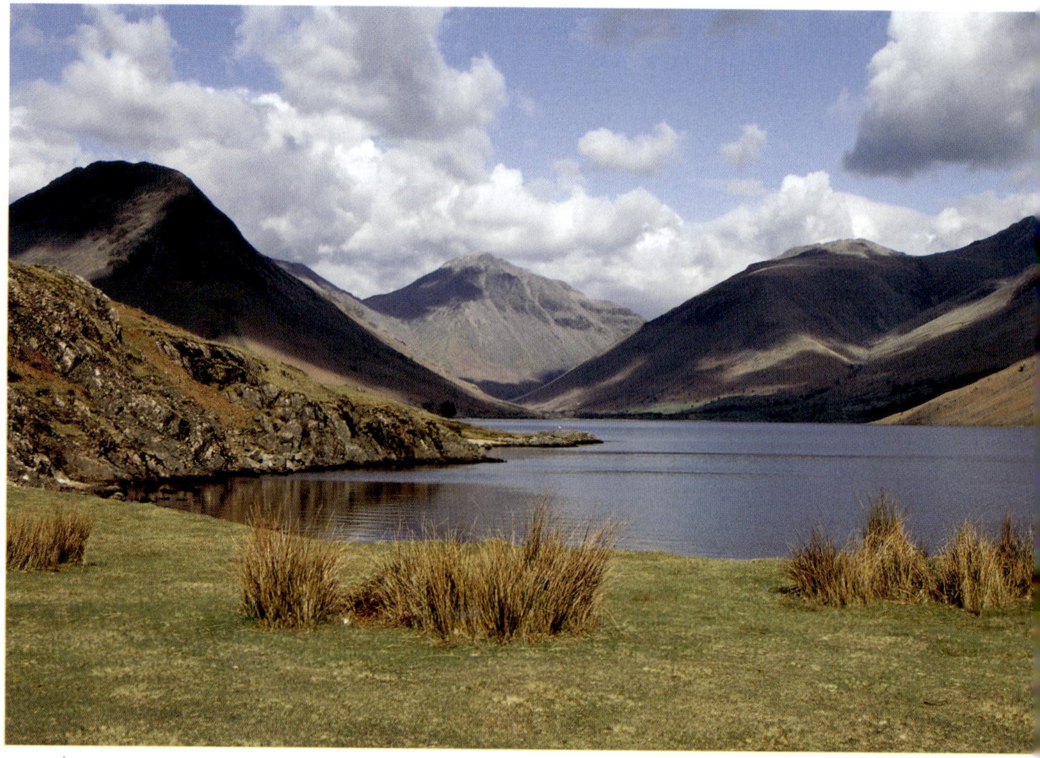

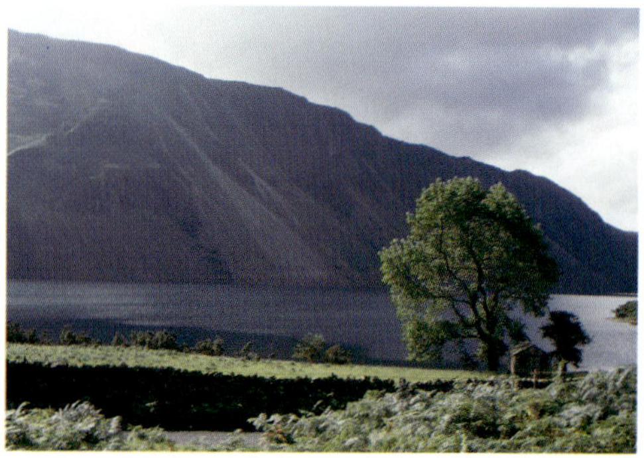

Springtime light spills into Wasdale.

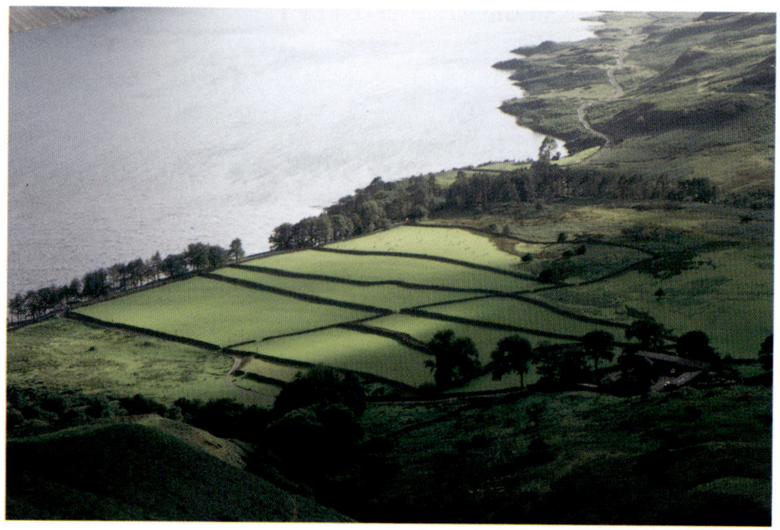

An aerial perspective of Wasdale, seen from the slopes of Yewbarrow.

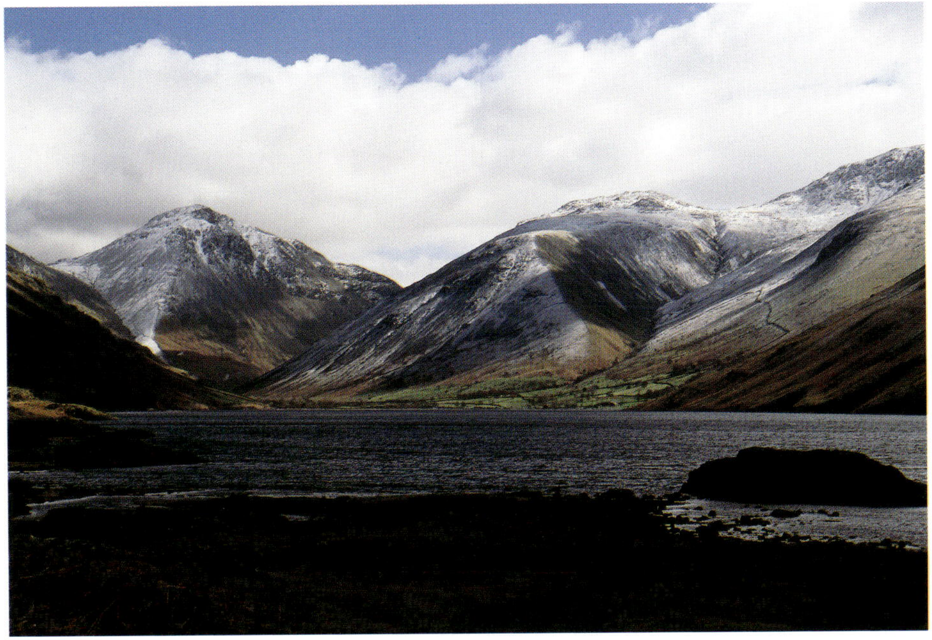

Early winter snows cap Great Gable and Lingmell.

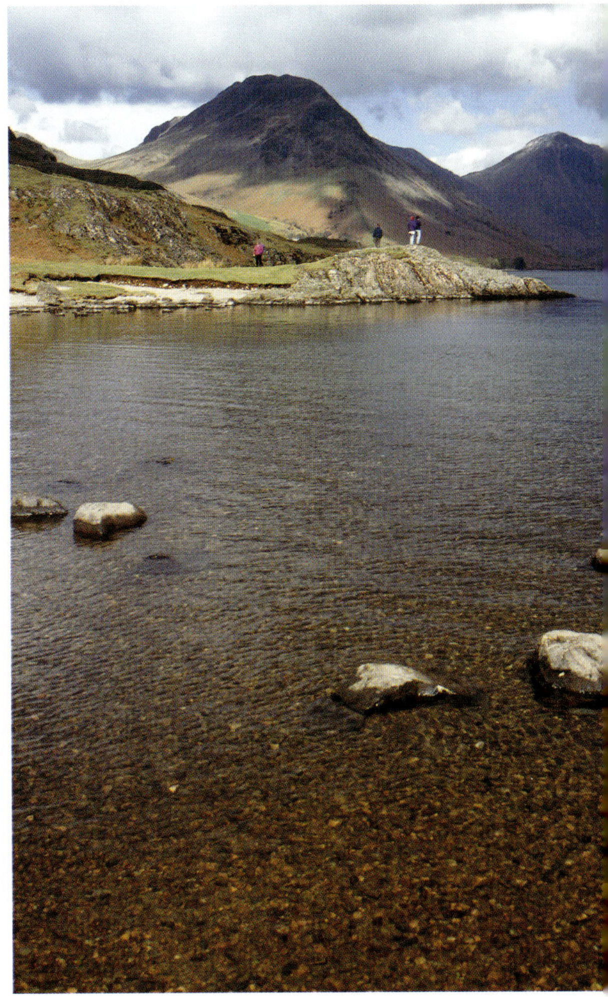

Wast Water shores and Yewbarrow.

Wasdale was, and still is, isolated, and is all the better for it. Even in the mid nineteenth century, the schoolmaster was able to enjoy the privilege of 'whittlegate', a tradition that allowed him to board at the different farmhouses in turn.

It used to be said of Wasdale that it had the highest mountain, the deepest lake, the smallest church, and the biggest liar. The liar was one Will Ritson, who was born in 1808 at the Wasdale Head Hotel. He was a friend of Wordsworth and de Quincey, a famed huntsman, wrestler and raconteur, who became the uncrowned king of Wasdale. But for most of the nineteenth century, he was a one-man tourist attraction, famed for his tall stories, textured with his own dry wit. He was a regular entrant in the competition for the Biggest Liar in the World, and won one competition when, having listened to a range of lies, it came to his turn. To everyone's surprise he asked to be withdrawn from the competition. 'Why?' they asked. 'Because I can't tell a lie,' came the reply.

At the southern end of Wast Water, the dale frees itself from the surrounding fells and has much less of a 'valley' feel about it. The river here is the Irt, which finds a winding course across the now pastoral landscape past Nether Wasdale to Santon Bridge. The church of St Paul in the tiny hamlet of Holmrook

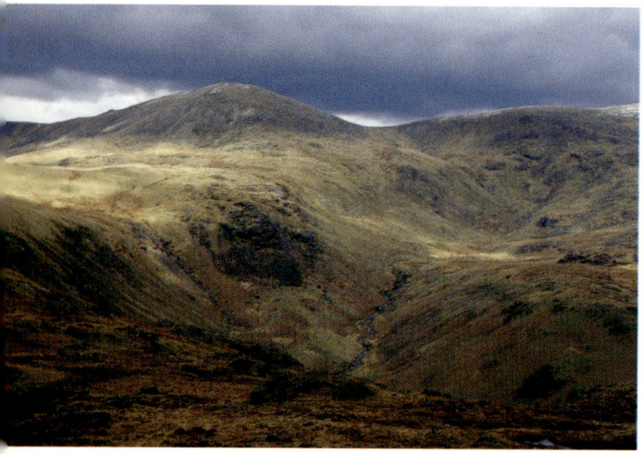

Weak sunlight on Haycock at the head of Nether Beck in Bowderdale.

contains memorials to the Lutwidges, cousins of Lewis Carroll (Charles Lutwidge Dodgson (1832-98)), who lived at Holmrook Hall, now demolished.

Three minor dales spring northwards from the main body of Wasdale. Mosedale is the most easterly, a rough-and-tumble dale that culminates in the rocky headwall of Pillar, and also provides an excellent walkers' through-route across the Black Sail Pass into the wilds of upper Ennerdale. Bowderdale is the name given both to the working fell sheep farm set amid emerald pastures at the confluence of Nether Beck and Over Beck, and to the valley of Nether Beck.

Both Nether Beck and Over Beck provide excellent ways onto the fells, the former graced with some lively waterfalls and a more-or-less direct route onto Haycock, the latter containing the Bowderdale Boulder on which rock gymnasts practice when they can't get onto the tops. The final dale, Greendale, rises abruptly from the farmlands of Nether Wasdale passing the delightful ravine scenery of Tongues Gills into a lovely sanctuary in which reposes Greendale Tarn, a great if rather boggy bowl suspended beneath the heavens. Middle Fell, modest in height but a craggy maze for anyone crossing it, rises to the east, and the immense bulk of Seatallan and Nether Wasdale Common to

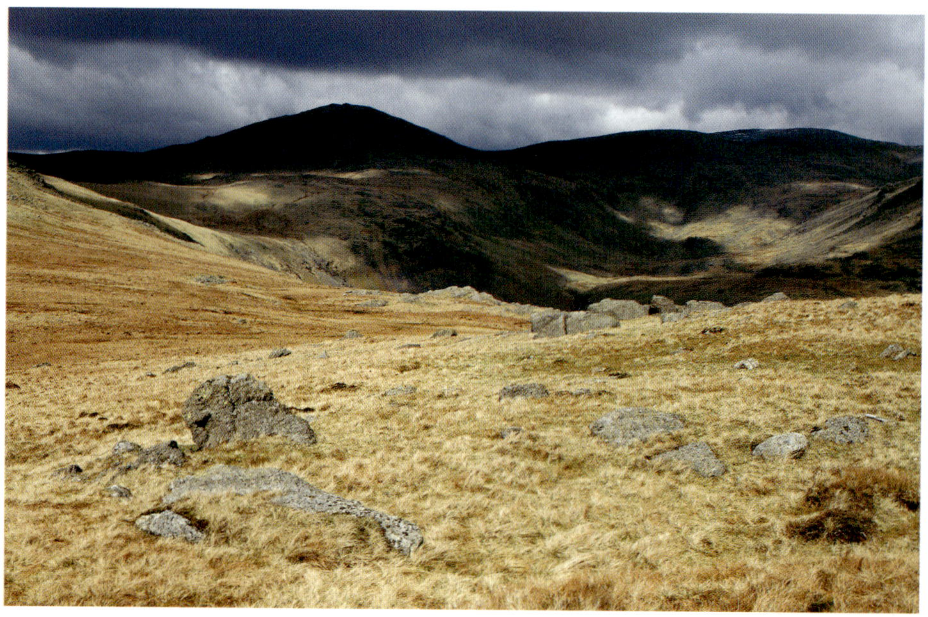

Stormy light over Haycock and the upper reaches of Bowderdale.

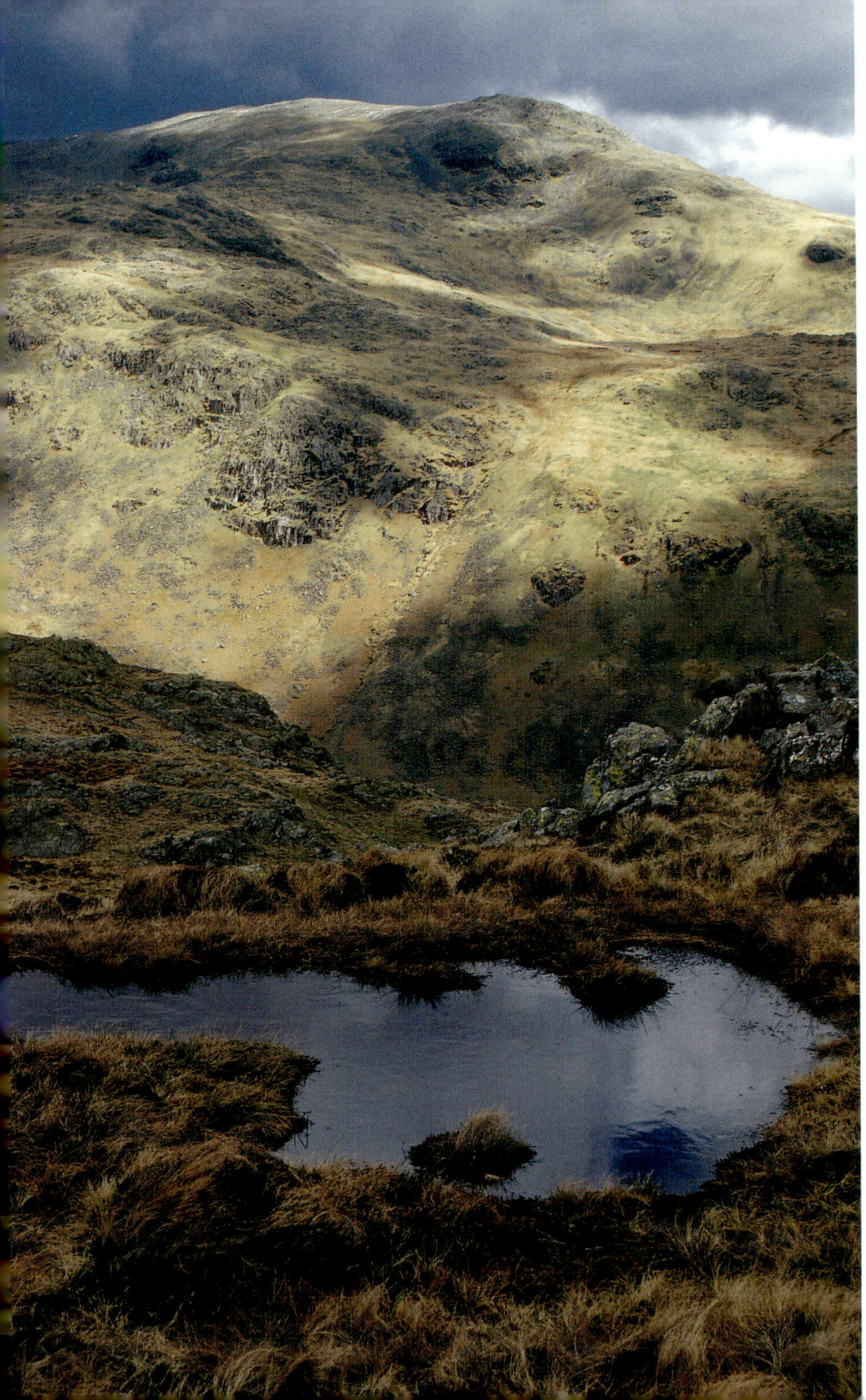

Red Pike viewed across Nether Beck (Bowderdale) from Middle Fell.

Greendale Tarn lies in an austere amphitheatre below Middle Fell and Seatallan.

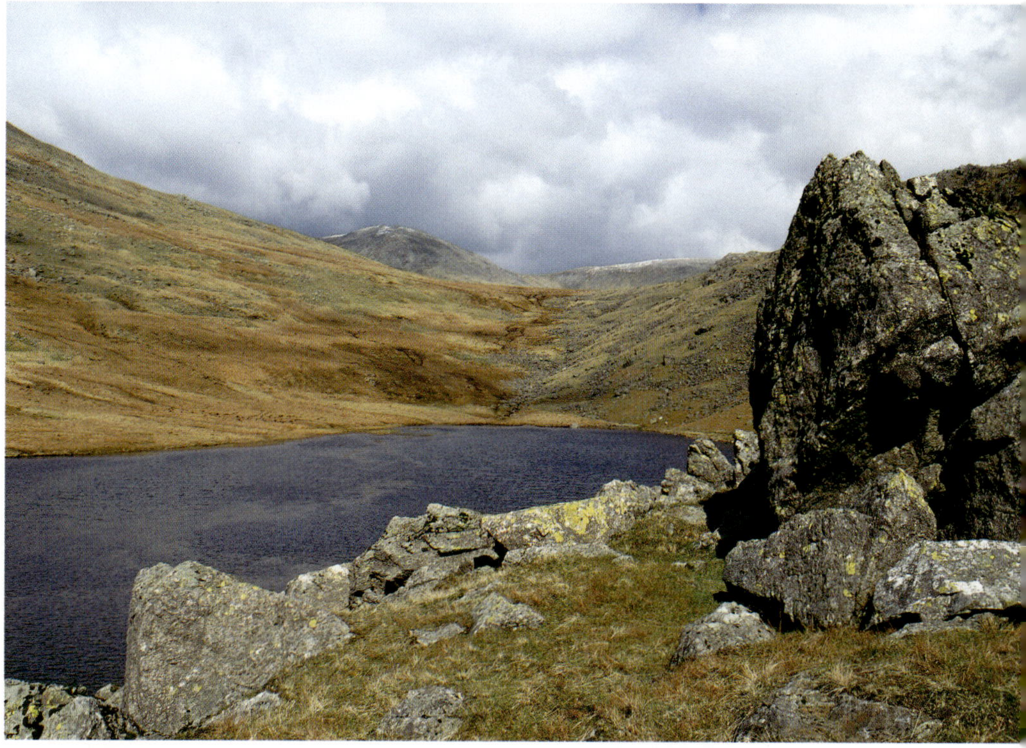

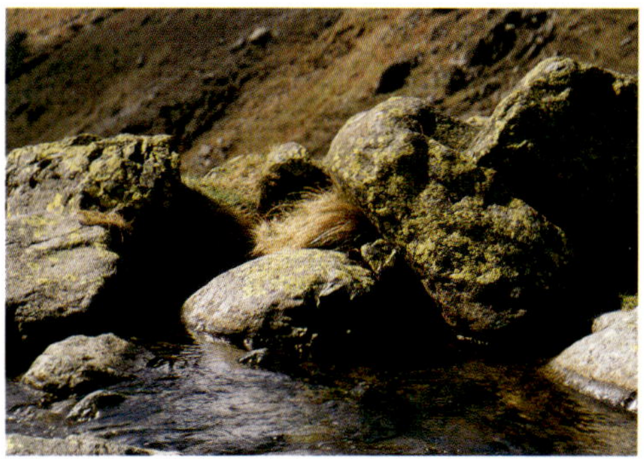

A rock detail at the head of Tongues Gill, Greendale.

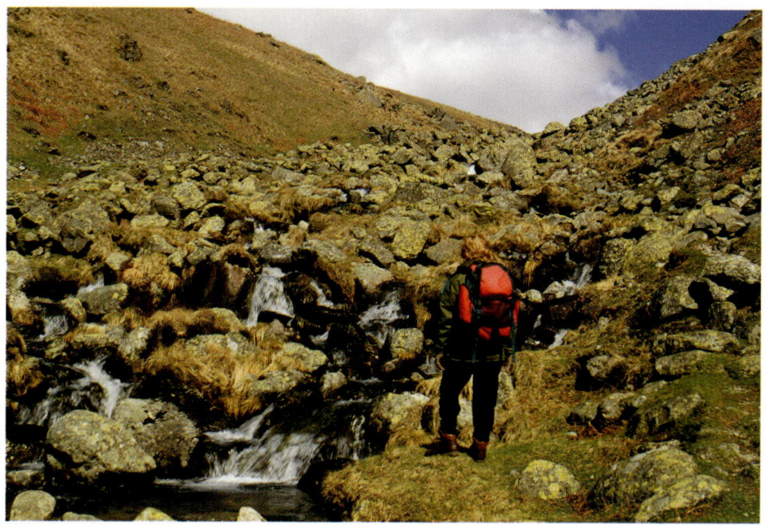

Ascending alongside Greendale Gill.

the west. Unimagined from below, Greendale is one of Lakeland's most peaceful places, and the tarn a sufficient objective in itself.

Further west lies one of Lakeland's secret dales, Blengdale. Few venture into its clutches, few even know where it is, but it reaches roughly north-eastwards from the village of Gosforth into the folds of Nether Wasdale Common and Stockdale Moor. A good track leads up the valley into the pinewoods of Blengdale Forest, a favoured spot for red squirrels. Above, the spread of Stockdale Moor has numerous relics of prehistoric man, including the long barrow that rejoices in the name Sampson's Bratfull. In spite of its proximity to Gosforth, Blengdale is as remote and peaceful as you can imagine. It provides the key to ascents of Ponsonby Fell and Swainson Knott.

At the entrance to Blengdale, Gosforth is the gateway to Wasdale and the ancient Forest of Copeland, and an interesting and busy village that combines old and new dwellings. In former times, Gosforth was a key staging post, where stagecoaches changed horses, but its principle economy was based on agriculture, and the village had its own group of trades, enough to make it self-sufficient. Gosforth is, however, mainly known for its Viking cross, fishing stone and other carved stones built into a toolshed, which is now a listed building. The oldest buildings in Gosforth date back to 1628.

At 14 feet (4.5m), the Gosforth Cross, in the churchyard, is the tallest sandstone monolith in Britain. It is carved with pagan and Norse symbols on one side and Christian motifs on the other; both relate the story of the triumph of good over evil. The cross is believed to date from the late tenth century, and thought to be a relic of the Vikings or their descendants. The base of the cross is carved to represent a tree bole, Yggdrasil, the ash tree of Norse mythology, that supported their universe.

Calderdale

Calderdale lies at the extreme western edge of the National Park, its river rising on the bleak fells of Whoap and Lank Rigg and the rough, grassy expanse of Kinniside Common. It has two major headwater tributaries, the Little Calder and Worm Gill, and flows across a variety of solid geology. The Calder is used as a source of water for industry and for public water supply by United Utilities.

Calder Bridge, a former agricultural village, between Gosforth and Beckermet, is now largely a residential area for workers at the Sellafield Nuclear Power Station. Here, as Collingwood describes, '...the river tumbles over flat tables of sandstone, very picturesque in its quiet, lowland way'.

During the twelfth century, Calder Abbey, just outside the village, was founded by Ranulph fitz William de Meschines, Lord of Copeland, for the Order of Savigny, an order that united in 1148 with the Cistercians. The abbey is now in ruins, and on private land. In 1138, less than four years into the monks' possession of the site, raiders burned down the abbey and drove them away. They walked to Furness Abbey, but apparently met with a less than welcoming reception, so continued into Yorkshire where, at Byland, they founded another abbey.

The oldest packhorse bridge in Cumbria (Monk's Bridge) spans the river Calder and was built for the Calder abbey monks. It is also known locally as Matty Benn's Bridge.

Ennerdale

The River Calder is joined on meeting the Irish Sea by the River Ehen, a river with its source high on the slopes of Green Gable from where it flows through afforested Ennerdale to the village of Ennerdale Bridge. Described by Jack Cunningham, the MP for Copeland, as 'the most numinous dale in Lakeland', Ennerdale is the most westerly of the lakes, and the most remote. It is a deep glacial lake, 4km (2½ miles) long and 1.2km (¾-mile) wide and 45m (148 feet) deep. The water is exceptionally clear, and serves as a reservoir for the coastal towns of West Cumbria.

Progress has been slow coming to Ennerdale: until 1989 it lacked electricity and even today it is the only lake without a public road running alongside it. In spite of that, Ennerdale is probably the most changed Lakeland dale, having been blanketed in the 1930s beneath ranks of dark conifers, a development that raised a tumultuous hue and cry so vociferous that the strength of the objections may well have been instrumental in saving other Lakeland dales from a similar fate.

Opposite page: *Crag Fell and Anglers' Crag across Ennerdale Water.*

In 1883, plans were laid to push a railway line through the dale. Not surprisingly it was also fiercely opposed, notably by Canon Rawnsley and the Lake District Defence Society (the forerunner of The Friends of the Lake District),

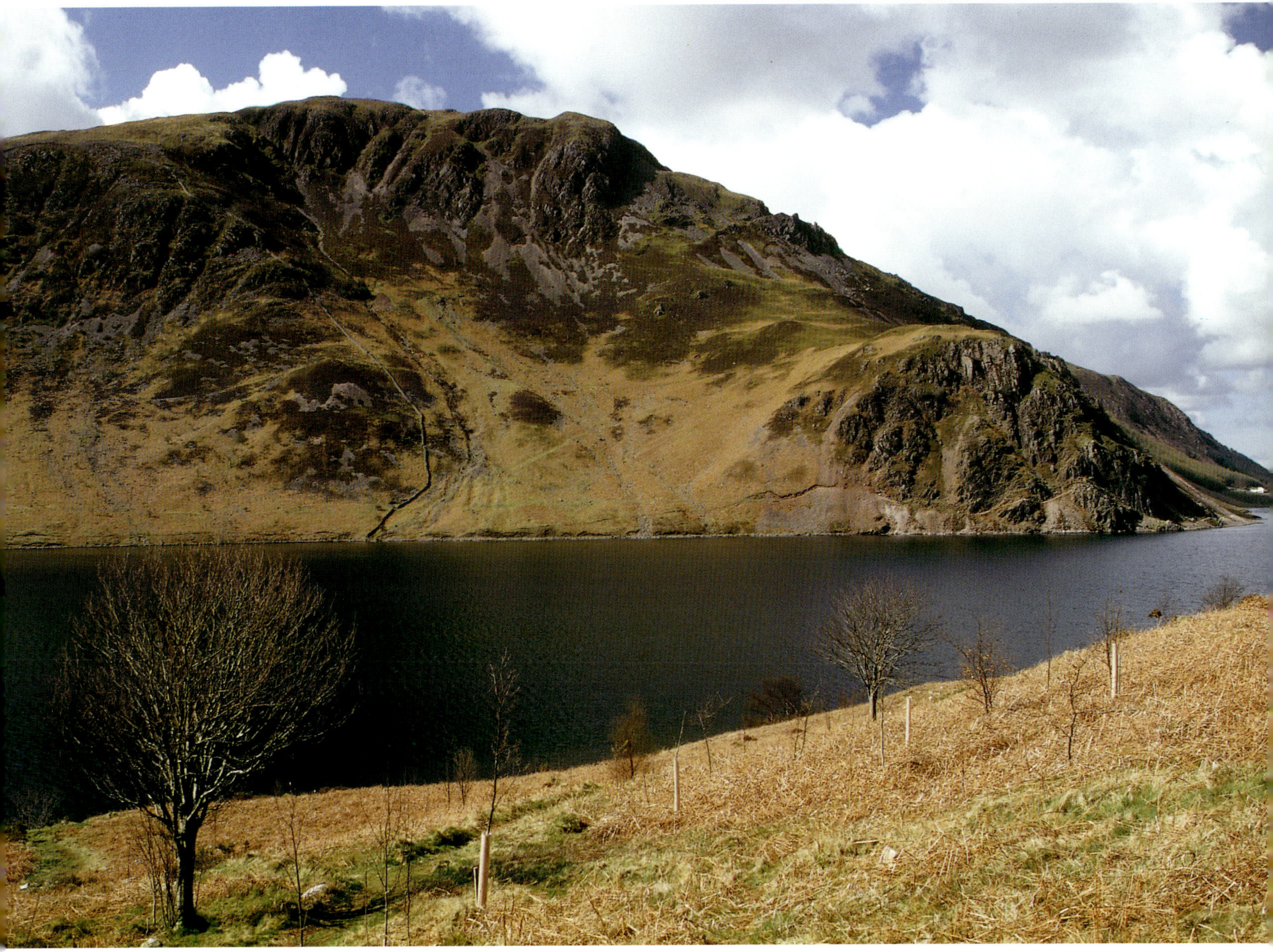

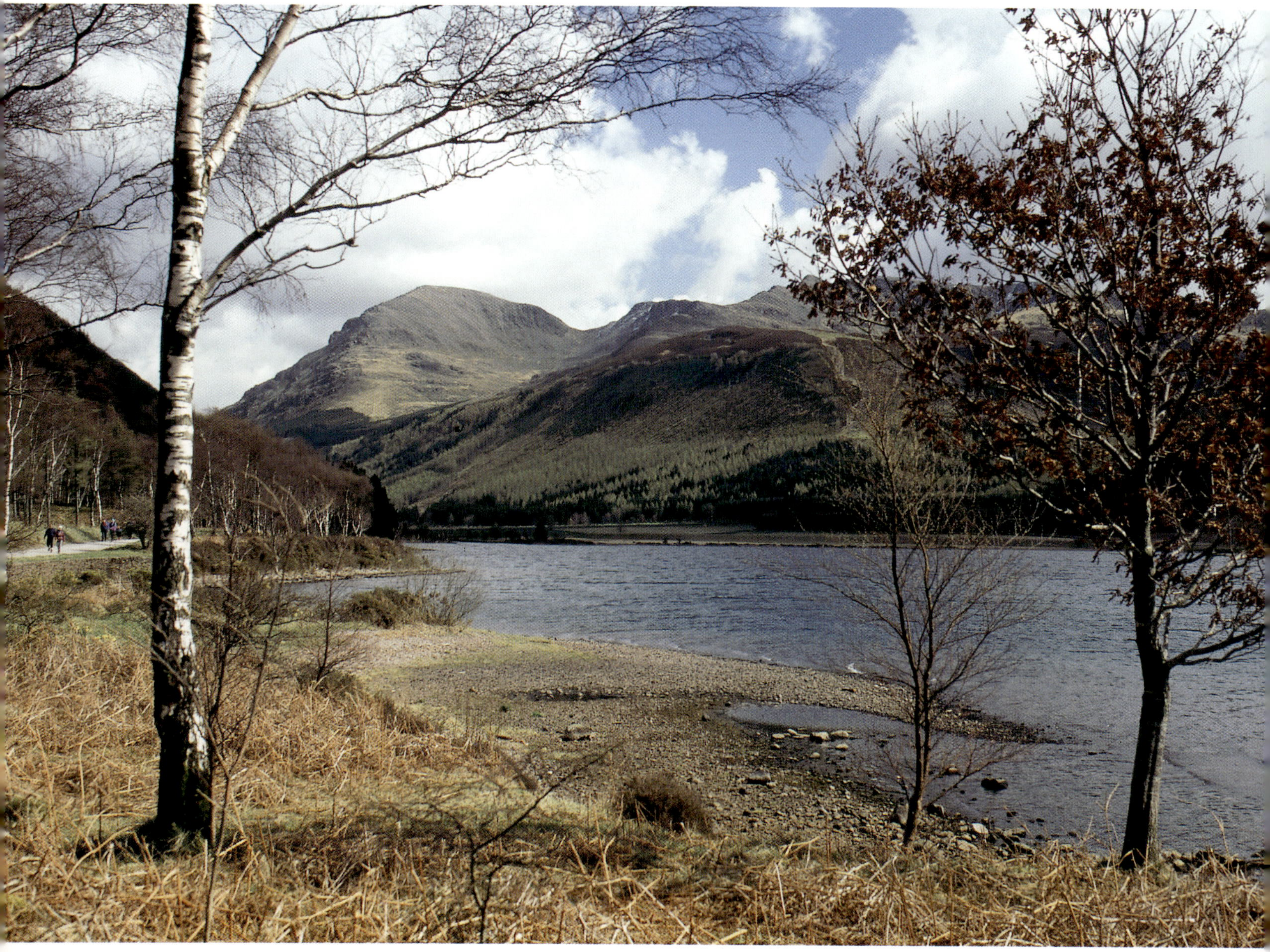

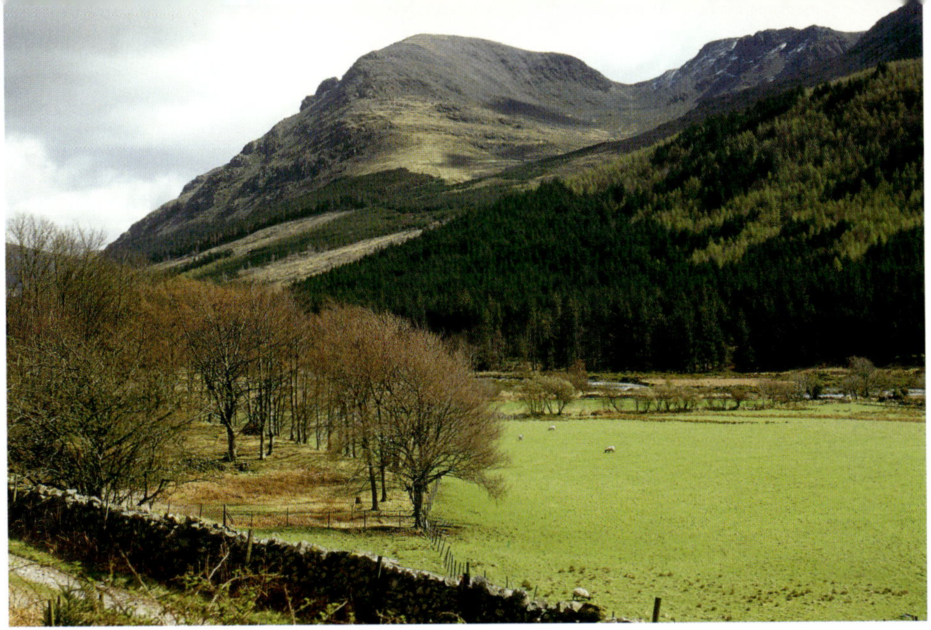

Pillar rises above the plantations and pastoral landscape of Ennerdale.

which had among its members Tennyson, Browning, Ruskin and the Duke of Westminster. The *Pall Mall Gazette*, an evening newspaper founded in February 1865 by Frederick Greenwood and George Smith with the original idea of digesting the news from the morning papers and to publish substantial articles on political and social questions, published a *Poetical Lamentation on the Insufficiency of Steam Locomotion in the Lake District* with the rousing lines:

Wake, England, wake! 'tis now the hour
To sweep away this black disgrace—

The River Ehen leaves the National Park at Ennerdale Bridge. In prehistoric times, iron was smelted here, and much later haematite was mined along the valley. There were also a number of small industries here related to weaving, and the village of Ennerdale Bridge grew as a result.

In Victorian times, the rare black freshwater pearls found along stretches of the River Ehen were sold for a King's Ransom. Today they are protected by the river's designation as a Site of Special Scientific Interest (SSSI). The freshwater mussels on the River Ehen are said to be the only ones breeding in Britain; each can live to be 120 years old.

Opposite page: *Silver birches flank Ennerdale Water.*

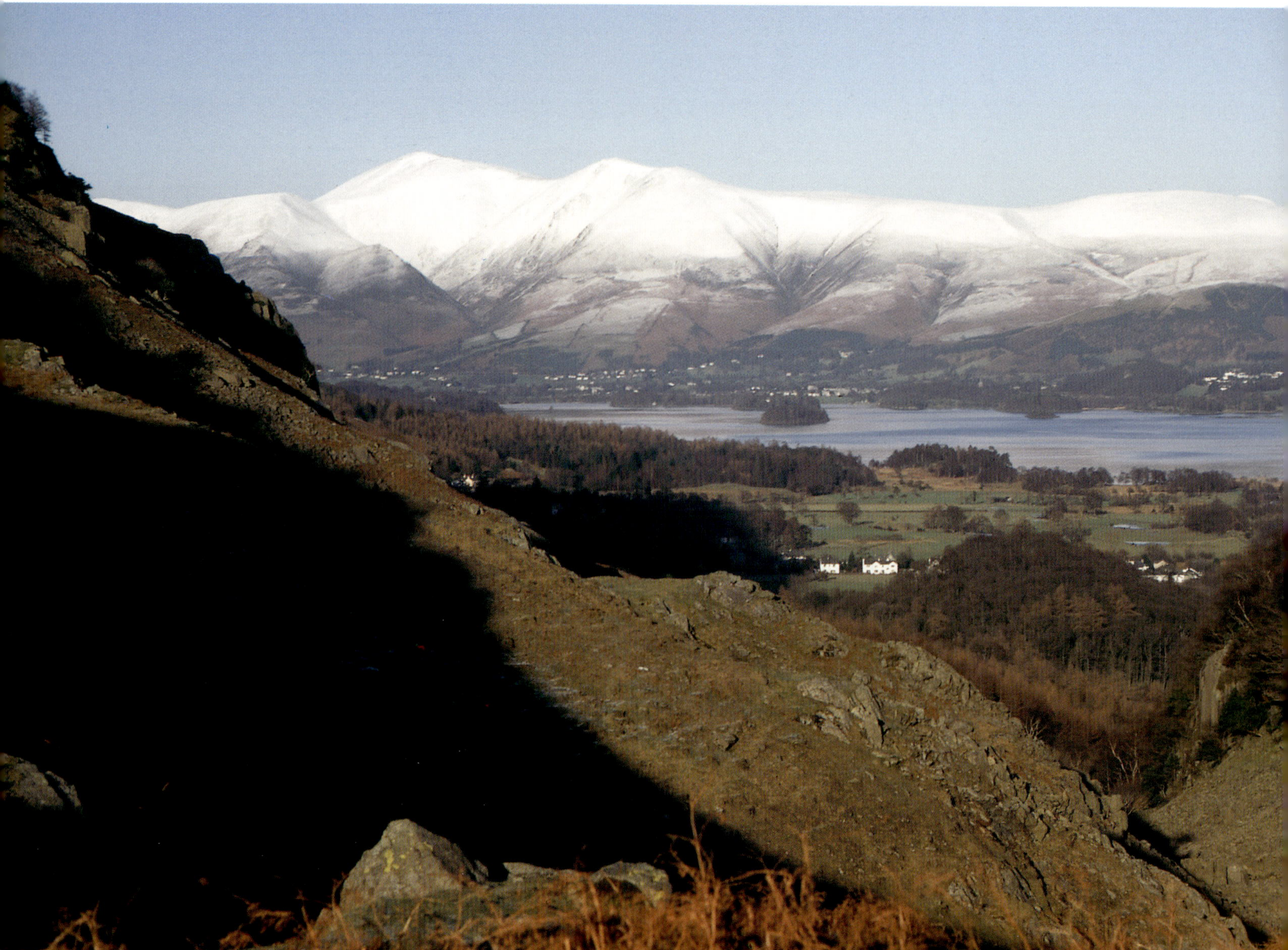

In the company of the Derwent

Borrowdale penetrates to the very heart of Lakeland, its watery thread reaching far into the 'turbulent chaos of mountain behind mountain, rolled in confusion...' that greeted Thomas Gray when in 1769 he ventured into the valley in the company of his Keswick landlord. Gray, a shy, delicate man, unsure of himself, found himself ridiculed by later writers who portrayed him as so terrified by what he saw that they said he drew the blinds of his chaise. Had that been entirely true, he could not have witnessed the hillsides 'clothed all up their steep sides with oak, ash, birch, holly &c... in a place where no soil appears by the staring rock, and where a man could scarce stand upright.'

What Gray unwittingly unleashed on the Lakeland scene was a great measure of curiosity, and an almost indecent haste among writers to jump onto an early nineteenth-century bandwagon. Typical of the time was John Housman's *Descriptive Tour and Guide to the Lakes, Caves, Mountains and other Natural Curiosities in Cumberland, Westmoreland, Lancashire and a part of the West Riding of Yorkshire*, in which he writes of Borrowdale:

> *The verdure of grass, and foliage of trees, now give way to the terrific glare of naked rocks, which overspread the surface with horrid grandeur, and burst out in various huge distorted figures, as if, in this corner of the universe, old Nature had deposited her rubbish during the formation of some happier district*

Gray was not the first outsider to venture into Borrowdale; a minister, Dr John Brown, paved the way for an influx of the curious in his *Description of the Lake and Vale of Keswick*, published in 1767. Brown's 'sensational' prose – 'rocks and cliffs of stupendous height, hanging broken over the lake in horrible grandeur...woods clinging up their steep and shaggy sides, where mortal foot never yet approached' – influenced later writers, though not all allowed their imaginations to get the better of them as Brown had done.

Opposite page: *The Skiddaw Fells in winter from the top of Castle Crag, above Borrowdale.*

Thomas Pennant, usually a reliable observer, paid Borrowdale a fleeting visit on the way to Scotland in 1772, yet even he succumbed to describing the southern end of Derwent Water as 'a composition of all that is horrible', adding:

> *...an immense chasm opens in the midst, whose entrance is divided by a rude conic hill, once topped with a castle, the habitation of the tyrant of the rocks; beyond, a series of broken mountainous crags..., soar one above the other, overshadowing the dark winding deeps...*

Derwent Water

Derwent Water is nowhere better seen than from the slopes of Cat Bells, but one of the most delectable spots here is Friar's Crag, which became 'Darien' in Arthur Ransome's *Swallows and Amazons*, the place that 'dropped, like a cliff, into the lake.' Atop the crag is a memorial to John Ruskin, who first visited Friar's Crag with his nurse at the age of five.

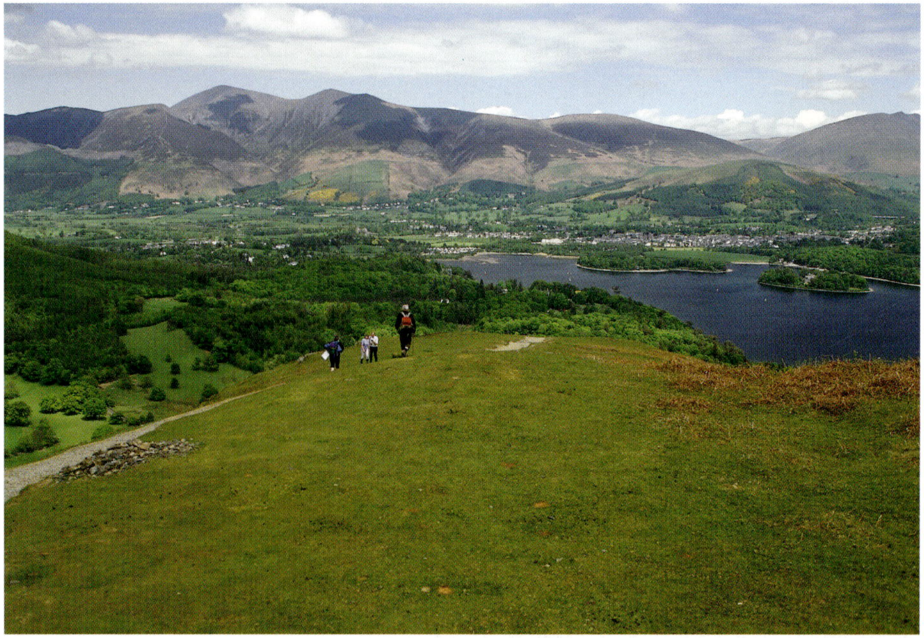

Skiddaw, Derwent Water and the Vale of Keswick viewed from the slopes of Brandlehow.

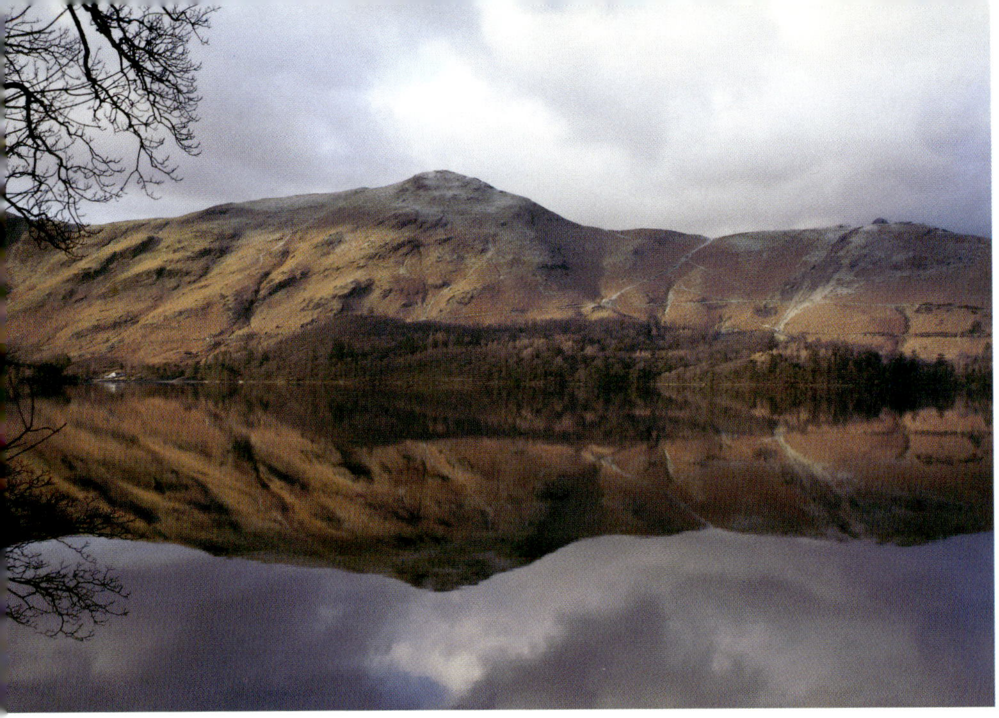

A mirror-like Derwent Water reflects Cat Bells.

The many islands on Derwent Water have played a varied part in local history. Lord's Island was the seat of the Radcliffe family, noted in 1539 by Leland as 'the Head Place' of the family. It still remained in 1653, but by 1709 the house and its gardens were described as destroyed. There is evidence of a bloomery on Rampsholme Island, but nothing now to show of the cell of Saint Herbert who once inhabited St Herbert's Island as a hermitage, and about which Wordsworth penned *The Hermit of Derwent Water*.

From Derwent Isle, the German miners of Elizabethan Keswick, originally imported to work the mines of the Newlands valley, ran all manner of businesses, including a 'brewhouse, a windmill, a pigeon-house, garden and orchard, and a drying-floor for corn.' Local eccentric Joseph Pocklington lived on Derwent Isle for a time, before moving to Barrow House (now a youth hostel), on the shores of the lake. Pocklington, known as 'Lord Pocky', was responsible for staging annual regattas on Derwent Water, and was described as 'a man of ebullient fancy who never understood the concept of restraint.'

The tiny island of Otters Bield means 'otter's sanctuary' and must once have been home to this rare species of animal. At the southern end of the lake lies the occasional spectacle of the floating island. This curious island of peat and roots appears only when the marsh gases on which it rests at the bottom of Derwent Water, contrive to boost it to the surface.

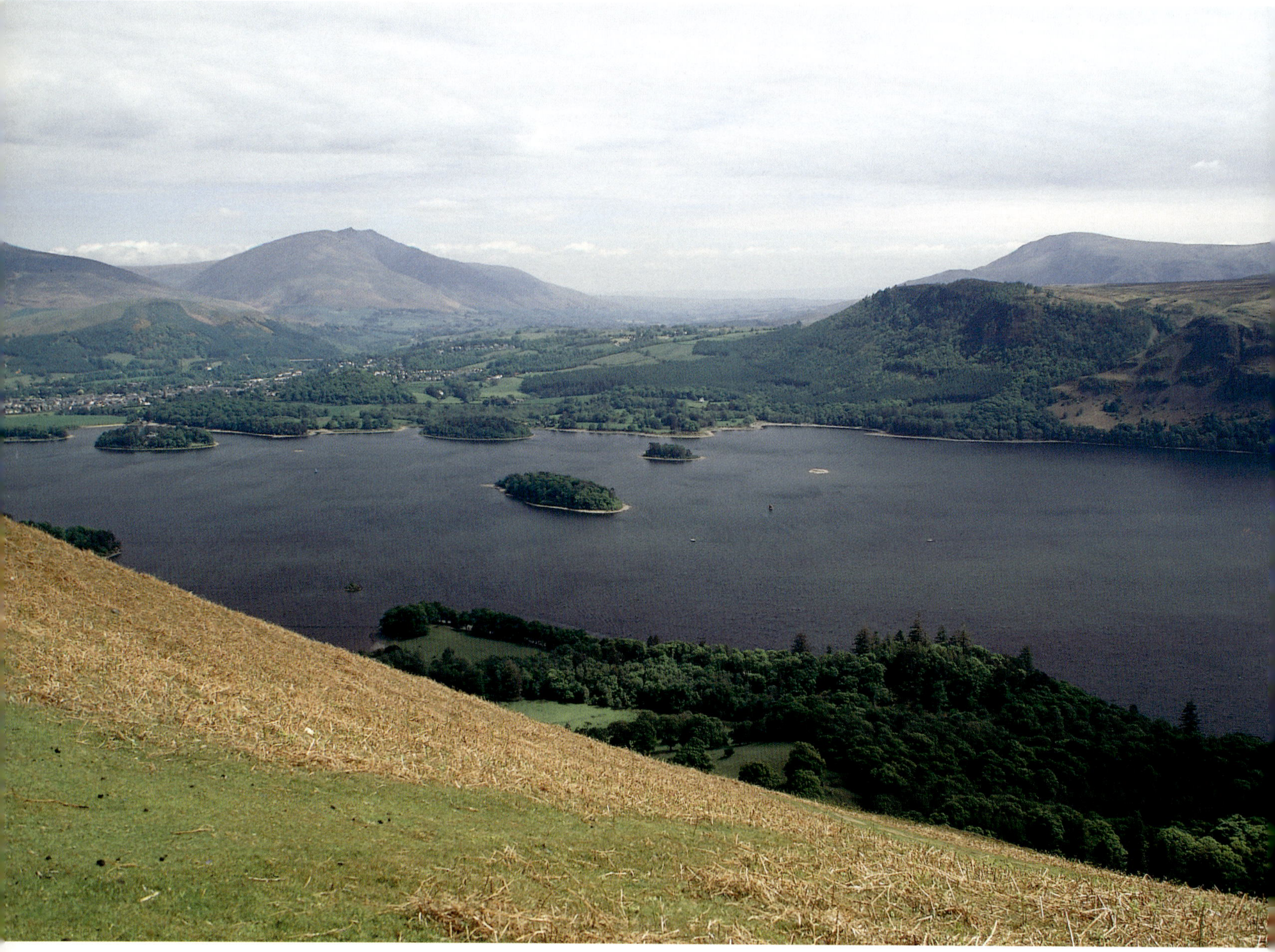

The dale of the fortress

Borrowdale, the 'dale of the fortress', is a lush green vale of contrasts, from luxurious woodland to craggy headlands. As Ann Radcliffe, the English romantic novelist, describes in *A Journey made in the Summer of 1794*, 'Dark rocks yawn at its entrance, terrific as the wildness of a maniac.' Admittedly, Radcliffe and Gray were both writing at a time when it was fashionable to portray places in horrific terms. No one, surely, venturing into Borrowdale today would regard it in such a light. But in the eighteenth century, superstition and the fear of evil and primitive forces was rife, and the people of Borrowdale were thought to be so lacking in intelligence that they had yet to discover the wheel. Once, it is said, they built a wall across the valley to keep in the visiting cuckoo, and so ensure everlasting springtime.

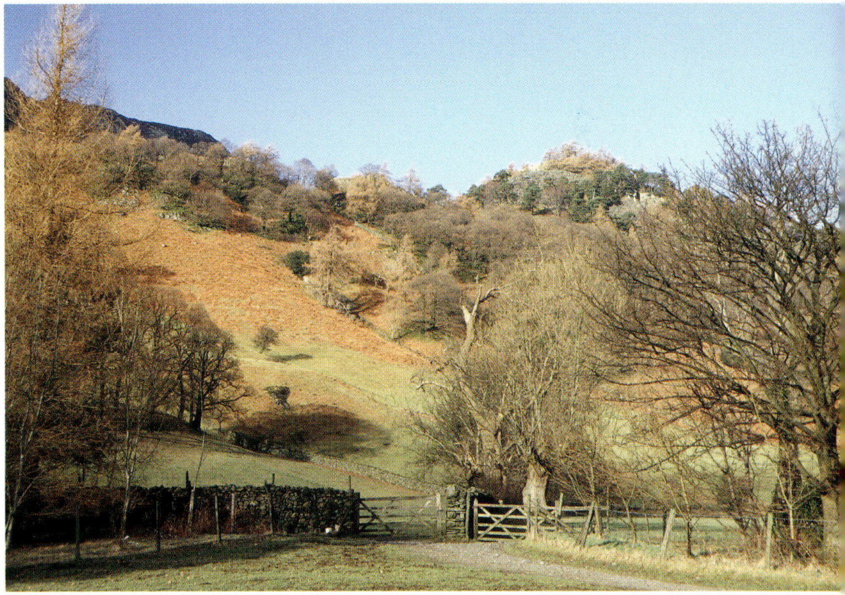

Castle Crag, Borrowdale, from beside the River Derwent.

The woodland in which Borrowdale abounds is probably the greatest expanse of native trees in Lakeland. Of course, the original trees were long since cleared for timber and charcoal production, and what survives today is known as semi-natural woodland, formed by replanting native species, and, arguably, re-creating the character and form of the original natural woodland. Many of the Borrowdale woods are hanging on steep, well-drained slopes, based on the underlying rocks of the Borrowdale Volcanic Series. Most of the trees are a mix of sessile oak, sycamore, rowan, holly, hazel and birch, with alder and willow finding especially favourable conditions in the valley bottom.

Once owned, from the head of Derwent Water to Sty Head, by Alice de Rumelli, heiress of the Barony of Allerdale, Borrowdale is a rather stage-set landscape where everything has its place, positioned to show every feature of the dale to its best advantage, as if an artist had worked on the blueprint. In 1209, the monks of Furness Abbey bought the greater part of the dale, but parts – Watendlath and Langstrath – were given to the monks of Fountains Abbey in Yorkshire. As a result, a huge swathe of central Lakeland was used from the thirteenth century onwards by monasteries for grazing cattle and sheep.

Opposite page: *Derwent Water and its isles.*

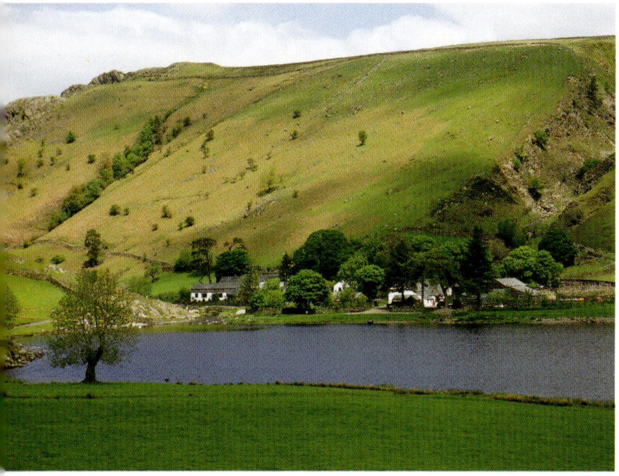

Tucked away among the fells, Watendlath was made famous by Hugh Walpole, who used it as the setting of his Rogue Herries *novels.*

Up Watendlath way

Before you reach the southern end of Derwent Water, a side road branches up towards the hamlet of Watendlath, crossing the lovely simple arch of Ashness Bridge on the way. Once almost legendary for its inaccessibility, the best approach to Watendlath is on foot from Rosthwaite, either direct, over Puddingstone Bank, or via Stonethwaite and up to Dock Tarn. The way up by car is often clogged with traffic, and not at all agreeable during the summer months.

In his *Herries Chronicle*, Hugh Walpole made Fold Head Farm at Watendlath the home of Judith Paris, and for a while there was the danger that Judith Paris might do to Watendlath what Kathy in *Wuthering Heights* did to the Haworth Moors, or Lorna Doone to Exmoor. Thankfully Watendlath, in its cradle in the mountains, needs no such support; in autumn it is a corner of Heaven burnished gold.

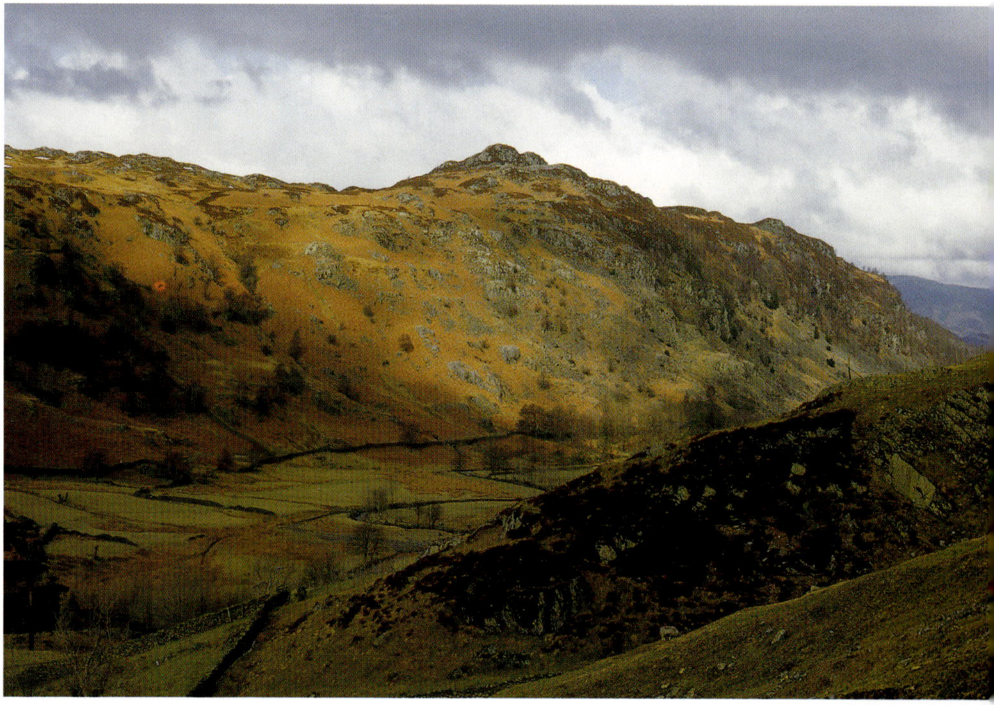

Craggy topknots crown the fellside road into Watendlath.

The setting is magnificent, and at its best as you descend on it in the dying sun from High Tove and Armboth Fell, or along the track from Rosthwaite. Smoke unfurls lazily from chimney stacks, sheep dot the hillside and swans preen themselves on the tiny lake. Fold Head Farm is a classic example of a traditional long house, one that has domestic and farm buildings in a single unit. Walpole describes it as being 'crouched into the soil as though it feared a blow.' One nineteenth-century author considered that any city dweller uprooted and transported to 'Watinlath', 'might sicken for society'. But the solitude which hangs over Watendlath does nothing to deter visitors – quite the opposite.

Not far into Borrowdale, the road meets a unique packhorse bridge, double-spanned and leading visitors to the grey cottages of Grange, which rest amiably in harmony with themselves against the backdrop of High Spy, Maiden Moor and Cat Bells. The name 'grange' is an old monastic term for an outlying farm.

To the south of Grange, lies the wooded constriction known as the Jaws of Borrowdale. Here the River Derwent – its name means 'abounding in oaks' – is pressed in on from both sides, giving the appearance to those timid eighteenth-century explorers that the route was a thinly disguised highway to Hell. Not surprisingly, most travellers were more than happy to view it from a distance, preferring not to venture further into the upper part of the valley.

Had they done so, they would have found that above the wooded gorge the land rises steeply to Castle Crag, an impressive viewpoint and one of the vantage points endorsed by Thomas West in his 1778 *Guide to the Lakes*:

> *From the top of Castlecrag in Borrowdale, there is a most astonishing view of the lake and vale of Keswick, spread out to the north in the most picturesque manner…a beautiful mixture of villages, houses, cots and farms, standing round the skirts of Skiddaw, which rises in the grandest manner from a verdant base and closes this prospect in the noblest stile of nature's true sublime. From the summit of the rock the views are so singularly great and pleasing that they ought never to be omitted… This truly secreted spot is completely surrounded by the most horrid, romantic mountains that are in this region of wonders; and whoever omits this coup d'oeil hath probably seen nothing equal to it.*

To the west, Castle Crag drops dramatically into a narrow valley before rising steeply onto Low Scawdell and Lobstone Band. Like a similar 'valley' a short way to the south, near High Doat above Seatoller, this was probably created by

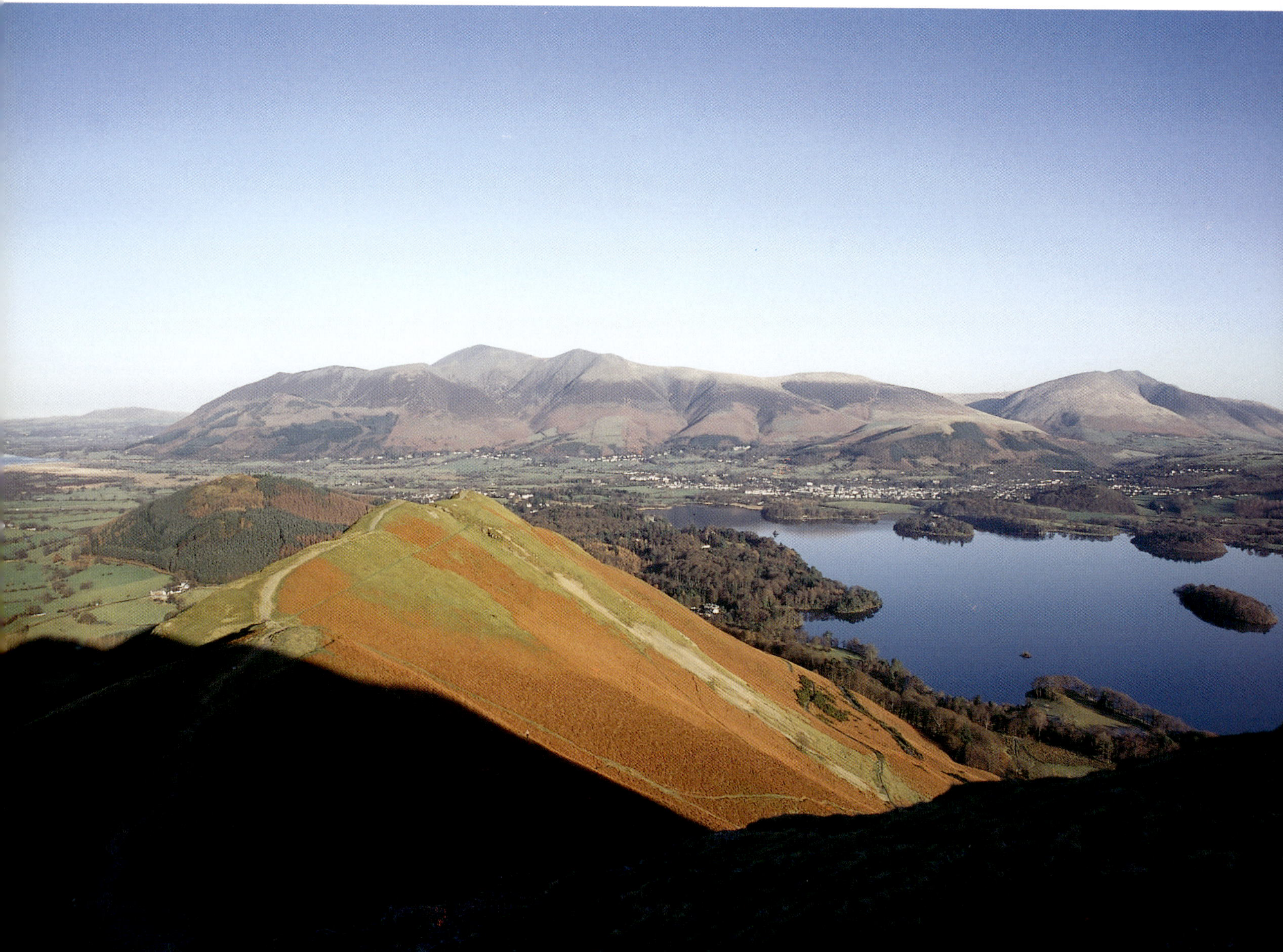

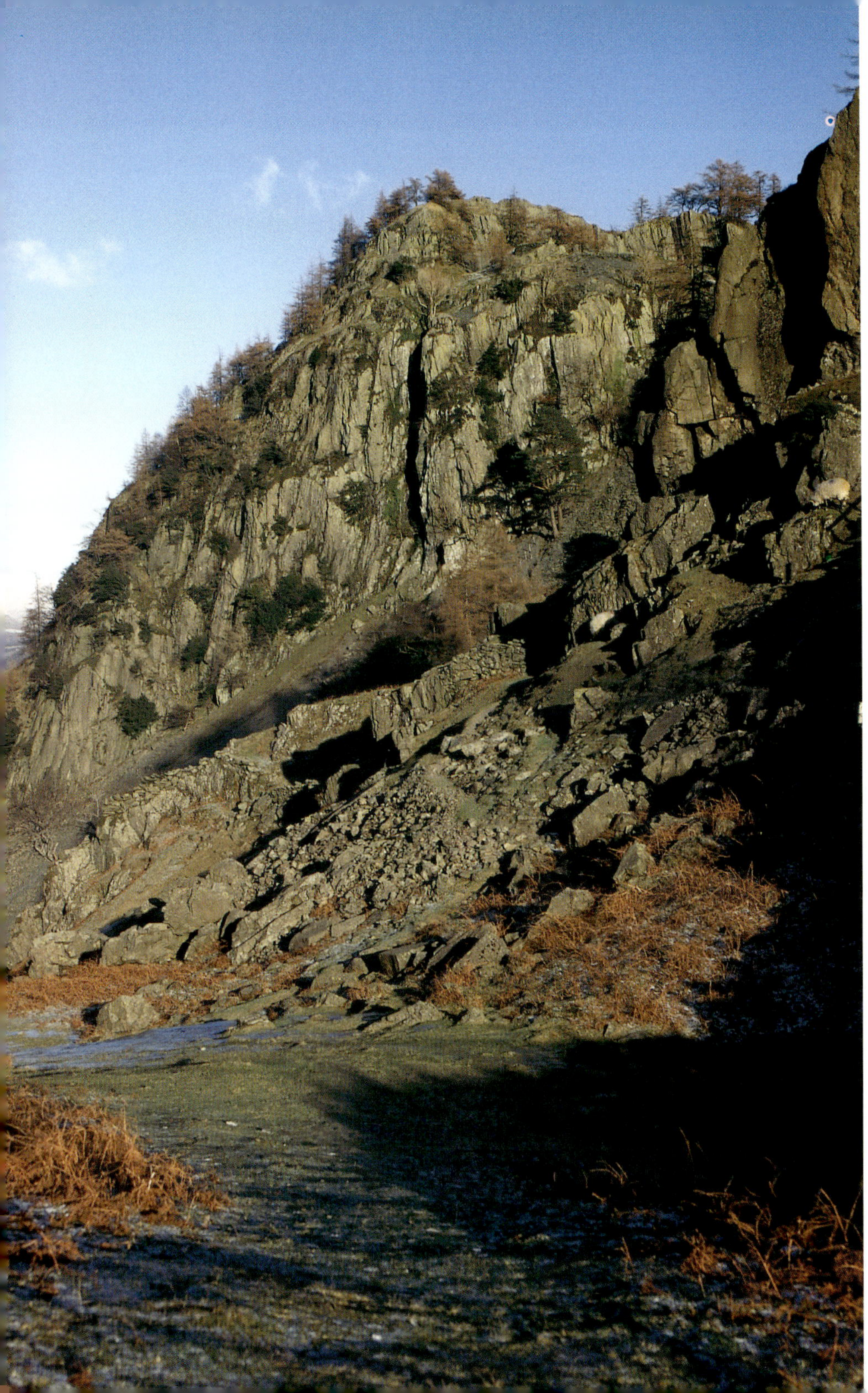

Castle Crag, the tooth in the 'Jaws of Borrowdale'.

Opposite page: *A fine view of Skiddaw, Blencathra and Derwent Water from the slopes of Maiden Moor above Borrowdale.*

a stream running along the upper edge of the glacier that filled Borrowdale during the Ice Age. The valley is now used by the Allerdale Ramble, an 80km (50-mile) hike that begins in Seathwaite and follows the course of the River Derwent, more or less, to reach the coast at Maryport, and thence northwards to Grune Point on the Solway Firth.

A short way on lies a Lakeland favourite, the Bowder Stone, said to be the largest 'self-stone' in England. 'Self-stones' are described as having been primevally formed with little or no link with the surrounding strata. In reality, they are what we know today as erratics, huge boulders dumped by retreating glaciers. The name comes from the Middle English *bulder-stan*, meaning 'a large boulder'. Close by this huge stone, a small cottage built by Joseph Pocklington at the end of the eighteenth century housed a guide employed by him, with the unusual responsibility of shaking hands with visitors through a small hole at the base of the stone.

Near where Rosthwaite now lies, a shallow lake once existed, punctuated, like Derwent Water, by small rocky islets. At the edge of the village stands the Hazel Bank Hotel, the fictional 'Herries' owned by the hero of Hugh Walpole's *Rogue Herries*, and to which David Herries comes, tired from the long journey from Doncaster, in the first pages of the novel. By the time Walpole has penned *Vanessa*, the hotel has assumed its true identity as a 'comfortable little Victorian house' amid, as A G Bradley describes in *Highways and Byways in the Lake District*, 'old-fashioned nooks of ancient cottage masonry and grey moss-grown roofs, ...barking collies and soft, swishing sound of travelling sheep'.

At Rosthwaite, the main thrust of the Derwent valley is joined by the side dale of Langstrath, a narrow, wild and rugged route that rises to the Stake Pass and thence into Langdale. Here the lush greenness of Borrowdale gives way to a no less dramatic but rather more craggy landscape. North of Eagle Crag – a sure indicator that eagles were once plentiful in the Lakes – Stonethwaite Beck is joined by Greenup Gill, flowing down from Greenup Edge, beyond which lies Far Easedale and the way down to Grasmere.

Prehistoric man would have seen the long neck of Stonethwaite as a lake. A collection of moraines near Rosthwaite effectively isolated Stonethwaite from the main glacial trough of the valley, impounding water behind them. Even now, Stonethwaite Beck has to wriggle a little to find its way into the Derwent.

Opposite page: *Early winter snow covers the fellsides of Borrowdale and Stonethwaite.*

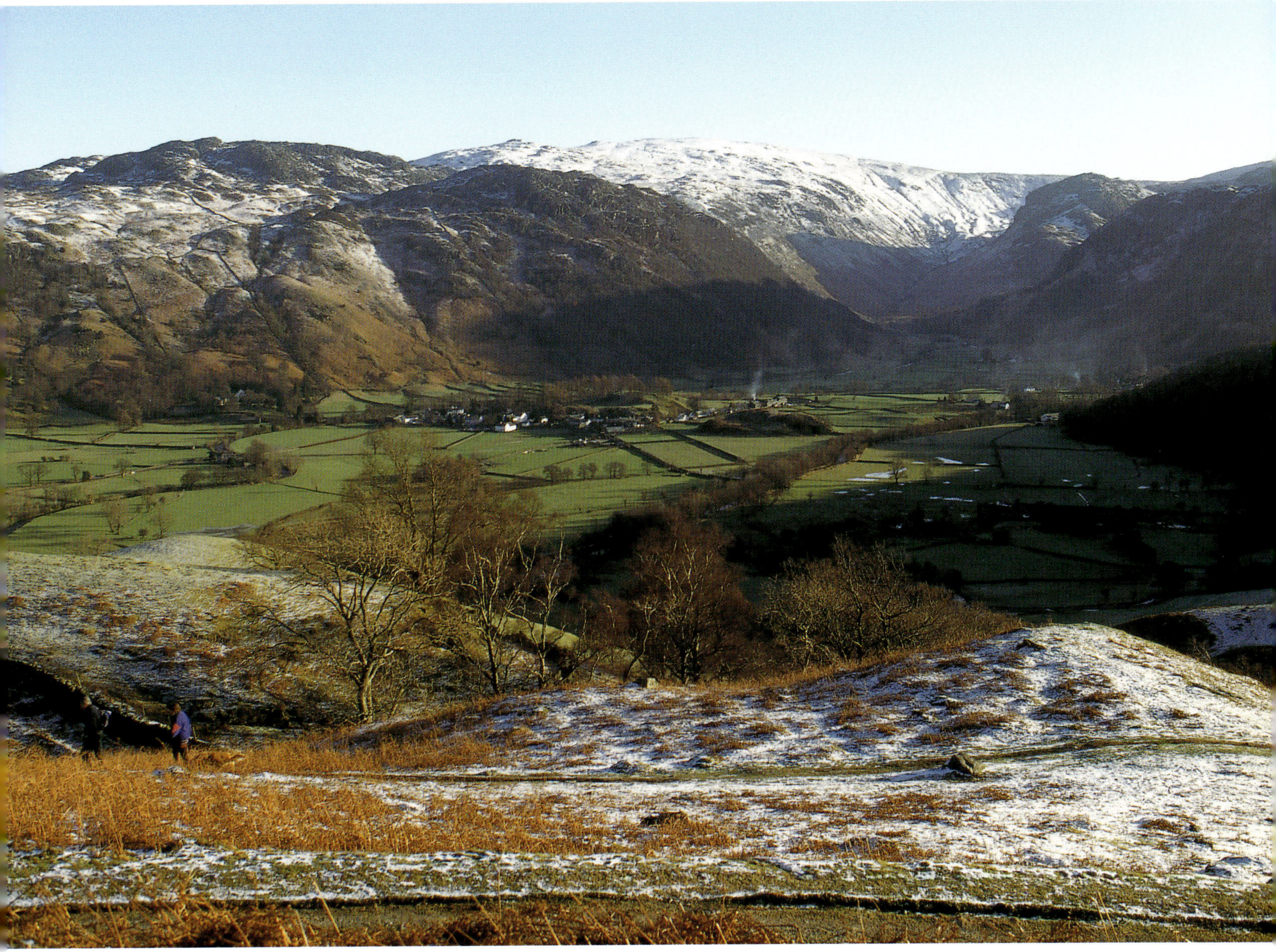

Man Hunt

At Seatoller, perched at the edge of another Ice Age lake, the dale gathers the hanging valley of Little Gatescarthdale, through which flows Hause Gill. The climb to the top of the valley, to the Honister Pass and its slate quarries, is always better on foot than by car. Initially, this is narrow and steep, but then the gradient eases, the bends of an old roadway are encountered, and the route climbs steadily, passing through hummocky drift left by a retreating glacier.

Seatoller, a huddle of cottages, means 'the summer pasture (*saetr*) with the alder tree'. Alders, of course, like water, which is just as well, because Seatoller, Seathwaite and Styhead vie with one another for the dubious distinction of being England's wettest place.

Concealing its history behind a modest façade, Seatoller House, now a guest house, has interesting connections. The earliest extant visitors' book contains an entry, dated 1887, by 'an old visitor for 10 years', and there is a suggestion that the artist John Constable (1776-1832) may have stayed at the house. It was certainly popular with a group known as the Cambridge Apostles, including among them the young historian George Macaulay Trevelyan, the composer Ralph Vaughan-Williams and philosopher George Edward Moore, who held a reading party at Seatoller House at Easter 1895.

In 1898 three Cambridge undergraduates, Trevelyan, mountaineer Geoffrey Winthrop Young and one Sidney McDougall, devised the 'Man Hunt' – a game of hare and hounds over the central Lakeland fells, inspired by the great man hunt in Robert Louis Stevenson's *Kidnapped*. The hunt crosses the fells above Seatoller, over Sty Head Pass to Wasdale Head, then up Mosedale Beck over Looking Stead, to Scarth Gap and on to Gatesgarth, up and over Honister Pass to Seatoller. The Hunt split in 1901, one thereafter being organised by Trinity College, Cambridge and the other by the Trevelyan family. Both hunts still continue to meet at Seatoller House every year.

Before the Second World War, many of the guests were politicians and university men, but a frequent visitor was a keen mountaineer by the name of Charles Edward Montague, sometime staff writer for the *Manchester Guardian*, who found Seatoller House 'Uncommon good'. He is best-known among the climbing fraternity for his story *In Hanging Garden Gully* (1923).

At the head of the dale: among mountains

The farm that at Seatoller developed into a small hamlet for the workers at the Honister Quarry, has no counterpart at Seathwaite. Here, just a farm and a few cottages exist, the launch-pad for excursions into the surrounding fells, including Scafell Pike which, arguably, has its finest line of ascent from Seathwaite.

Just above the farm to the right of Sour Milk Gill are the remains of old mines where graphite – 'wad' or 'wadd' as it was known – was extracted. Known also as black cawke, plumbago and blacklead, it was discovered here sufficiently long ago for it to be mentioned in Camden's *Britannica*. At the end of the eighteenth century, these mines were largely responsible for the development of the Keswick pencil industry. But there were other uses for graphite: for marking sheep, rust-proofing, making metal castings, cannon balls, for 'blackleading' stoves and, consumed with a modicum of ale, as a panacea for just about everything.

To the right of the mine is a strip of woodland, and at its base the dark shape of yew trees. These are the present-day 'Borrowdale Yews', replacements for those 'fraternal Four of Borrowdale, joined in one solemn and capacious grove', celebrated by Wordsworth in *Yew Trees*. The original specimens were badly damaged in a storm in 1883.

Sour Milk Gill reaches Seathwaite from its catchment in the hanging valley of Gillercomb. From the farm, a good path climbs beside the falls, presses through the glacial moraine at the corrie lip, and continues to reach Green Gable. Sandwiched neatly between Grey Knotts to the north and Base Brown, Gillercomb is a popular through route, but still offers the seeker of solitude a few places to perch in sheltered tranquillity.

From Seathwaite a packhorse trail follows the Derwent south through more hummocky moraine to Stockley Bridge, a neatly constructed single arch bridge, but one which in 1966 felt the full force of a flooded Grains Gill and was badly damaged. The name 'Stockley Bridge' has an unusual distinction in being formed from two elements of Old English, rather than the pre-dominant Scandinavian roots. The name means 'the place in the clearing', suggesting that lowland farmers brought their animals here for summer grazing.

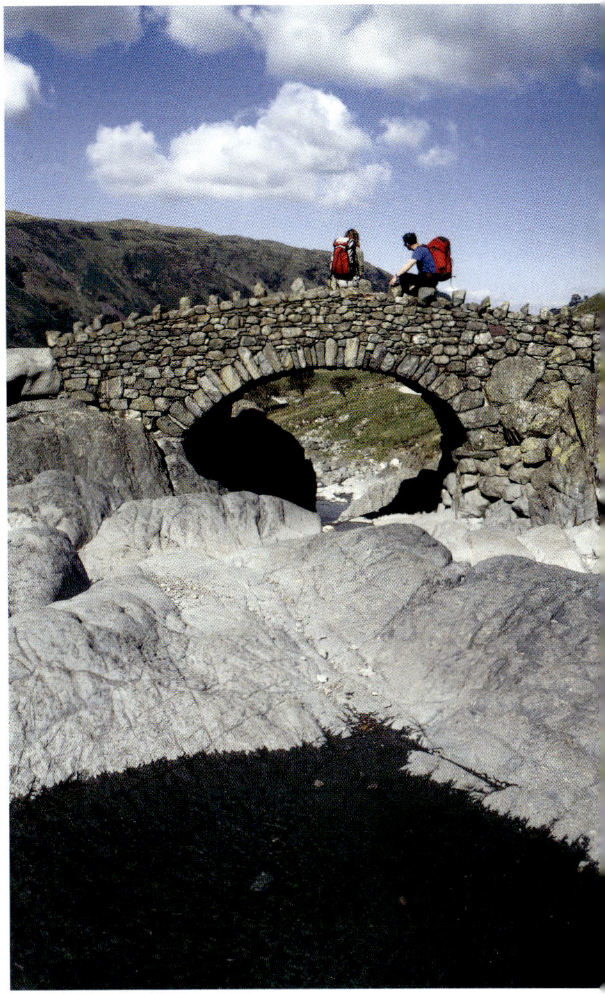

Demolished by floods in 1966, Stockley Bridge is one of the best-known single-arch bridges in Lakeland.

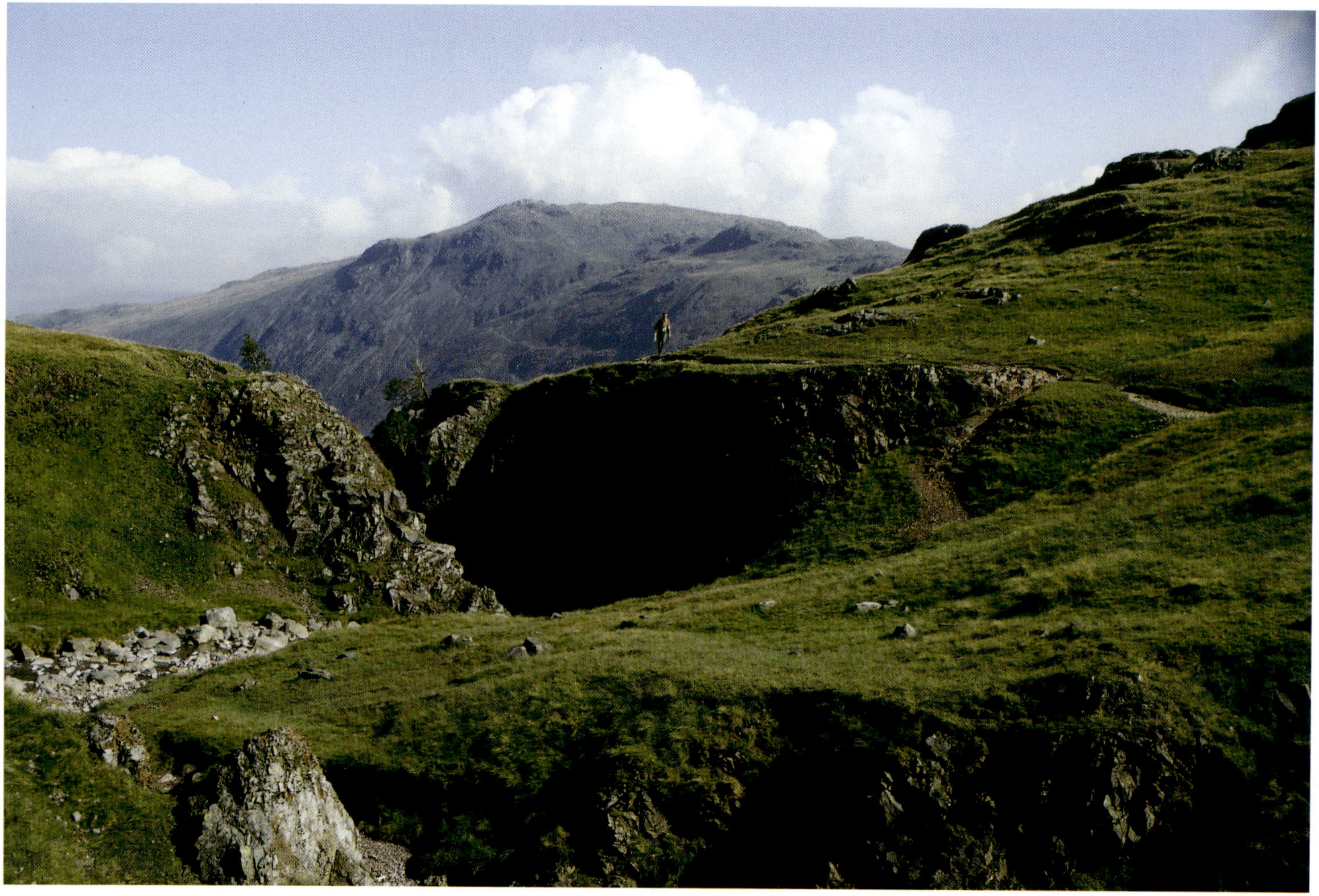

The infant River Derwent sets off down the ravine of Ruddy Gill.

Great End viewed across the still waters of Styhead Tarn.

Just below the bridge, the upper valley divides once more, sending one arm southwards along the course of Grains Gill and into Ruddy Gill below the stern crags of Great End, and another by way of Taylorgill Force and Styhead Gill to Styhead Tarn.

The Grains Gill branch eventually reaches Esk Hause, the highest mountain pass in Lakeland and the source of the Derwent both here, where the land drains northwards, and to the east of Allen Crags, where it drains into Angle Tarn before spilling into Langstrath. Quite where the definitive source of the Derwent lies is probably an academic nicety – the summit of Great End, perhaps?

Up here crags encircle, and high fells, resting on a hazy blue-green landscape that ripples southwards to the sea, stand temptingly within easy reach. Dorothy Wordsworth, with her friend Elizabeth Barker, ascended to Esk Hause in October 1818 and saw 'The green Vale of Esk – deep and green, with its glittering serpent stream'. Without needing to continue into the upper reaches of Eskdale or to England's highest summit, it is a fine outing in itself simply to wander up to Esk Hause and from there back to Borrowdale by way of Sprinkling Tarn to Sty Head and so back to Seathwaite.

There are few places, if any, more inspirational than Sty Head. In poor weather it is awesome; on a good day, the incentive to move on is low. The tarn, beside which Charles Dodgson (Lewis Carroll) walked in 1856 on his tour of the Lakes, lies in a shallow bowl and its sensational setting has tempted many to pitch a tent nearby.

When darkness comes here, it comes with a vengeance; far from city lights, the sky is Stygian black, and the Milky Way an entertainment that can last all night. The tarn is, as Melvyn Bragg describes in *The Maid of Buttermere*, 'a small bleak pool like the last drop in the bottom of [a] gigantic bowl'. The place also features in Hugh Walpole's novel *A Prayer for my Son*, in which a group of friends, escaping from a deranged colonel climb to Sty Head and watch the dawn from the tarn.

Along the Greta and the Glenderamackin

Scarcely does the River Derwent escape Derwent Water before it is joined by the Greta, the river that flows through Keswick, and which, in its infancy, not all that far distant, was the River Glenderamackin and a host of tributaries – St John's Beck, Mosedale Beck and Trout Beck. The name Greta means 'rocky river' from *griót á* (Old Norse). The great dale through which the rivers flows has long been one of the main arterial routes into Lakeland from the north, a route once taken by the much-lamented Penrith-Keswick-Cockermouth railway line.

Visitors entering the northern Lake District along the A66 from Penrith on breasting the slight rise at Troutbeck are greeted by the distinctive shape of Blencathra. To the right lies haunted Souther Fell, the entrance to Mungrisdale, through which the Glenderamackin fashions a lazy course, and the craggy upthrust of Carrock Fell.

To the left the eye alights first on the domed shape of Great Mell Fell, long since explained to me as being, like its sibling Little Mell Fell, simply a collection of 'pebbles' swirled together at the ebb of some Carboniferous sea, millions of years ago. Further round, the Dodds mark the skyline, reaching south to Helvellyn. The whole skyline – Grisedale Pike far ahead, the Newlands fells a little to the south – always arouses feelings of well-being and excitement. In the days of steam, with engines labouring up from Penruddock to Troutbeck puffing billows of cloud and steam into the stands of birch and alder, the train journey to Keswick must have been a memorable experience.

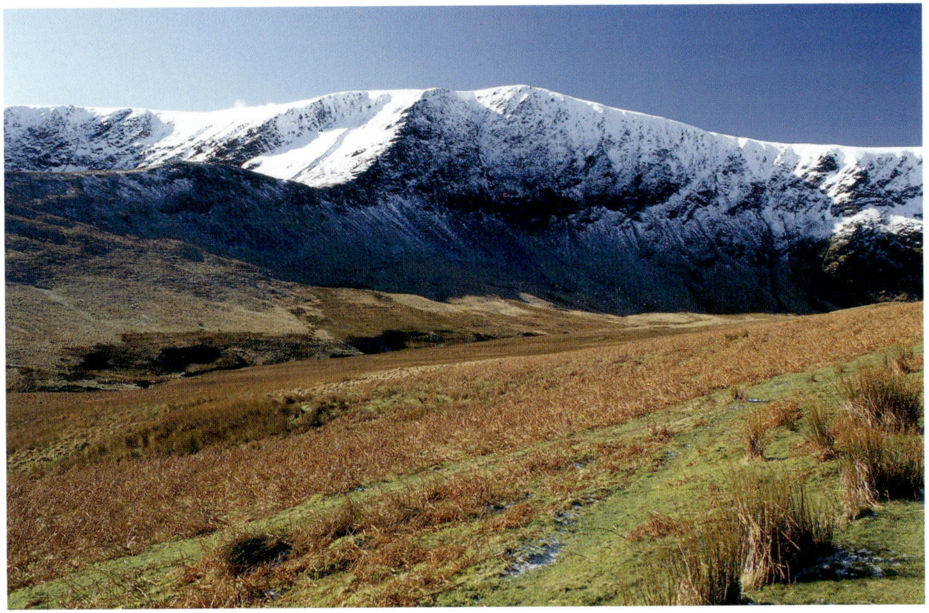

Crisp white crags rise above secluded Bannerdale.

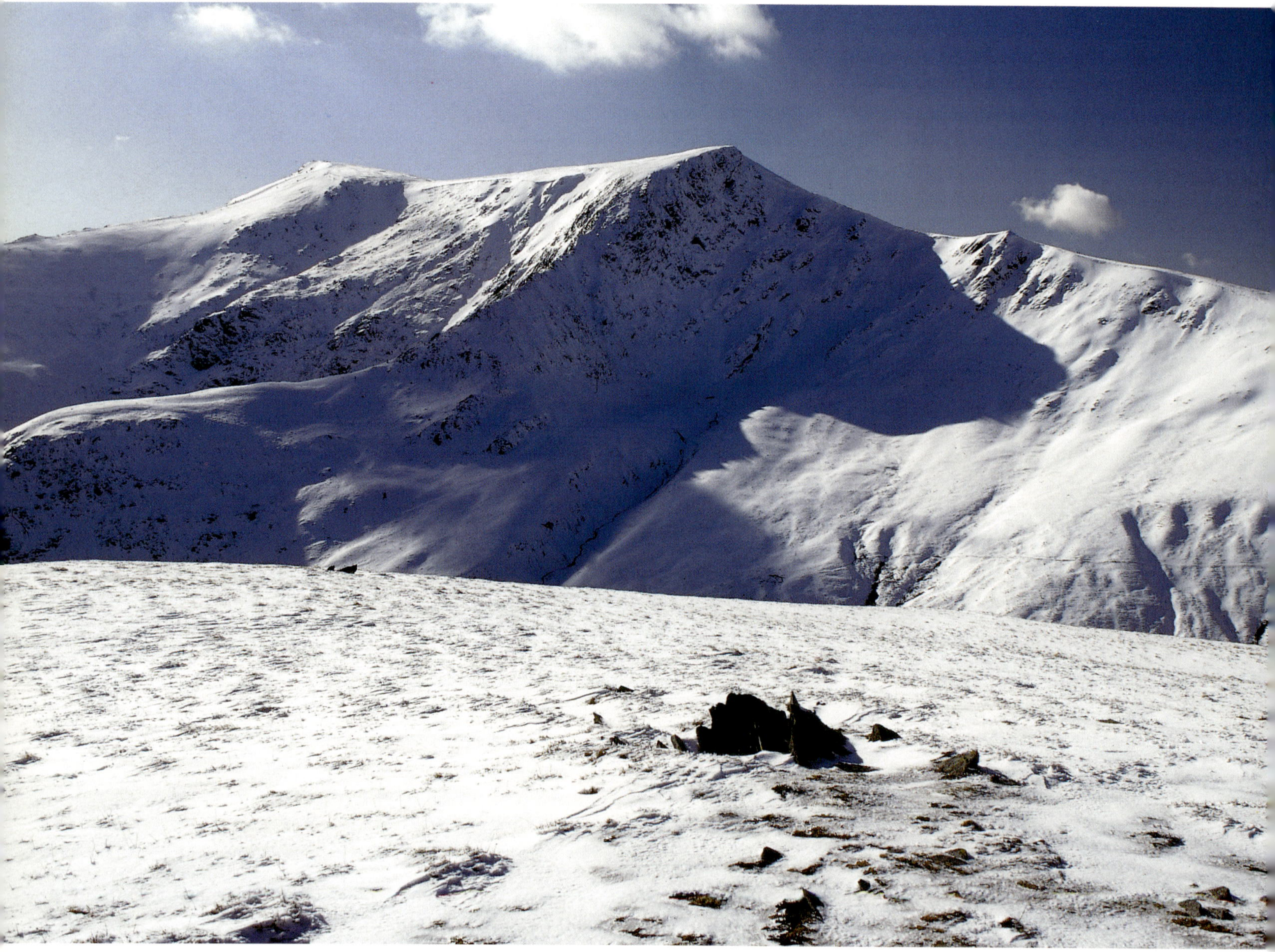

It is the Dodds that define the catchment of the eastern arms of the Derwent. The broad moorland ridge which spills north-east from Great Dodd over Matterdale Common is a watershed, gathering Groove Beck and Blake Sike into Thornsgill Beck at Cockley Moor, by-passing Deepdale and Aira Beck, which take a different course to the sea.

A little to the north, Thornsgill Beck becomes Trout Beck, shortly changing direction and heading west for Keswick. At Troutbeck, the Romans had two forts and three temporary marching camps. Although the exact date of the camps is unproven, the similarities between this site and the Flavian encampment at Oakwood in the Scottish Borders suggests that the two were contemporary, which would imply a Flavian foundation date (AD69-96) for the Troutbeck camp.

The thoroughfare to the Vale of Keswick looks less like a dale than any other in Lakeland. Its broad, fertile and green expanses spread back from its rivers before rising steeply into the fells. At Wolt Bridge, Trout Beck meets the River Glenderamackin, which untangles itself from the embrace of Blencathra and its birthplace on Mungrisdale Common only by dint of looping northwards around Souther Fell to emerge at the hamlet of Mungrisdale. En route, the Glenderamackin gathers in the outflow from Scales Tarn and Bannerdale, a soft green vale rising westwards to the rim of Bannerdale Crags.

It is one of the simplest and most agreeable of fell-walking pleasures to set off from Mungrisdale on a crisp winter morning bound for Bowscale Fell and from there south to Bannerdale Crags before locating the headwaters of the Glenderamackin and following its course back to the village.

Scales Tarn, sometimes also known as Threlkeld Tarn, occupies a crater-like depression below the ridge of Sharp Edge. The saying goes that here the sun never shines and you can see the stars at noon. Of course, it isn't true, but anyone who has descended from over Scales Fell into its sanctum, and seen its dark-eyed stare, will have a good idea where those sentiments originate. John Stuart Mill (1806-73), the English philosopher and social reformer came this way as a young man of twenty-five, and commented 'The water, which is of the deepest blue, seems hid, out of the reach of man; no trees or shrubs, nor even the smallest herb, overshadow it.'

Having rounded White Horse Bent, the Glenderamackin heads northwards, skimming along below the steep ground of Souther Fell, and so out to the

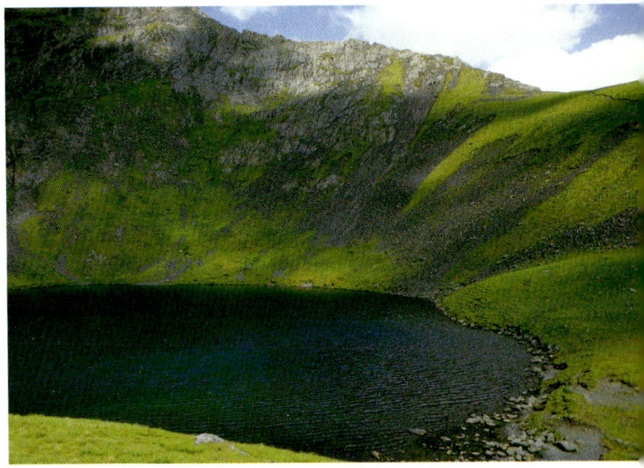

Scales Tarn.

Opposite page: *A winter's day on Bannerdale Crags, looking towards Sharp Edge and Blencathra.*

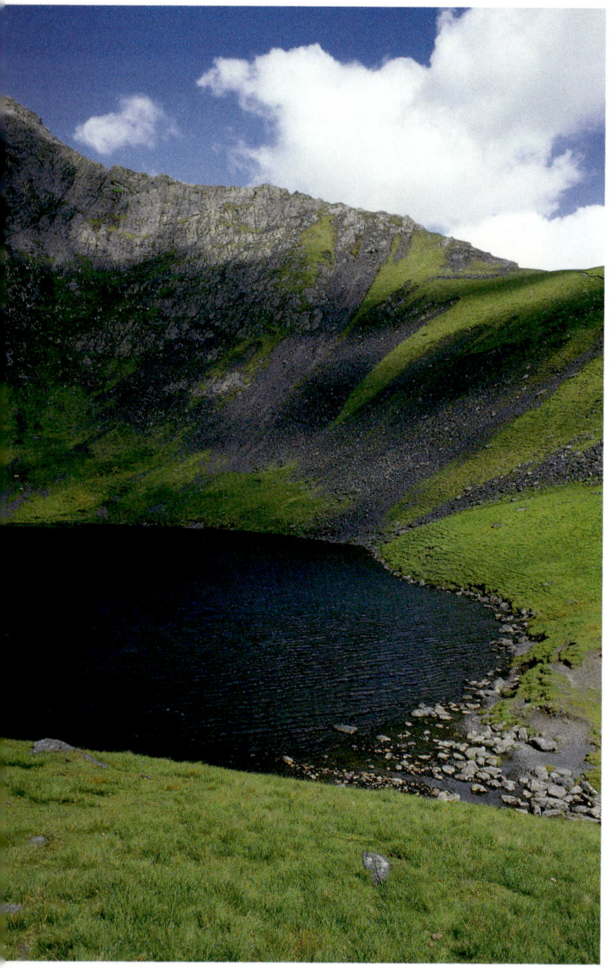

Scales Tarn where ' the sun never shines and you can see the stars at noon'

Hesket Newmarket road. Dorothy and William Wordsworth passed this way with Coleridge on their 1803 tour to Scotland, crossing 'the foot of Grisedale and Mosedale, both pastoral vallies...green, with scattered trees and houses, and each a beautiful stream.' In Wordsworth's day, the dale that runs westwards from the village of Mungrisdale was known as Grisedale.

Within half a mile, at Dobson's Bridge, the Glenderamackin collects Mosedale Beck, a long and sinuous tributary that rises in the grassy folds of Great Dodd and Clough Head. At Mariel Bridge, the beck is crossed by an old coach road, a superb jaunt across Matterdale and Threlkeld Commons from Dockray to St John's in the Vale. I came this way one winter's day many years ago and stopped to watch a fox emerging from a temporary den in the snow-clad fellside and pad purposefully across the slopes of Clough Head. Not until it crossed Randerside, about a mile away, did it pause, turning briefly to look back to where I sat, and then slipped out of sight. Foolishly, I thought it didn't know I was there.

All the land at this north-eastern end of the Lake District formed part of the Barony of Greystoke created by Henry I around 1120, and, for once, not handed to the imported Norman aristocracy, but granted to Forni, a descendant of the family that held the lands before the Norman Conquest. Rolling rushy moorland and blanket peat bog predominates. This is not the best walking country, which is what makes the Old Coach Road so invaluable, but there is a tremendous sensation of openness, undulating expanses and far views.

Below the truncated ridges of Blencathra, the village of Threlkeld overlooks the confluence of the Glenderamackin with St John's Beck which, having combined, then become the River Greta. It can be argued (successfully so, I think) that the Greta has its birth high among the Wythburn Fells above Thirlmere. But it is only at Threlkeld Bridge that the name customarily appears.

Thirlmere, set in a long and quite narrow valley, is different in origin to the other northern lakes. At the start of the twentieth century its two small lakes were dammed to create the present reservoir supplying water to Manchester through nearly 160km (100 miles) of tunnels, channels and pipelines. Sadly, it was not to prove enough for the Mancunian thirst, and before long the distant corporation was developing plans to submerge Mardale and Riggindale to create another supply at Haweswater. Thirlmere has the dubious distinction of

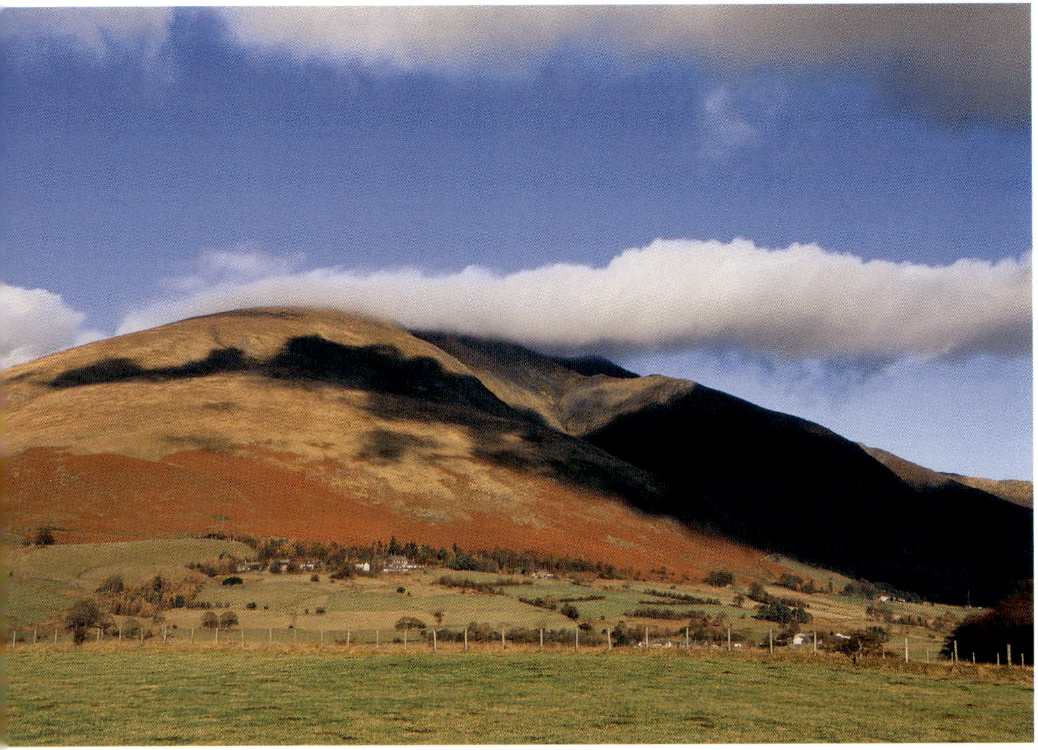

Early autumn clouds streak from the summit of Blencathra above the Vale of Keswick.

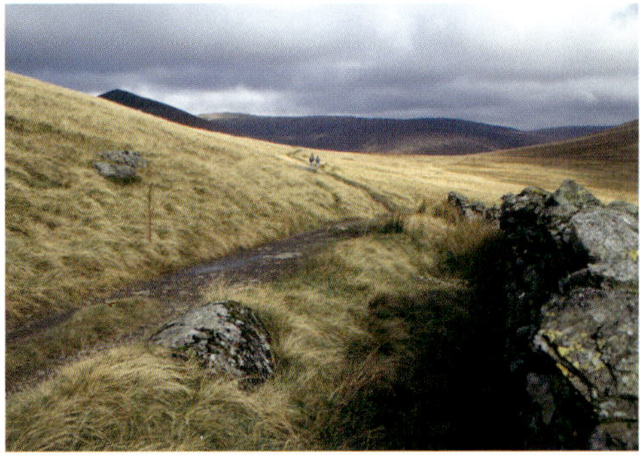

Heading along the course of Glenderaterra Beck into the wild moorland 'Back o'Skidda''.

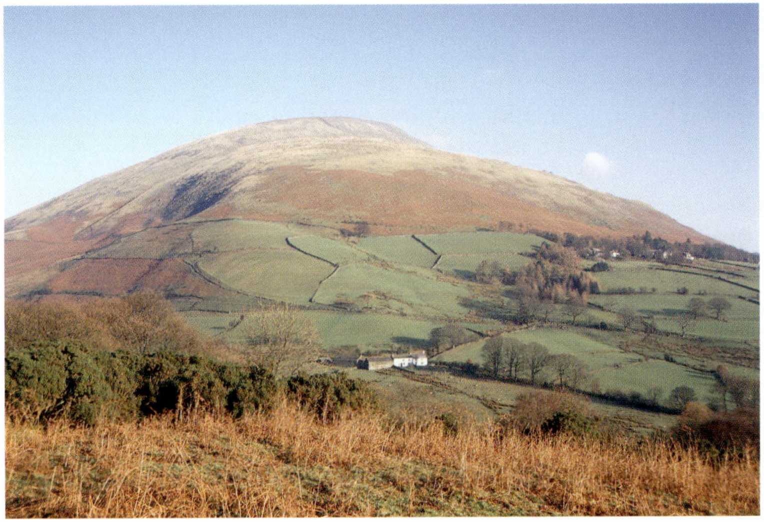

An autumnal view of Blencathra rising above the gap of Glenderaterra.

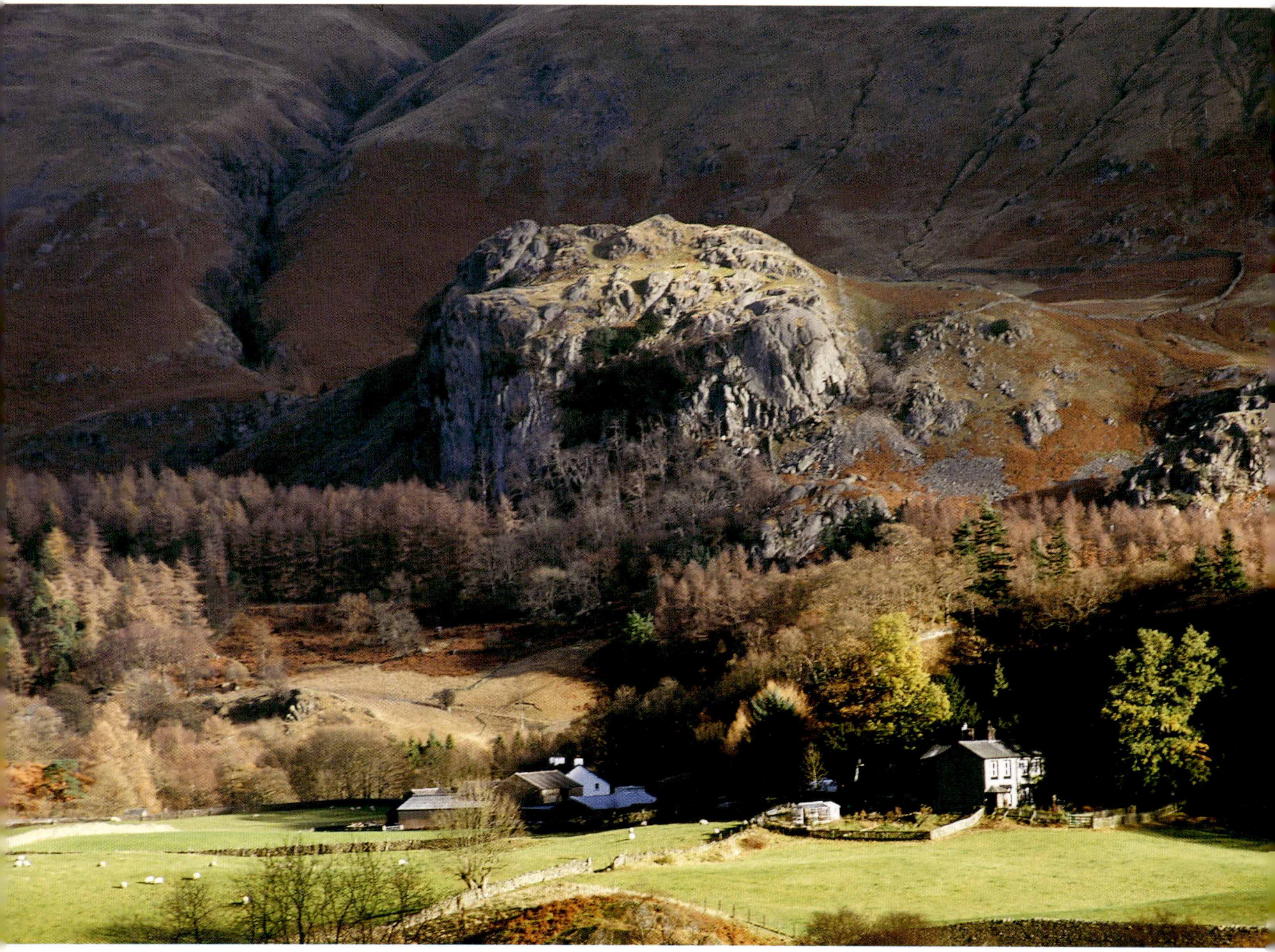

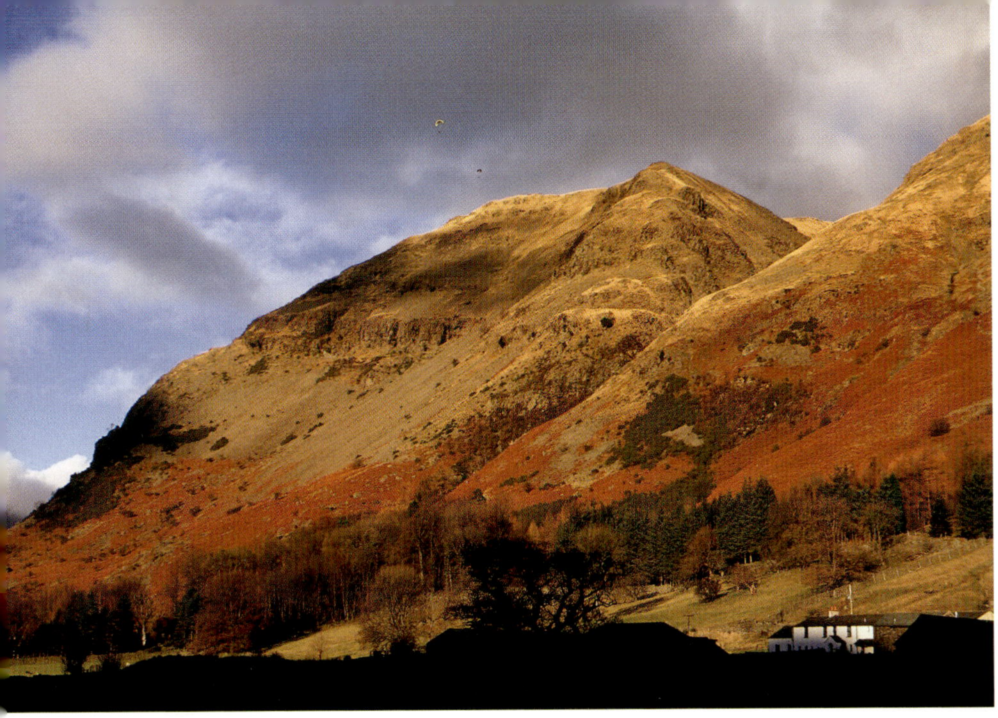

Parapente enthusiasts circle above Wanthwaite Crags, St John's in the Vale.

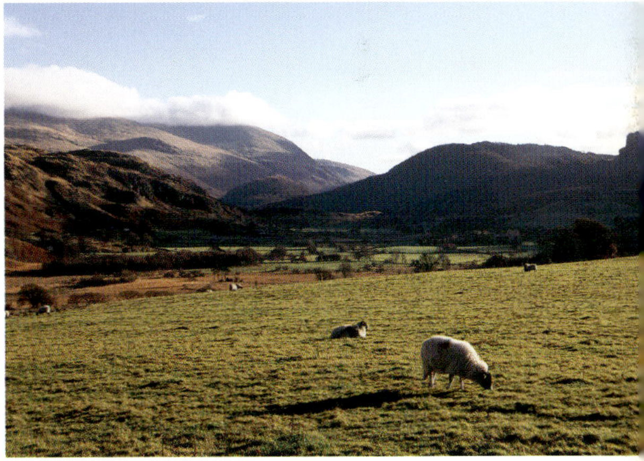

A lovely pastoral scene looking into the dale of Naddle Beck from near the Castlerigg Stone Circle.

being the first region in the Lake District to be planted mainly with evergreen conifers rather than larch, an intrusion on the traditional landscape that aroused great resentment.

St John's in the Vale is a study in simple beauty. At the southern end, crags constrict the valley, and here stands one of the legendary sites of Lakeland, Castle Rock, subject of Walter Scott's *Bridal of Triermaine* in which it becomes a subject of Arthurian legend. As the vale widens to the north of Castle Rock, so its beauty unfolds: fenced meadows dotted with farmhouses and stands of trees, twisting lanes and tumbling beck rest easy on the eye, but not enough to please William Gilpin, the English clergyman, writer and artist, and leader of the eighteenth-century cult of the Picturesque, for whom St John's failed to meet his expectations. He must have been a hard man to please, and I suspect few today fail to appreciate the loveliness of this brief dale.

To the west lies the knobbly ridge of High Rigg, which conceals the Victorian church of St John's in the Vale, and beyond, the marshy ground of Naddle Beck above which, on slightly raised ground, is the Neolithic Castlerigg Stone Circle, regarded as one of the finest stone circles in Britain and thought to pre-date Stonehenge.

Above Keswick, the huge blocks of rock are now gone that once spurred the

Opposite page: *Castle Rock, St John's in the Vale, where fenced meadows dotted with farmhouses and stands of trees, twisting lanes and tumbling becks rest easy on the eye.*

Greta in flood to loud and awful noises, and inspired Wordsworth to write:

Greta, what fearful listening! when huge stones
Rumble along thy bed, block after block.

Gone, too, are the waterwheel-powered bobbin mills that ranged its banks. The new flyover built to ease traffic pressure on town-centre Keswick is an eyesore, but the dale remains no less beautiful, as anyone who walks the old railway trackbed below Latrigg will testify. Better still, climb Latrigg, and see for yourself. In his *Colloquies*, Southey agrees: 'The scenery upon this river where it passes under the woody side of Latrigg, is of the finest and most rememberable kind.' The Greta, however, is short-lived, and to the west of Keswick becomes lost in the greater force that is the Derwent.

The Vale of Keswick

When Thomas Gray visited Keswick it was nothing more than a single street, with a courthouse presiding over the Market Square at one end and a tithebarn at the other. Indeed, its name simply means the village where cheese was made, a place described by Leland in 1540 as 'a lytle poore market town'.

Run-down cottages flanked the cobbled street in between, along with grimy little pot houses, one such the Queen's Head where John Hatfield the impostor and central character of *The Maid of Buttermere* stayed. Melvyn Bragg draws a picture (set about thirty years later) of 'packhorses ambling the broad main street, the gigs and carts, the chaises and carriages constantly flowing in and out of the winding side thoroughfares, and everywhere the heartening signs of solid prosperity.' Keswick by now was an industrial town, and it soon became the world centre of the pencil industry (though the process of making pencils was first developed and patented in 1795 by a Frenchman, Nicolas Conté).

Today, those signs of prosperity remain, but now it is tourism that bolsters the economy of the town. It is generally accepted that Keswick was 'opened up' to the outside world by the first poets – Gray, Coleridge, Keats, Southey, Scott, Tennyson, Ruskin and Stevenson. Coleridge and Southey lived at nearby Greta Hall, but Keswick can boast only one indigenous writer of note, Eliza Lynn Linton, an emancipated careerist who argued passionately that the role of the woman was that of domestic anchor.

Lakeland's only lake

It was Eliza Linton who commented that 'Not one tourist in a hundred knows anything of the real beauty of Bassenthwaite.' That probably still holds true today; this broad lake, sandwiched between the smooth fellsides of the Skiddaw massif and the afforested flanks of Lord's Seat, seems only to serve to draw the visitor out of Lakeland, away from all the action.

There is a great openness about Bassenthwaite – technically the Lake District's only 'lake' – with which I made a close acquaintance some years ago as I trotted painfully round it during a marathon race. This is Skiddaw Slate country and the landscape is markedly different from the earlier stages of the Derwent. Here, there are no dramatic overhanging cliffs and scarcely any admirable vantage points. The River Derwent continues its course across the low-lying fenland north of Keswick – it would once have been submerged beneath a much

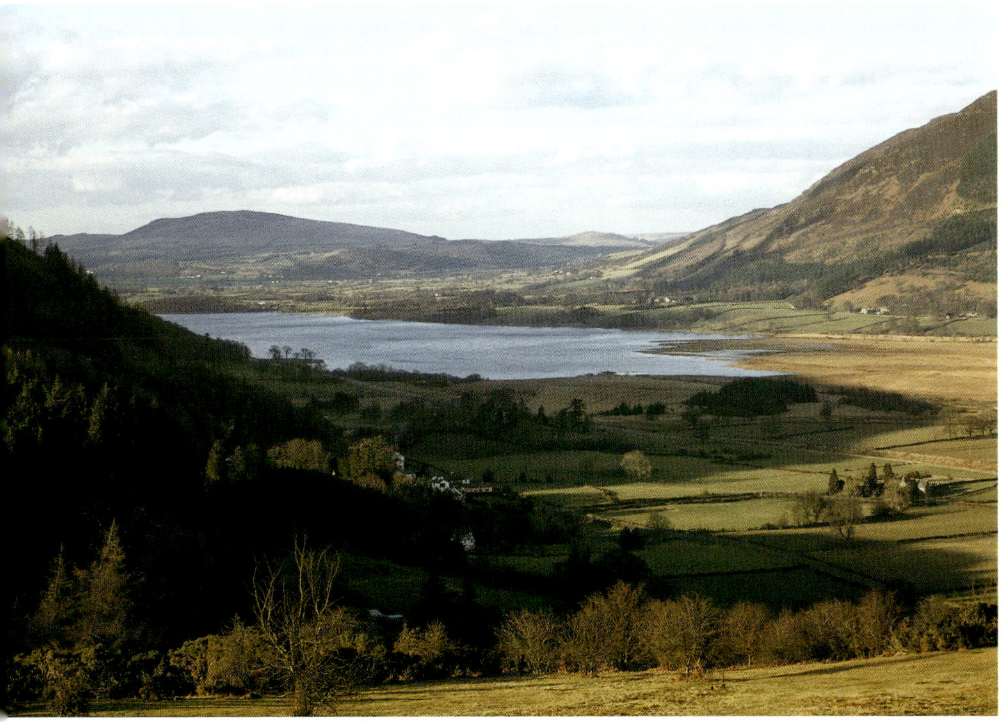

The wide dale which accommodates Bassenthwaite Lake rises to the distant summit of Binsey.

larger lake – into Bassenthwaite at Derwent Foot. Here, tiny woodlands, and fields that have their origins with prehistoric farmers, pattern the morning shadow of Skiddaw.

Like its sibling, Bassenthwaite is a shallow lake, and contains pike, perch and trout. The two are also the only lakes to have a species of whitefish, the vendace (*Coregonus albula*), one of only three whitefish native to the British Isles. Towards the southern end of the lake stands Mire House, renowned as a literary centre and attended by Southey, Tennyson and Wordsworth. It was during one of Tennyson's visits that he worked on *Idylls of the King* in which he describes the passing of Arthur. Here it was that Sir Bedivere cast Excalibur, and here that the black barge bore away the dying king.

Near the village of Bassenthwaite, Roman and ancient British remains have been found, evidence that the area around Bassenthwaite was settled more or less permanently from the time of the Vikings. Like many Lakeland villages, nineteenth-century Bassenthwaite was self-sufficient, and had a wide range of tradespeople living and working there, as well as corn mills, mines and shops.

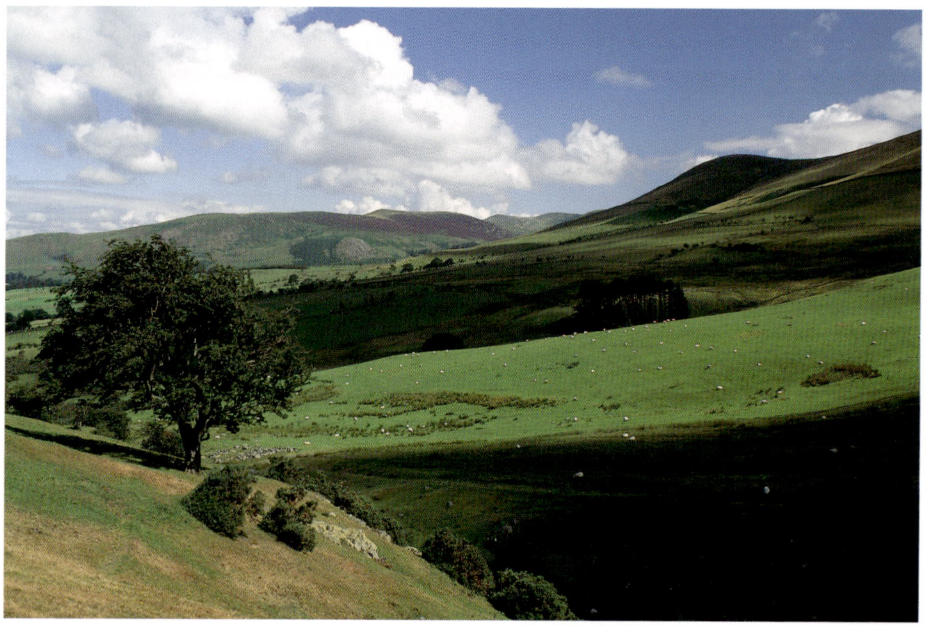

The fertile landscape of Barkbethdale, on the north-western slopes of Skiddaw.

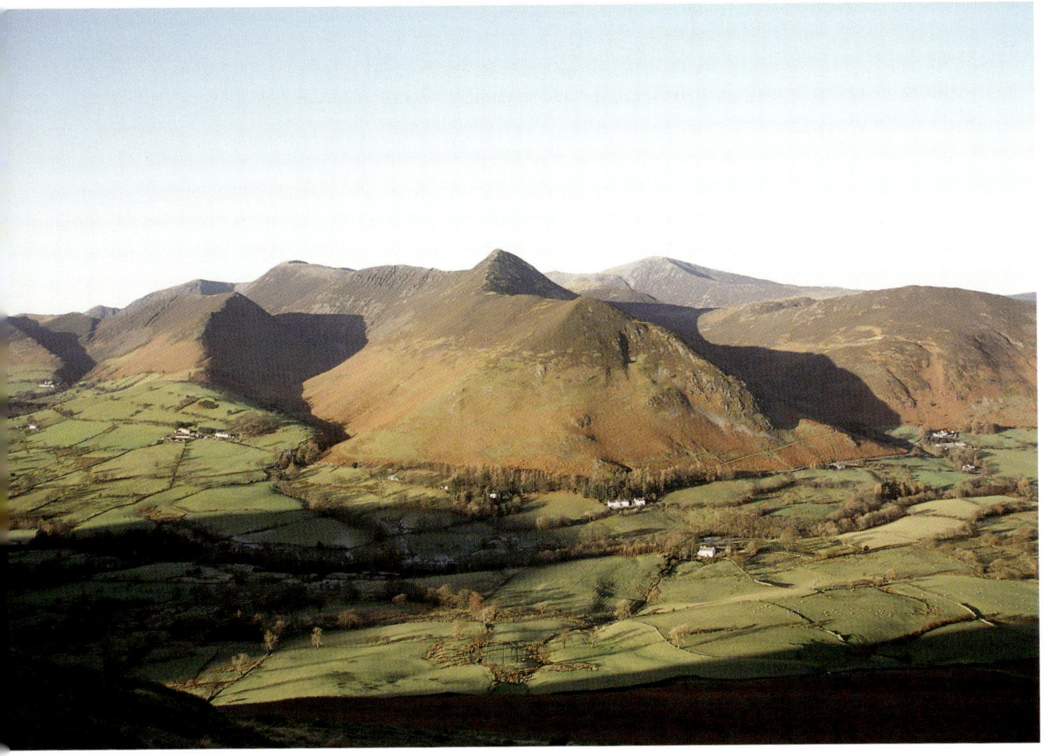

The broad base of Newlands Valley seen from the slopes of Cat Bells.

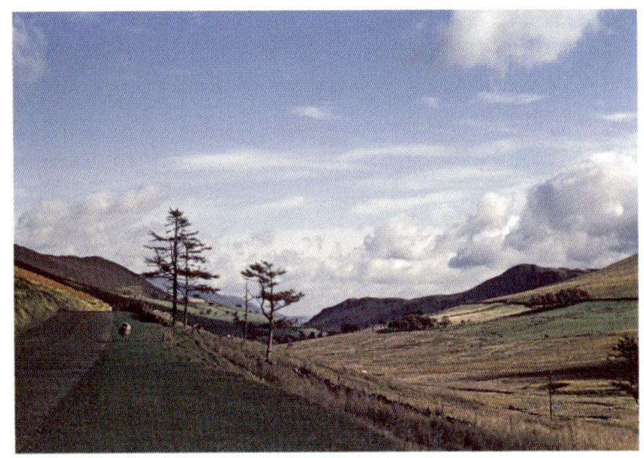

The Newlands Valley as it was forty years ago: not much has changed.

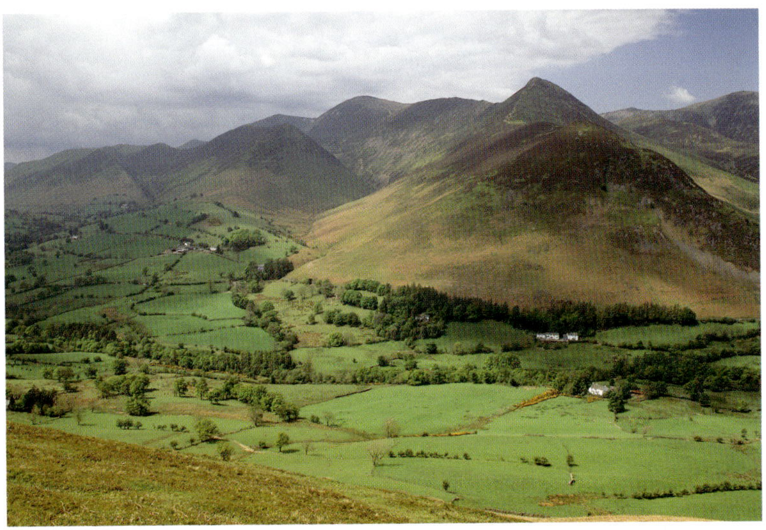

The lush green of the Newlands Valley in springtime.

The catchment area of some rivers is much wider than often imagined. The Derwent is a worthy example, having not yet finished gathering delectable dales.

East of Bassenthwaite Lake, and emptying into it not far from the village, Dash Beck, which has its source somewhere up on the north-eastern slopes of Skiddaw, makes a presentable show at Whitewater Dash before looping round to Bassenthwaite village. Before reaching the lake, it acquires Barkbethdale, a retreat only ever visited by shepherds and walkers passing to or from the northern slopes of Skiddaw. This tiny dale is largely enclosed by walls, but above the walls lies Bassenthwaite Common. Although this is a true common where traditionally there are no restrictions on how it may be grazed, some commons, and this is one of them, are known as 'stinted' – which means that there are limits to the number of animals a farmer may graze.

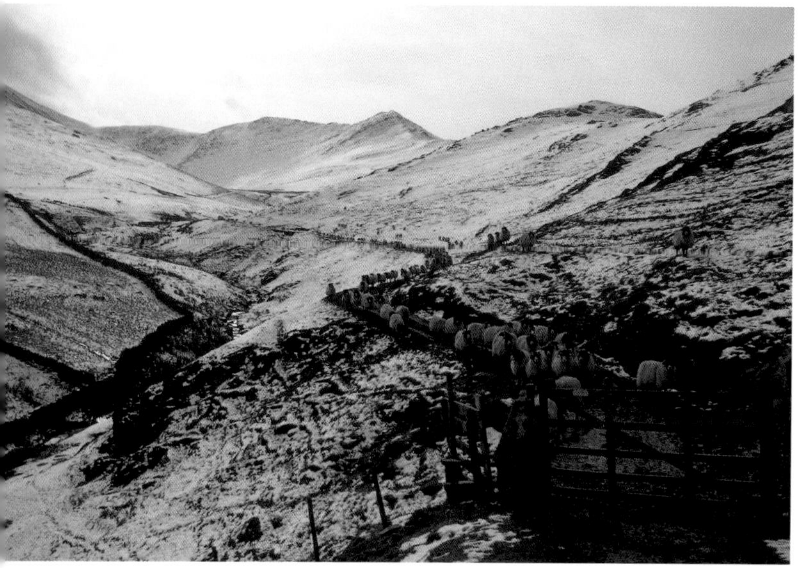

Southerndale and Ullock Pike, part of Longside Edge, in winter.

Bassenthwaite Common has been stinted since the time of the enclosures, around the end of the eighteenth century, and, as a result has good quality grassland no better seen than in the lovely green Southerndale, framed between the scree slopes of Skiddaw and the long ridge of Longside Edge that runs from Ullock Pike to Carl Side. If ever there was a truly quiet place in the Lake District, this is it, with only the sound of running water and bleating sheep to break the silence.

Into Newlands Vale

Before heading out of central Lakeland, one of the most sublime dales and its tributaries needs exploring; the Newlands valley just cannot be ignored.

The main thrust of Newlands lies south from Braithwaite, through Little Town to the dale head, but it is the branching Keskadale that takes the road up to Newlands Hause and over to Buttermere. Above the road stands a small group of trees, part-screened by bracken. Keskadale oak wood has the appearance of a very old coppice and may have supplied oak bark for tanning. It is tempting to think that this isolated stand of oaks form a relict woodland that has contrived to escape the devastations of Man.

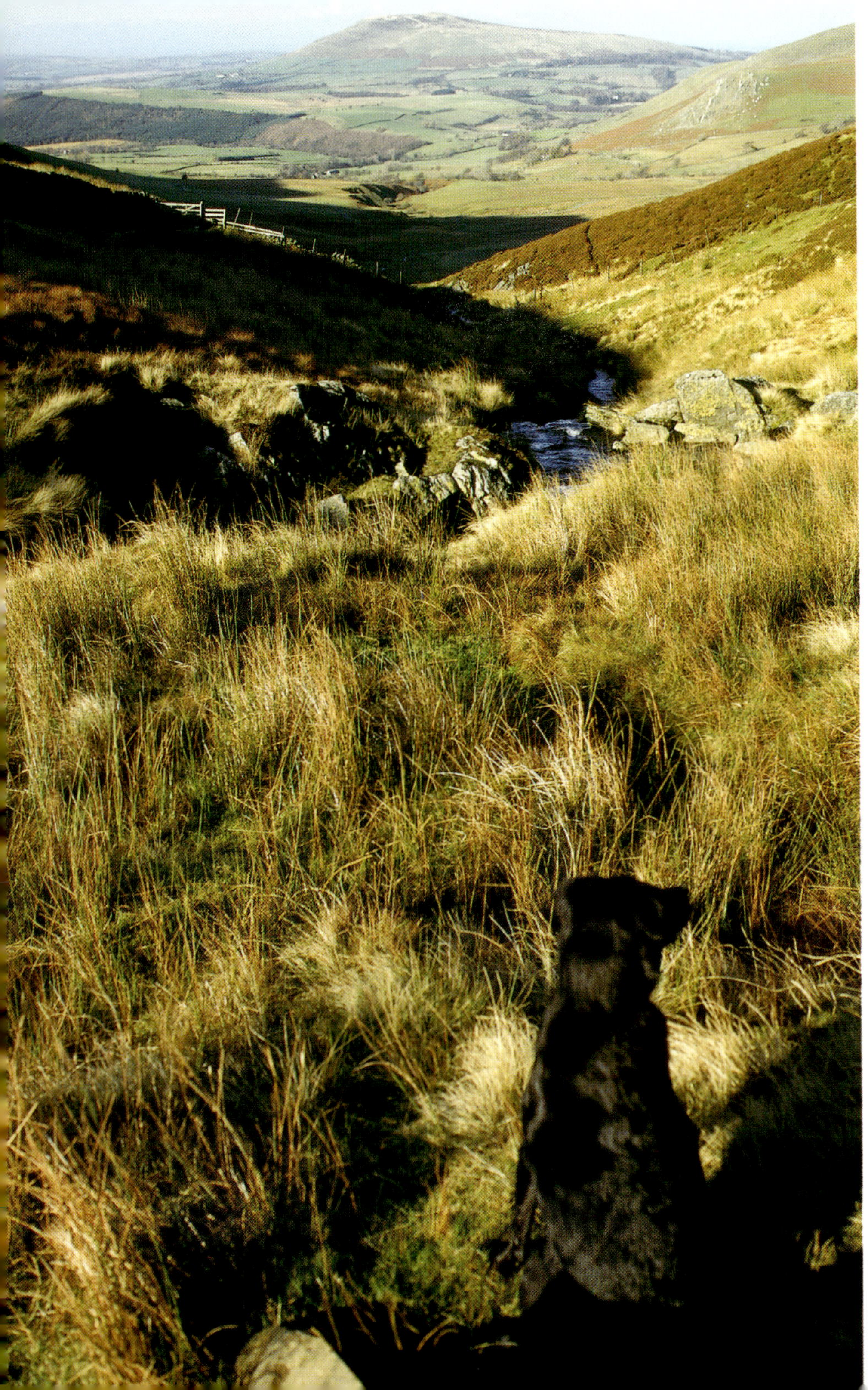

Lucy takes in the view of Binsey from Dash Falls.

A view into the rough bounds of Little Dale, between Hindscarth and Robinson.

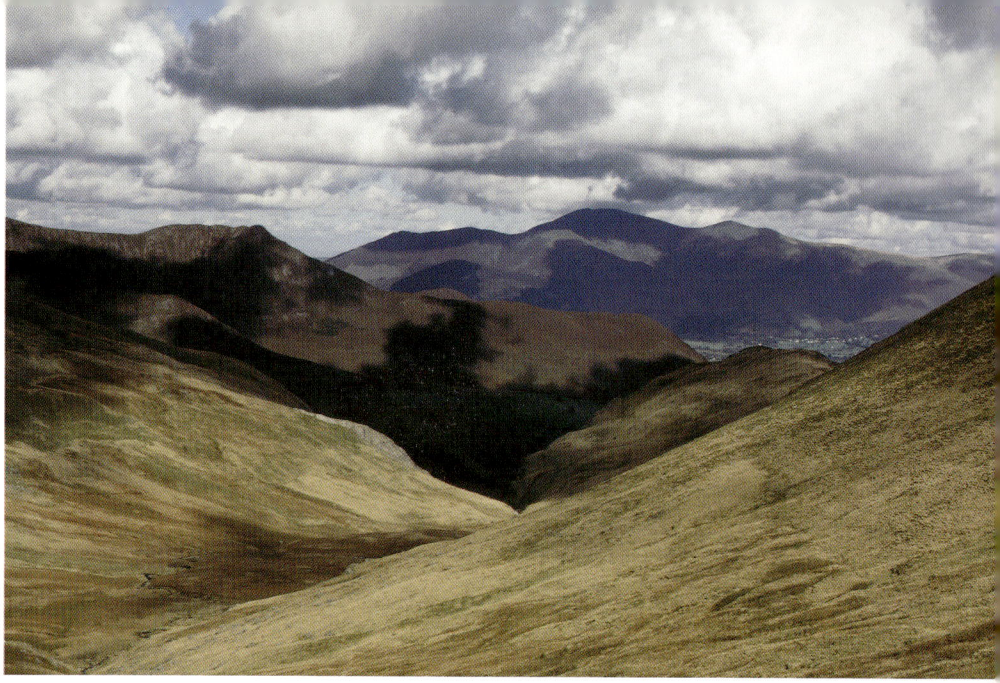

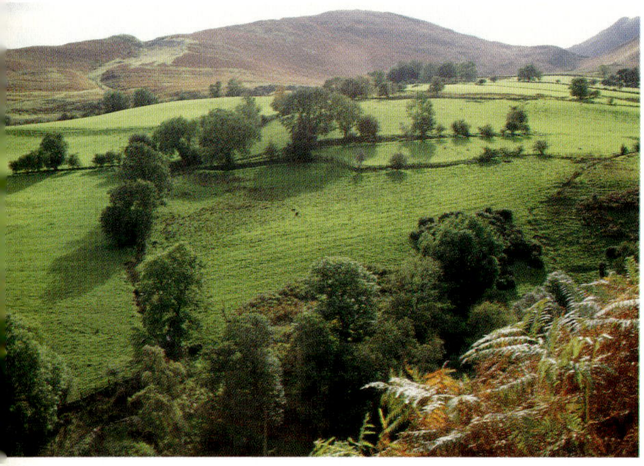

The bracken-covered summit of Barrow rises above the fertile fields of Coledale.

At the head of the dale lie three huge fells 'overflowing', as Thomas West describes, 'with the purest water, that foams down the craggy brows': Dale Head, the diminutive Dalehead Tarn feeding north to Newlands Beck; Hindscarth and, separated from it by the rough hill pasture that is Little Dale, Robinson. During Elizabethan times, colonisation was active around Newlands with the arrival of German miners imported to work the copper veins at the Goldscope mine, a name first appearing as *Gottesgab* or God's Gift because of the wealth of minerals extracted from it.

The energetic among the walking fraternity will think nothing of launching themselves onto Cat Bells from Hawes End, and then by way of High Spy to Dalehead Tarn, up onto Dale Head and across to Robinson, before descending towards Newlands Hause. From here, taking a moment to admire the splash of Moss Force, Knott Rigg, Ard Crags and Aikin Knott, they amble back along red-squirreled lanes to Hawes End. This watershed of the Newlands is a demanding route, but one that displays the beauty of this enclosed arena of craggy peaks, patterned fields, fecund greenness and isolated farmhouses to good advantage.

Opposite page: *Braithwaite and Bassenthwaite Lake.*

North of Ard Crags, Rigg Beck forms an unobtrusive link with Buttermere, a secret way through the fells below the steep slopes of Causey Pike and Scar Crags. At Stair, Newlands Beck breaks free of surrounding fells and flows on to Braithwaite where it gathers Coledale Beck.

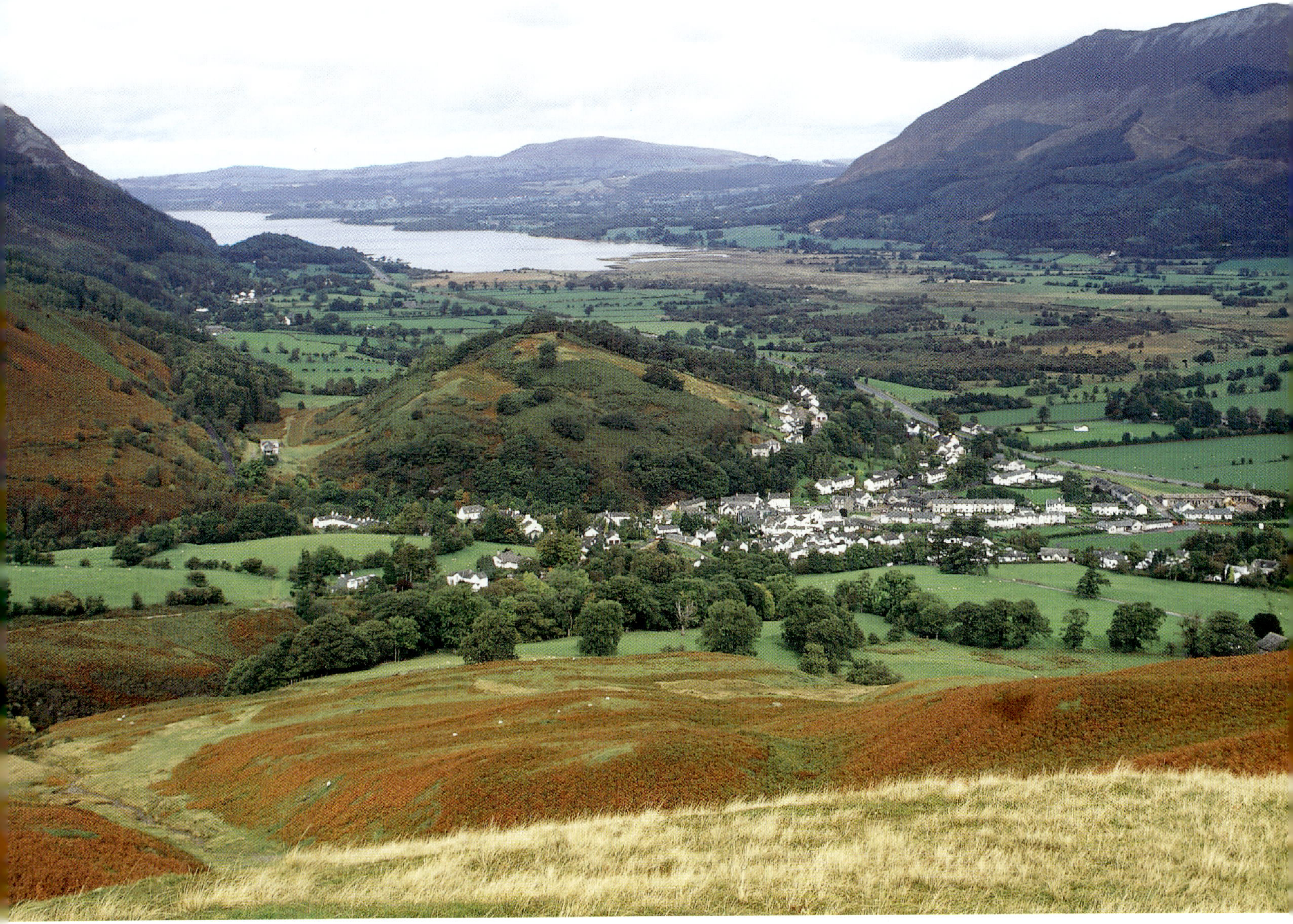

Grisedale Pike rises steeply above the grassy sides of Hobcarton Gill.

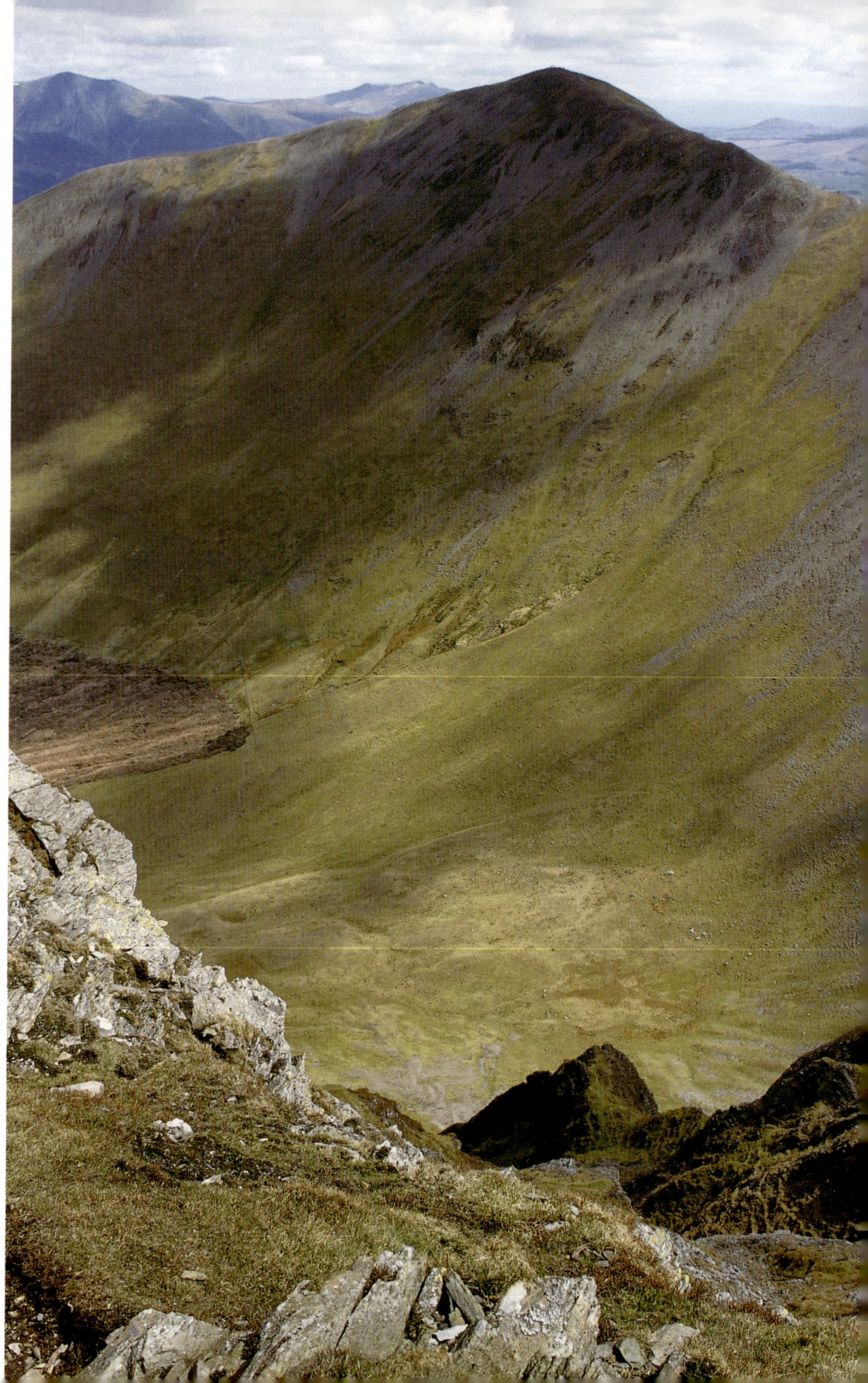

Braithwaite today is a quiet place with few residents employed locally, but in the past it had more than 1,000 inhabitants and its own coterie of tradespeople – butcher, baker, blacksmiths, millers, shoemaker, grocer, joiners and builders. Formerly the scene of a thriving woollen industry, Braithwaite was the first location of the Cumberland Pencil Company.

The long Coledale is direct and uneventful until the lip of Force Crag is reached and with it the remains of Force Crag Mine. Here, between the cone of Grisedale Pike and Outerside, the landscape is wild and has a disproportionate sense of remoteness, given that Braithwaite is no more than three miles of uncomplicated walking away. Where Force Crag interrupts the flow of the land, it creates a series of cascades from High Force above Coledale Hause to Low Force near the mine. Most visitors here today follow the round from Causey Pike to Grisedale Pike; few opt out at Coledale Hause for the amble beside Coledale Beck.

If there is a Grisedale Pike it follows that there must be a Grisedale, and so there is. It doesn't amount to much and is largely lost beneath Hospital Plantation. But tiny Grisedale between two arms of Grisedale Pike flows down to reach Comb Beck, which drains the greater part of Whinlatter Forest Park. At Thornthwaite Comb Beck becomes Chapel Beck for the final mile into Bassenthwaite Lake.

And so to Cockermouth

Beyond Bassenthwaite, the Derwent changes course, heading for Cockermouth and the Roman fort at Papcastle, finally releasing itself from the fells of Lakeland. Oddly, Cockermouth was excluded from the Lake District National Park (as was Kendal), but it is a charming and historical town, and the birthplace of William Wordsworth.

The name comes from the River Cocker, which, though shorter than the Derwent, has no less a scenic journey to the sea; the two rivers combine in the town.

The route taken by the River Cocker is known as the Vale of Lorton, a sequence of lovely, peaceful dales that begin high on Honister. Here the infant Cocker – Gatescarthdale Beck – threads boulder beds and rocky buttresses, hemmed in by the incredibly steep flanks of Honister Crag and Fleetwith Pike to the south

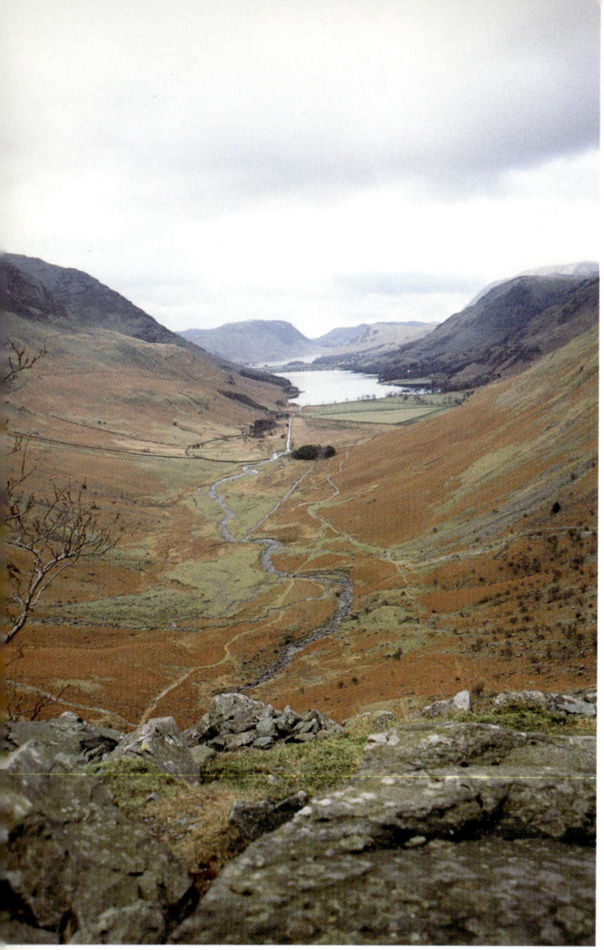

Buttermere and Crummock Water viewed over the length of Pasture Bottom.

and the bulky threesome – Dalehead, Hindscarth and Robinson – which rather turn their backs on Gatescarthdale, presenting their best sides to the Newlands valley. The conventional U-shape of a glacial valley has here been modified by scree downfall to give more of a V-form to the dale.

Before long Gatescarthdale Beck filters into Buttermere lake, and is joined by the streams that tumble from Fleetwith Pike and Blackbeck Tarn into Warnscale Bottom, a brief but sumptuous moment among the fells. At Gatescarthdale Farm the valley opens out significantly, and the beck takes a more sedate route across low-lying flats that once were part of an extended lake.

The name Buttermere applies not only to the lake, but also to the village that stands on the raised deposits which today separate Buttermere's lake from Crummock Water. The valley is, in the way of the dales that have to be accessed from the west, somewhat sheltered from the main pulse of visiting tourists, though it gets its fair share. The whole scene is one of Nature in her most benevolent mood: swelling peaks, wooded fellsides, grey crags, oases of vivid green, all endorse the view that this is one of Lakeland's most endearing dales. W G Collingwood, sometime private secretary to John Ruskin, wrote in his excellent book *The Lake Counties*, 'Buttermere and Crummock are Nature's art for art's sake.'

Many of the buildings in the village of Buttermere date from the seventeenth century, but the village is, however, renowned for something of a scandal that took place early in the nineteenth century. One of the village's hotels, The Fish, was kept by a couple called Robinson, who had a beautiful daughter, Mary, who used to wait at table. When only fourteen, Mary was remarked upon by Captain Budworth in *A Fortnight's Ramble in the Lakes*, as a result of which she became a local celebrity, known as the 'Beauty of Buttermere'.

Ten years later, Mary caught the eye of a personable visitor to Buttermere, the Honourable Alexander Augustus Hope, Lieutenant-Colonel in the 14th Regiment of Foot, and brother to the Earl of Hopetoun. The colonel wooed and won Mary, and they were married in Lorton church on the 2 October 1802, coincidentally two days before William Wordsworth and Mary Hutchinson were married. Coleridge, a long-standing admirer of Mary, wrote a piece about the wedding for the *Morning Post*, where it eventually came to the notice of the genuine Colonel Hope, who had been abroad all summer, for Mary's husband was an impostor, John Hatfield. He was already married, and eventually hanged at Carlisle, not for bigamy but for forgery. Mary eventually remarried and settled in Caldbeck.

Opposite page: *Buttermere village and Grasmoor.*

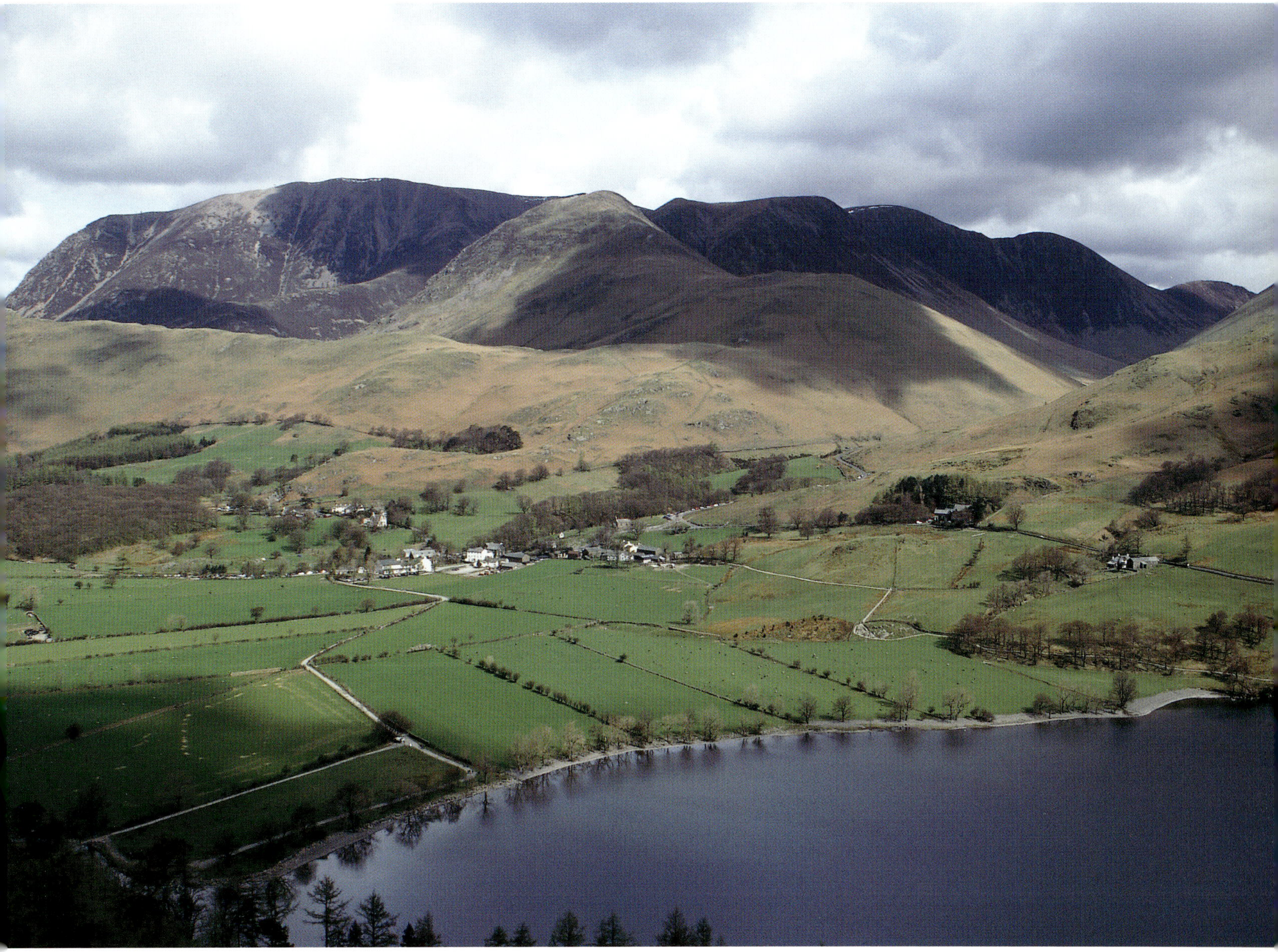

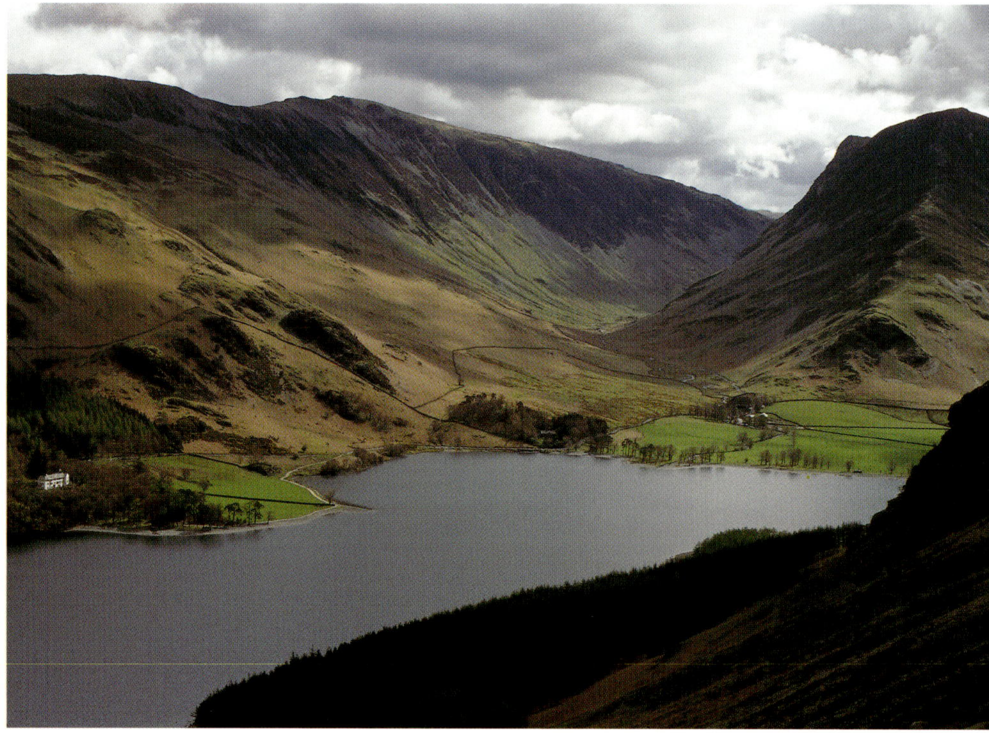

Fleetwith Pike and Robinson close the head of the Buttermere valley.

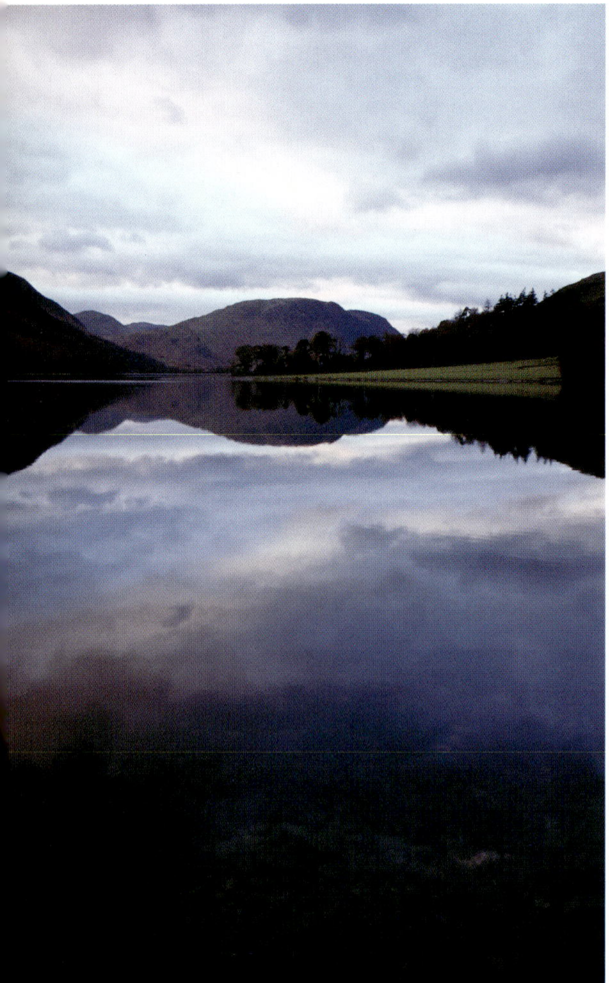

Buttermere, late afternoon.

Along the southern shores of Crummock Water, Scale Force is to be found, the highest waterfall in the Lake District with a single drop of 50m (170ft), and two others of about 6m (20ft). It is hidden away in a deep tree-lined gorge. Wordsworth described it as 'a fine chasm, with a lofty, though but slender, fall of water'. The force is a spectacular site even after dry periods, and has been an attraction from the earliest days of Lakeland tourism when Victorian visitors would journey across the lake to reach it.

Just north-west of the village, the road squeezes around the edge of Hause Point to reveal a surprise valley in Rannerdale, a long, gently ascending dale concealed behind the craggy upthrust of Rannerdale Knotts. Close by, the steep-sided Rannerdale Beck and Squat Beck combine to create a spread of low land, Cinderdale Common, so-called because it was here the ashes were tipped from the smelting that took place on the common.

In *The Secret Valley*, Nicholas Size tells how the men and women of Buttermere repelled Norman invaders at the end of the eleventh century, thought to be the

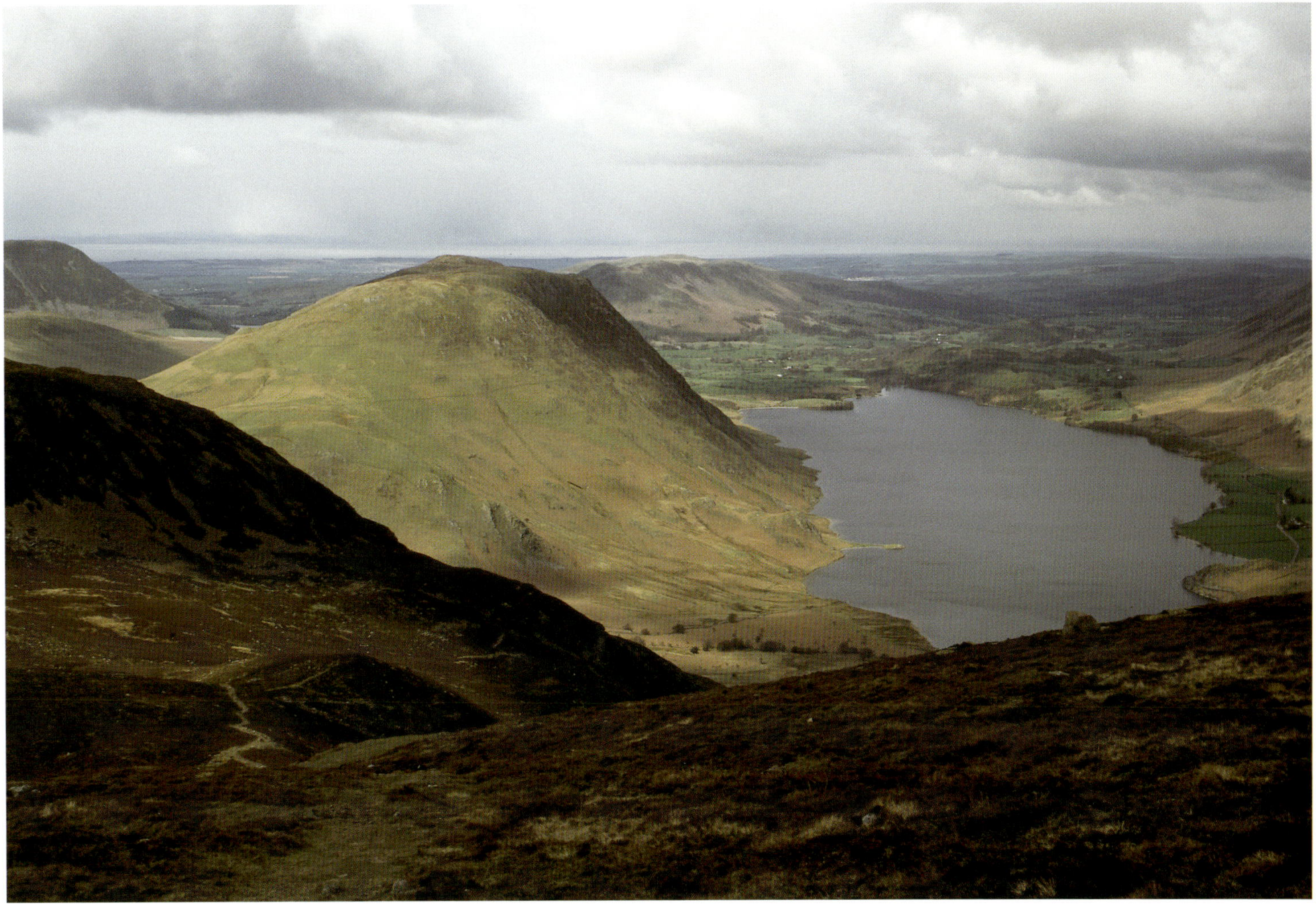

Crummock Water and Mellbreak; a lovely view from the slopes of Red Pike and Dodd.

Crummock Water and Rannerdale Knotts overtopped by the dark bulk of Grasmoor.

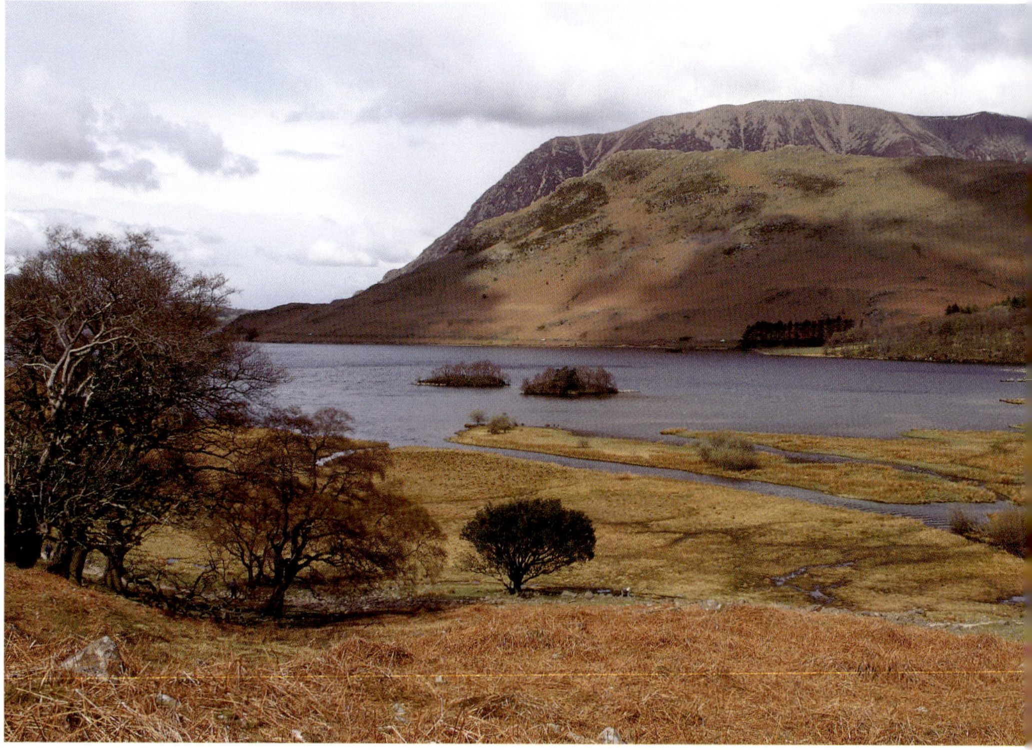

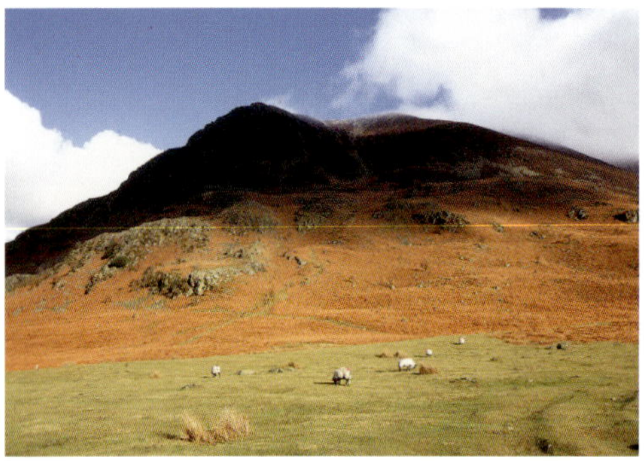

Cinderdale Common and Grasmoor.

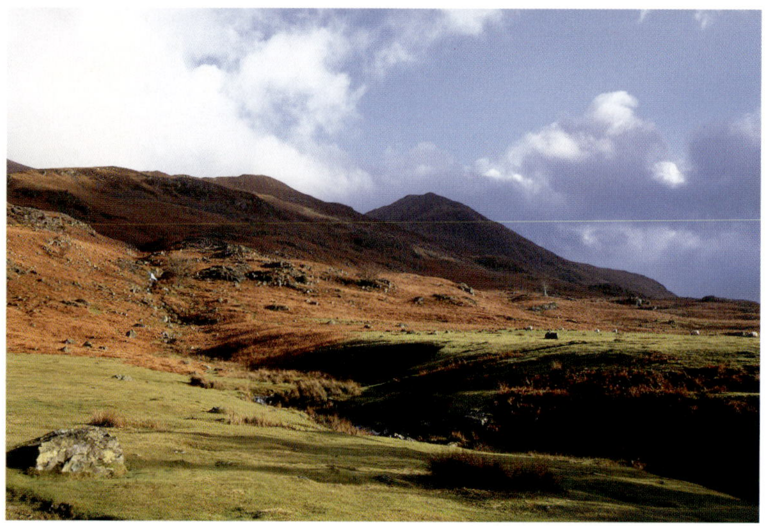

Cinderdale Common and Whiteless Pike.

last stand of the British against the Normans. The Normans had made many attempts to enter Buttermere without success and decided to try a route from Cockermouth. Anticipating their plans, the people of Buttermere had the road around Hause Point concealed and a new road apparently constructed which led the invaders into the narrow defile of Rannerdale, where, trapped, they fell victim of the archers of Buttermere. It is said that the bodies of the dead were left to rot in a huge pile, and at this spot each year Rannerdale puts on one of the finest displays of bluebells seen anywhere. Perhaps there is something in Omar Khayyám's notion that 'the loveliest flowers may spring from some dead Caesar's breast.'

In Lorton Vale

Heading northwards out of the dale, Gasgale Gill appears on the right. This is a narrow dale and a delight to walk, ascending rockily between the huge bulk of Grasmoor and the crags of Whiteside to Coledale Hause. Across the main valley, much less obvious, lies Loweswater, a tiny scattered hamlet and, sheltered by the

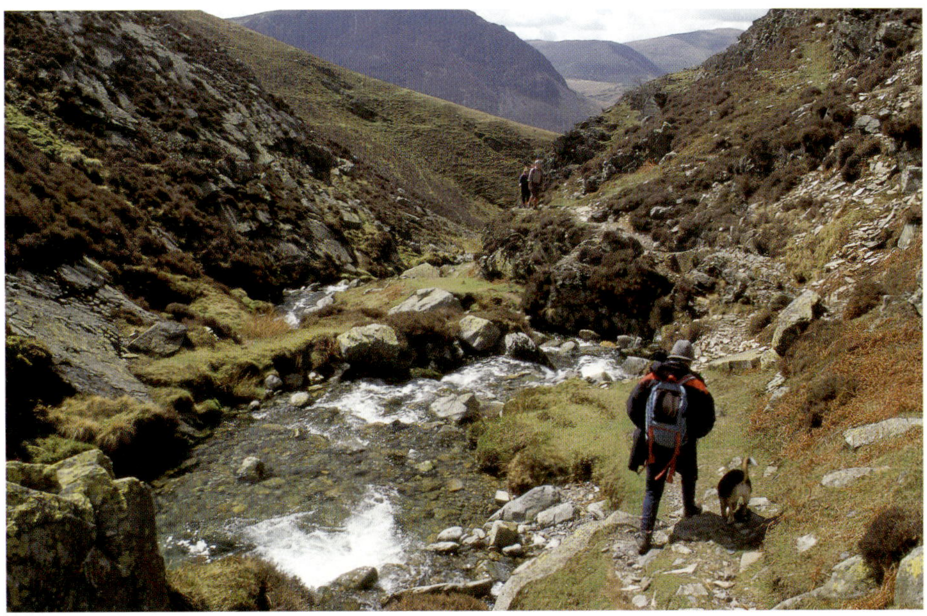

Sadie guides Ron Bickerton down Gasgale Gill.

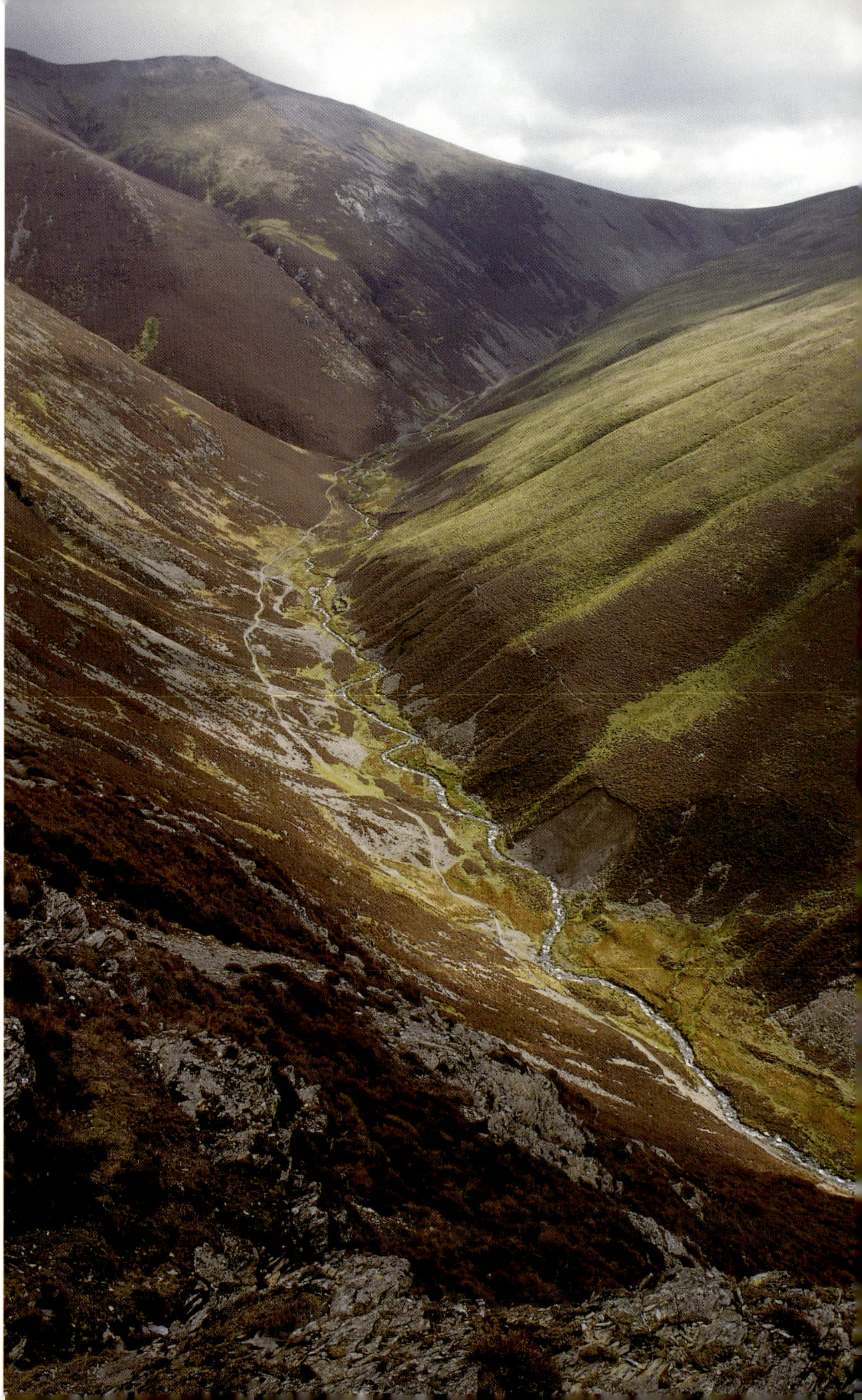

An aerial view of Gasgale, a superb, steep-sided dale flanked by Whiteside and Grasmoor.

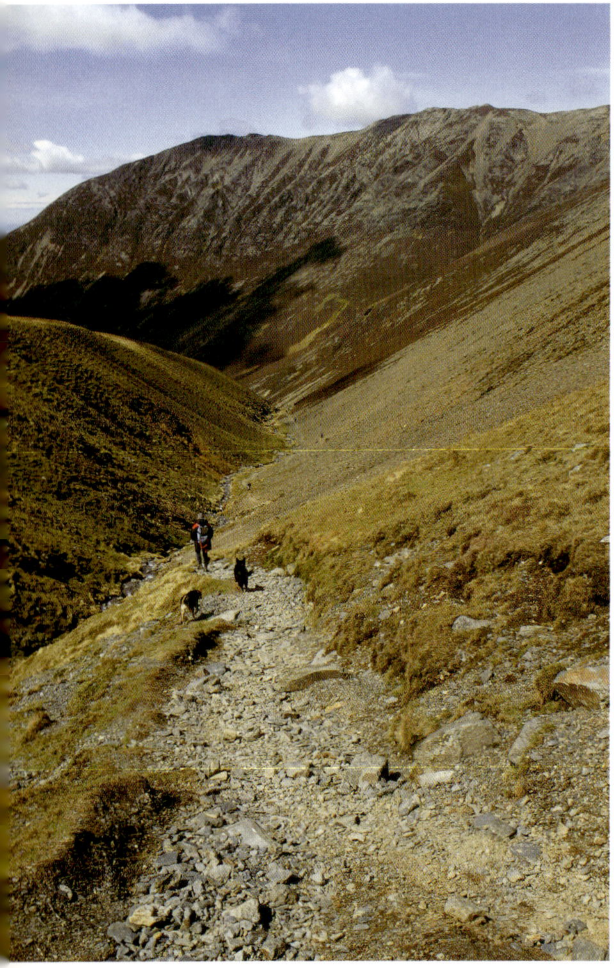

The craggy slopes of Whiteside rise above Ron, Sadie and Lucy.

mixed plantings of Holme Wood, an enchanting lake that, when water levels were higher, was joined to Crummock Water.

Loweswater, the leafy lake, is unique within the Lake District in being the only lake that drains towards the centre of the district, flowing into Crummock Water. The beck linking Loweswater and Crummock Water gathers Mosedale Beck, which flows through a hidden valley – one of many 'Mosedales' in Lakeland – slotted neatly between the bulk of isolated Mellbreak and Hen Comb. Mosedale Beck begins in Floutern Tarn below the crags of Great Borne, and then fashions a rather boggy course, northwards through Mosedale proper.

The whole of the Loweswater Fells, marking the western edge of Lakeland, tend to be neglected by walkers; height, or lack of it, may be one reason, lack of rights-of-way another. But the group deserves exploration, and is ideal for summer days when the rest of Lakeland is over-run.

Beyond the northern tip of Crummock Water lies Lanthwaite Green, site of an ancient British settlement with hut circles and enclosures. From here the valley

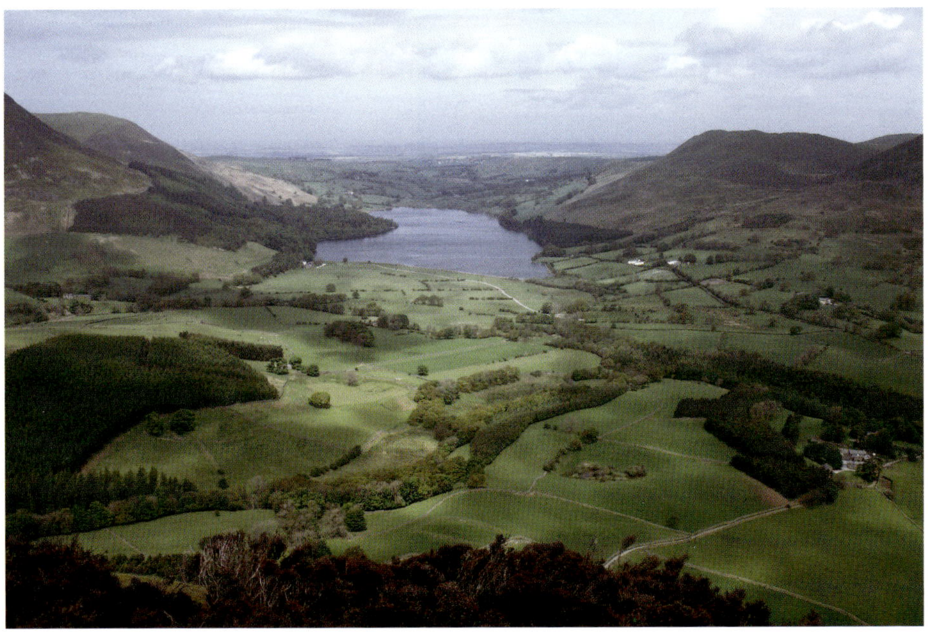

Loweswater, the leafy lake, is unique in Lakeland being the only one which drains towards the centre of the district.

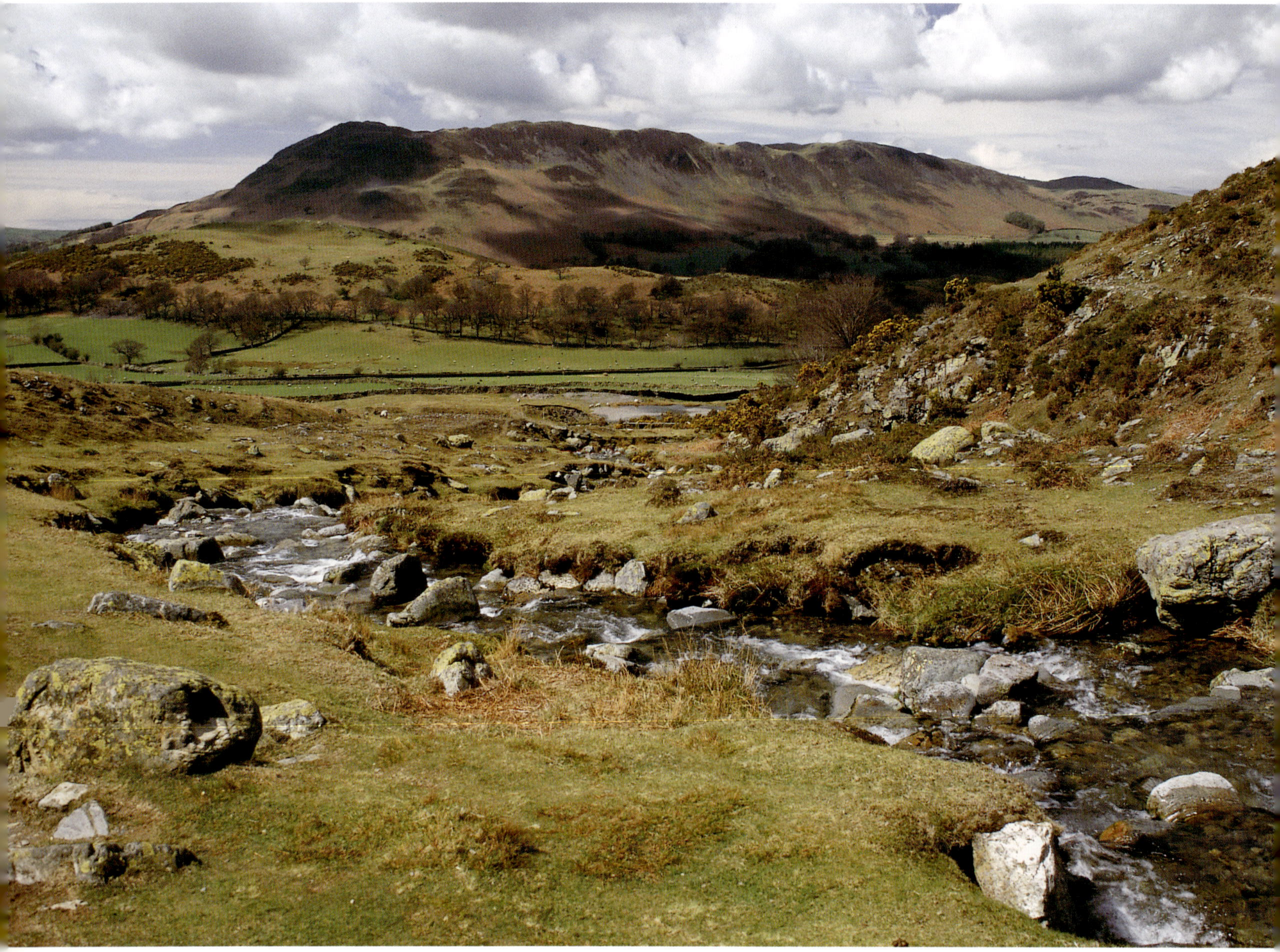

widens appreciably, the fells relax and start to keep their distance as the River Cocker works its way northwards through the two-part village of Lorton, High and Low. Lorton Hall once had two pele towers, now only one remains. The body of St Cuthbert, bound for Durham, was given sanctuary here in the ninth century, and both Malcolm III of Scotland and Queen Margaret are believed to have visited the hall in 1089. Lorton Hall was a loyal stronghold, and later became a place of recusancy.

During the eighteenth century, the fast-flowing streams of the Cocker were used to power mills producing flour and linen. The buildings adjoining Boon Beck bridge were a linen mill, but later became the site of the Jennings family brewery. The village hall was formerly the brewery malt house.

Behind the old brewery stands what's left of Wordsworth's yew tree:

> *the pride of Lorton Vale,*
> *Which to this day stands single in the midst*
> *Of it own darkness…*

half-concealed behind a wall, on the edge of Hope Beck behind the village hall, rather the worse for a beating it received during a storm in 1855 when half of the tree was torn away. Some accounts contend that the original tree has vanished and has no successor, but there is a tree, thought to be over 1,000 years old, and many believe it is the one beneath which the Quaker George Fox, preached to a large crowd, as did John Wesley, the founder of Methodism. The mayor of Cockermouth's chair is made from wood taken from the broken half of the storm-damaged tree.

Once the fells are left behind, the Cocker hurries on to its meeting with the Derwent on the northern edge of Cockermouth, from here bound for the sea at Workington, where the Derwent's 56km (35-mile) journey ends.

Opposite page: *Looking across Lanthwaite Green to the Loweswater Fells from the foot of Liza Beck.*

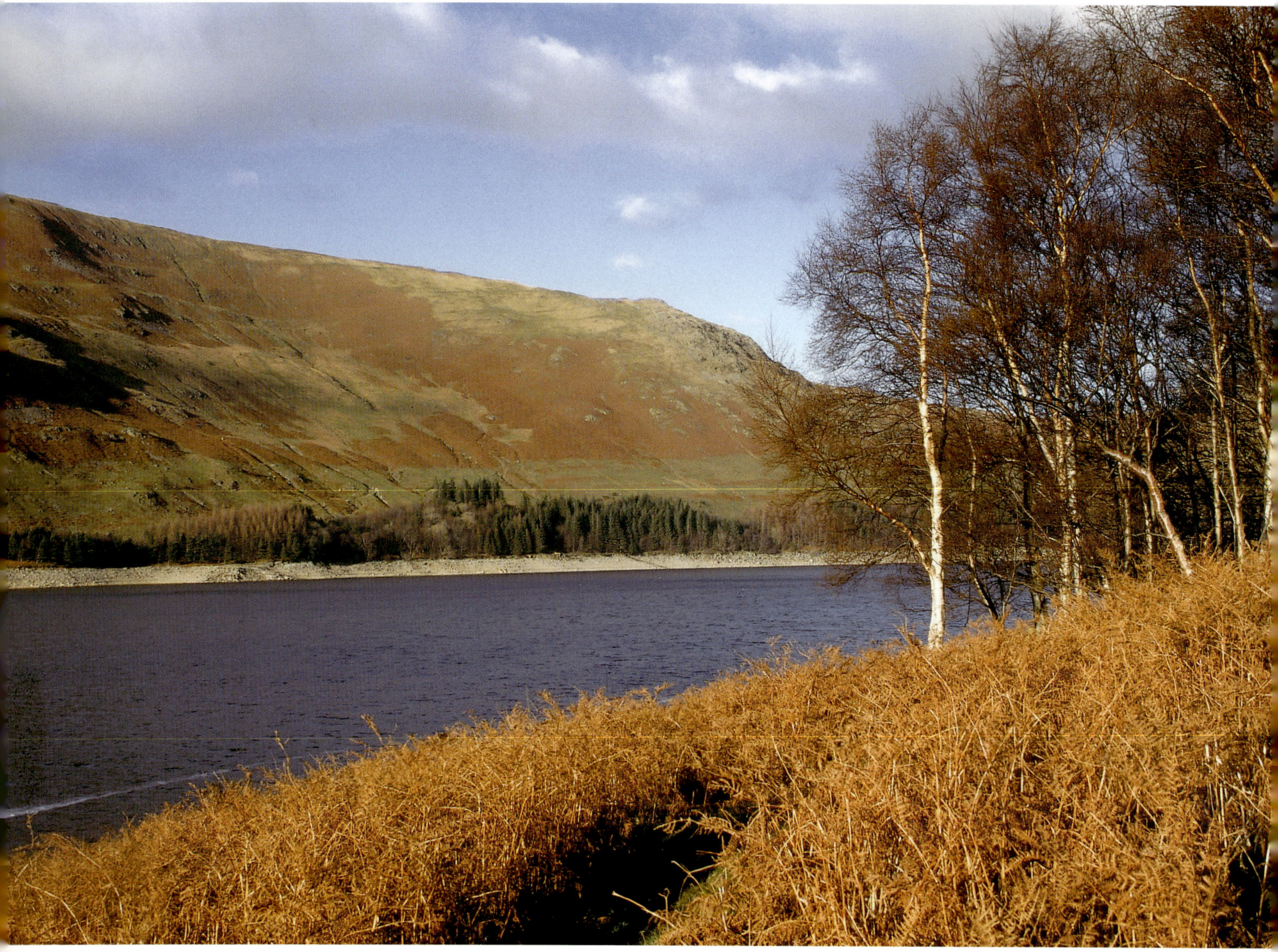

The land of the Lowther and the Eamont

Two main rivers combine to drain the fells and dales of north-eastern Lakeland, the Lowther and the Eamont, yet their tributaries are such that the area produces by far the largest number of dales. The Lowther begins its journey as three tributaries among the Shap Fells: one rises at the head of Wet Sleddale, another in Mosedale draining Harrop Pike, Tarn Crag and Branstree, and the third flowing through the Haweswater Reservoir and the drowned valley of Mardale from two stunning tarns, Blea Water and Small Water that lie tucked beneath the slopes of High Street and Mardale Ill Bell.

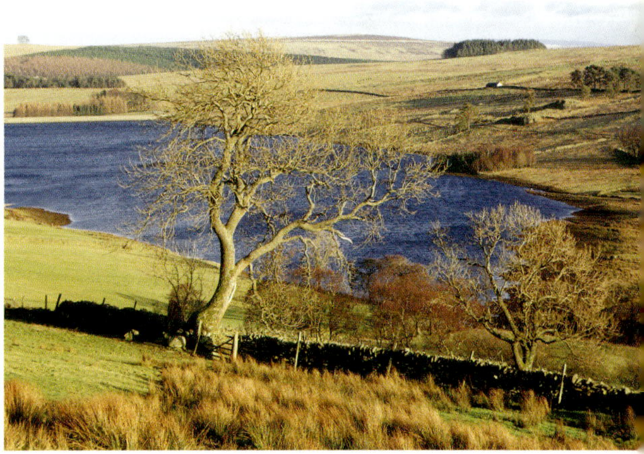

In the right light, Wet Sleddale is remote, wild and beautiful.

The scenery around Shap is austere, wild and woolly with a great sense of remoteness. To the west it rises emphatically to meet the Roman road, High Street. Beyond lies the catchment of the Eamont and the popular central fells of Fairfield and Helvellyn, running north to meet a watershed on Great Dod.

This is an area of two distinct halves: the valley of the Eamont, which contains Ullswater and its tributary dales is hugely popular and is in marked contrast to the tranquillity of Haweswater, which by comparison is rarely visited. The reason is simple: Ullswater has a through-road, Mardale does not. And the effect is remarkable. Haweswater is a reservoir and in a sense a protected area; Ullswater and Patterdale have become a tourist trap, the lake plied by paddle steamers and private yachts and its shores patrolled by countless walkers.

Lowther lands

The upper reaches of the Lowther are made for lovers of isolation. Sleddale Beck flows eagerly north-eastwards through Wet Sleddale and into a reservoir

Opposite page: *Haweswater birches.*

slaking the thirst of Manchester before being discharged into the infant Lowther. Old maps show nothing here before the dam was built.

Sleddale Hall was the unlikely setting for the 1980's cult film classic, *Withnail and I*, which featured two unemployable actors, fed up with damp, cold piles of washing-up, mad drug dealers and psychotic Irishmen, who decide to leave their squalid Camden flat for an idyllic holiday in the countryside. But when they get there it rains non-stop, there's no food, and their basic survival skills turn out to be somewhat limited. Wet Sleddale was perfectly typecast, and Sleddale Hall became Crow Cragg in the film. In springtime, huge flocks of black-headed gulls gather and whirl in mutual stimulation above Sleddale, or launch in sudden 'dreads' as they all take to the air.

Anyone who has ventured further west will know that lonely Mosedale Cottage, surrounded by its stand of trees, would have been equally suitable for the role. It must rank as one of the most remote cottages in Lakeland, tucked in beneath the grassy slopes of Branstree at the head of Mosedale Beck. The beck flows through a wide, V-shaped moorland dale between Selside Pike and Seat Robert before spilling energetically over Forces Falls and into Swindale, 'the valley of the swine'.

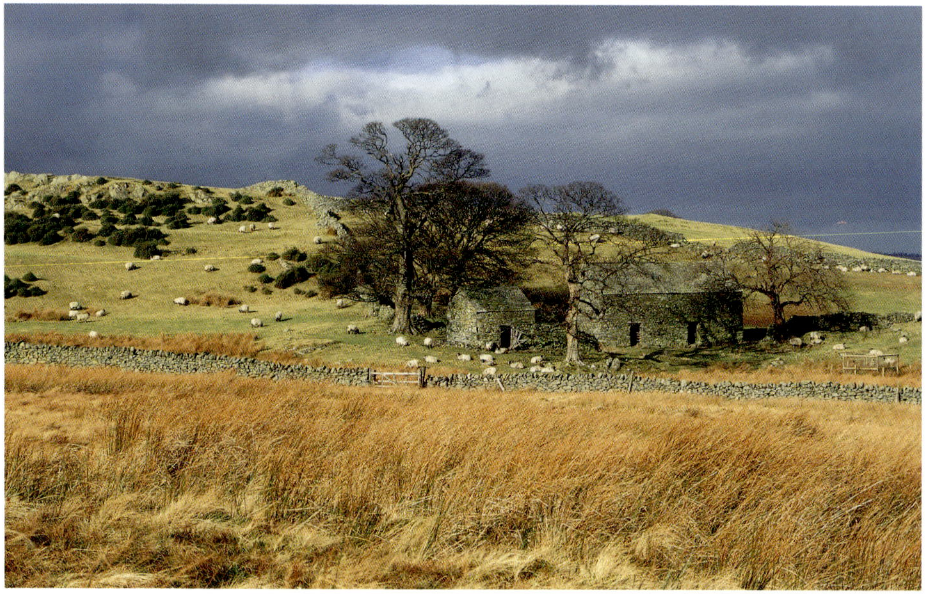

Fields barns are typical of the eastern side of Lakeland; seen here at Dog Hill, Tarbert, near Swindale.

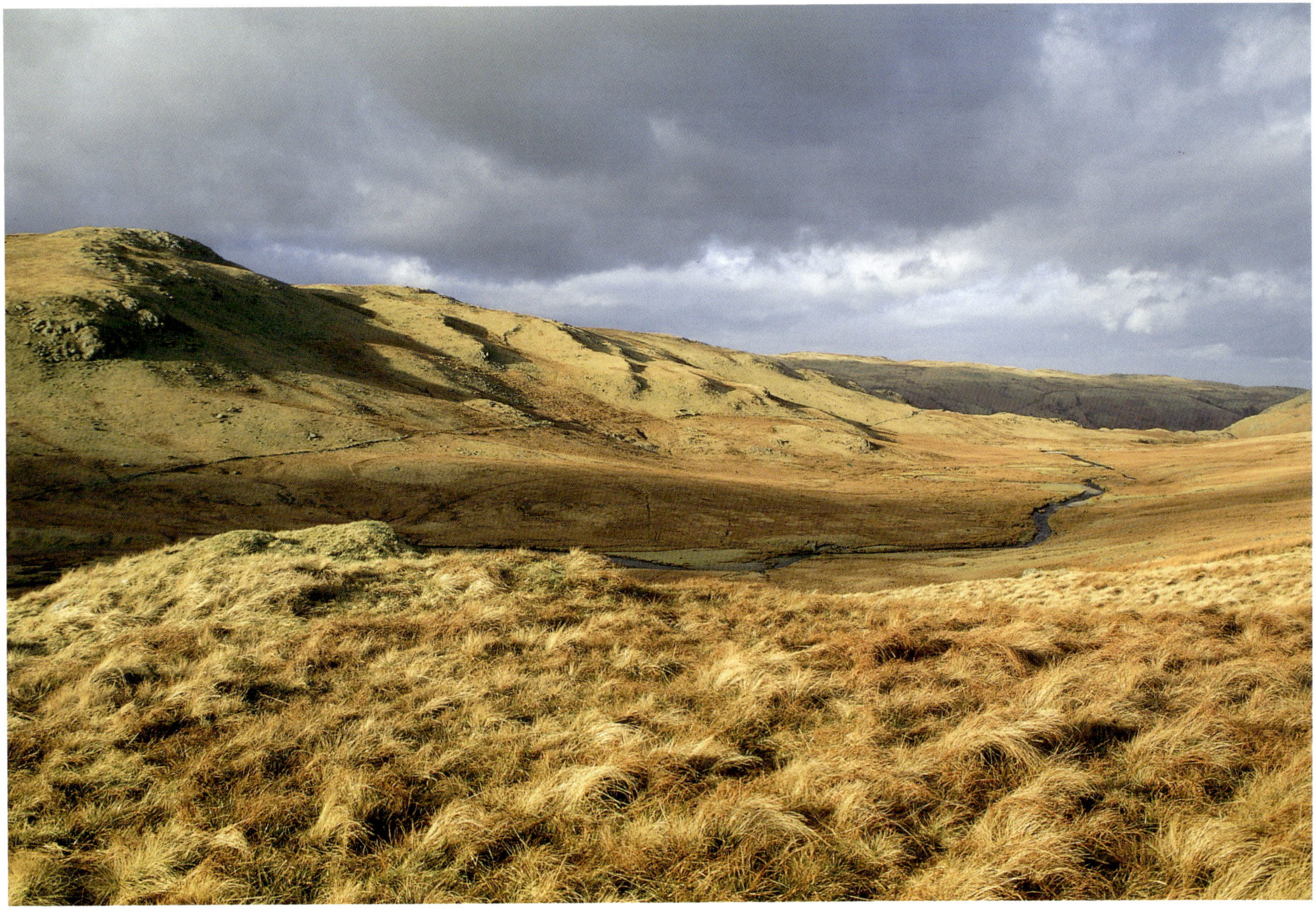

Howes and Selside above the austere moorland of Mosedale.

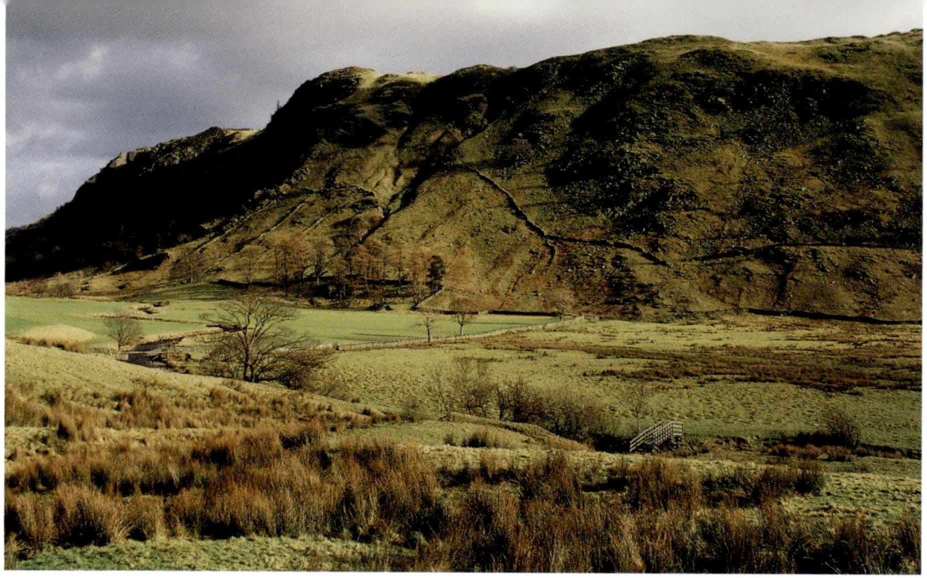

A place where Viking chiefs once met, Swindale is only rarely visited by walkers, but it offers a lovely walk through into the even more remote Mosedale.

Mosedale is an empty, wild, barren place, where only resilient sheep's fescue and common bent grasses seem to thrive. Red deer roam freely across these moorland tops. Pass this way in autumn and you will hear the 'belling' of stags at the rut. Now as Swindale Beck, the stream is joined by the cascade of delightfully-named Hobgrumble Gill before threading through the narrows at Truss Gap to meander out to join the Lowther. Old records show the name 'Thengeheved' below Gouther Crag, for this was an ancient meeting place of Viking chiefs who would gather beneath the crag to settle the affairs of their communities.

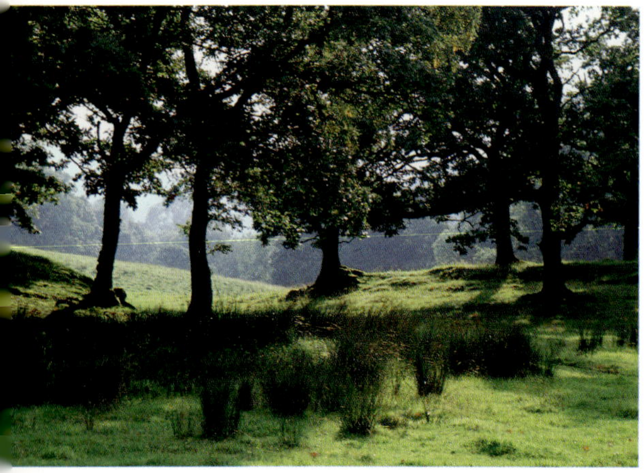

A quiet spot among the trees of Burnbanks.

Swindale and Sleddale Becks unite at Rosgill, a tiny hamlet. This manor was held by a family of its own name from the reign of Henry III to that of Richard II, when it was carried in marriage to the Salkelds, one of whom sold it to Sir John Lowther, so that it now belongs to the Earl of Lonsdale.

Believed to have been visited by St Patrick, during the nineteenth century, the compact village of Bampton and its neighbour, Bampton Grange, were typically self-sufficient, having their own communities of tradespeople, from blacksmiths and clog makers to tailors and grocers. Nearby, the Lowther is joined by Haweswater Beck.

The small, and now partially derelict, village of Burnbanks was originally built to house the workers who constructed the Haweswater Dam.

Once described as a most primitive and secluded dale, but surely the most charming and restful in all Lakeland, Mardale, as the valley above Burnbanks is called, is now under water, flooded in 1936 to quench the thirsts of Mancunians.

In her *Guide to the English Lakes*, Harriet Martineau describes the path to the drowned village of Mardale at the head of the valley, which 'winds…round the bases of knolls, past the ruins of the old church, and among snug little farms'.

Sheep and dairy cattle had been the mainstay of the dale community for hundreds of years, and early descriptions of the valley mention buildings with huge chimneys in which meat was hung to dry for winter food. It was these self-same farms that supplied butter and other produce to the distant cities, Manchester included.

But it was not enough. As Manchester grew, the need for water exceeded that which could be supplied by Thirlmere, and so Mardale and its farms, its popular Dun Bull Inn, its quiet lanes, and the church of the Holy Trinity (where the last service was held on 18 August 1935), were drowned. During subsequent droughts it is still possible to see the old village lanes and the ruins of its buildings.

The head of Mardale climbs to a splendid sanctuary where dark-eyed Blea Water and Small Water nestle below High Street. Here eagles really do dare,

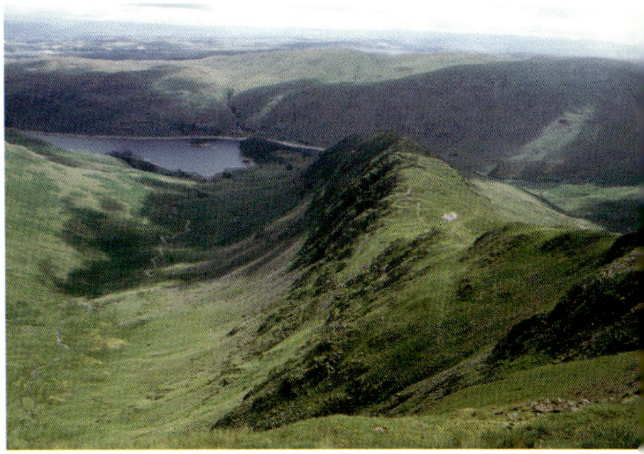

Rough Crag from the Straits of Riggindale.

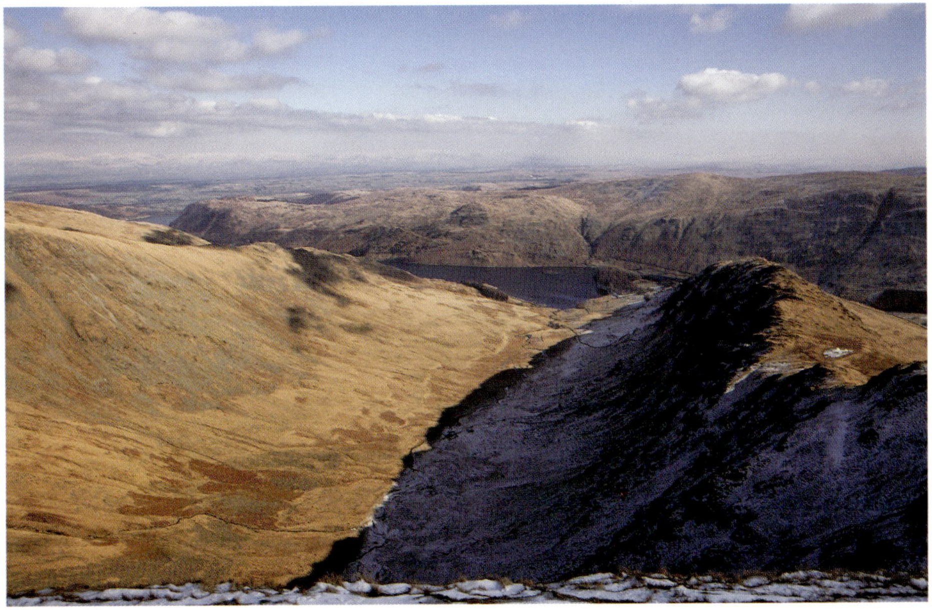

Riggindale.

Small Water and the southern end of Mardale, from Mardale Ill Bell.

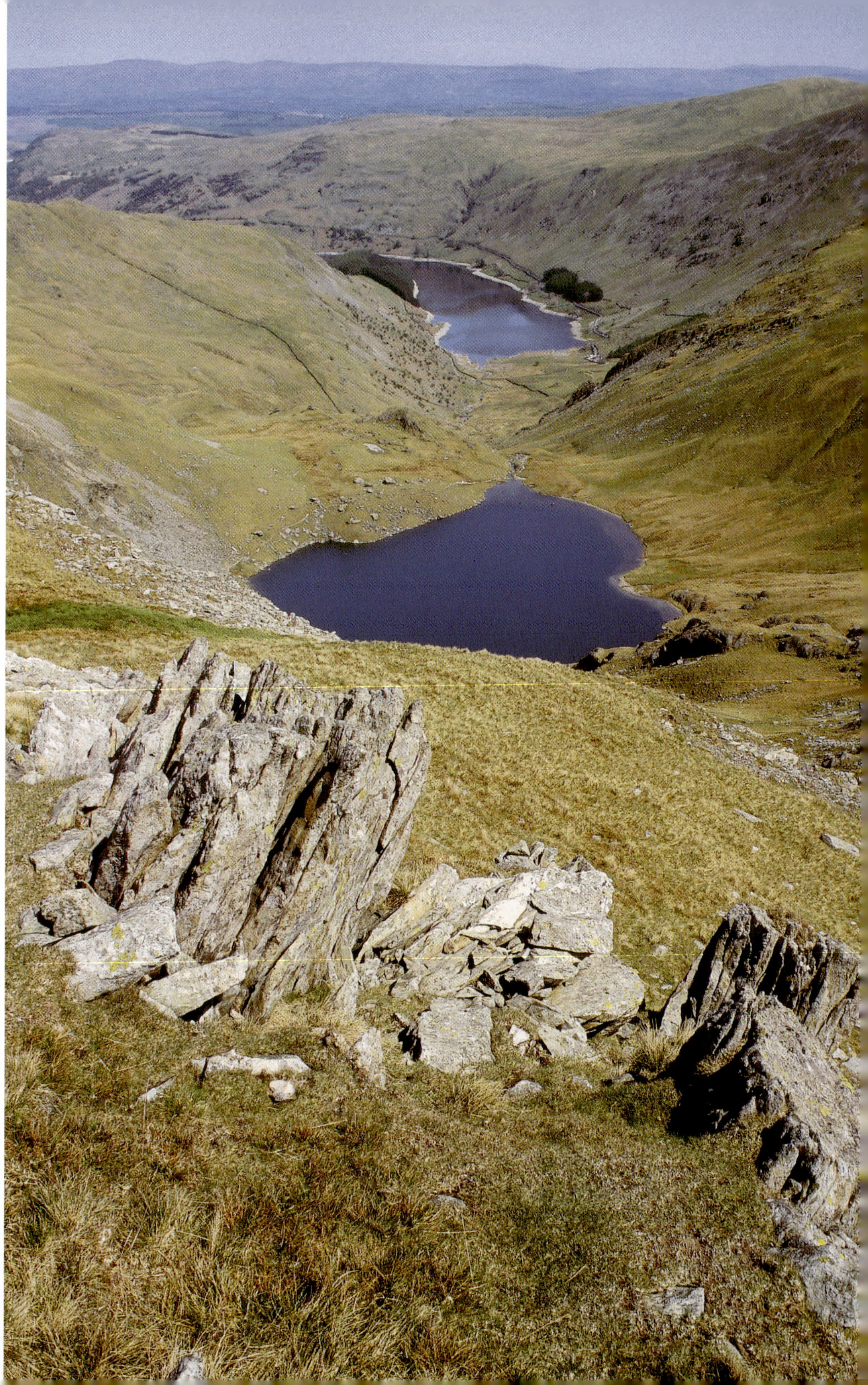

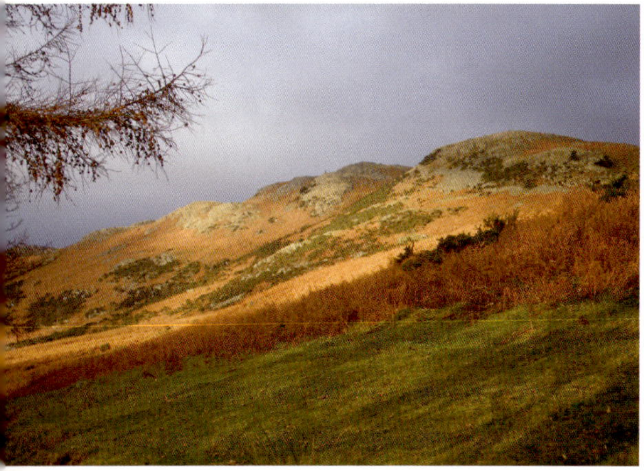

Autumn light on the slopes of the Haweswater Fells near Burnbanks.

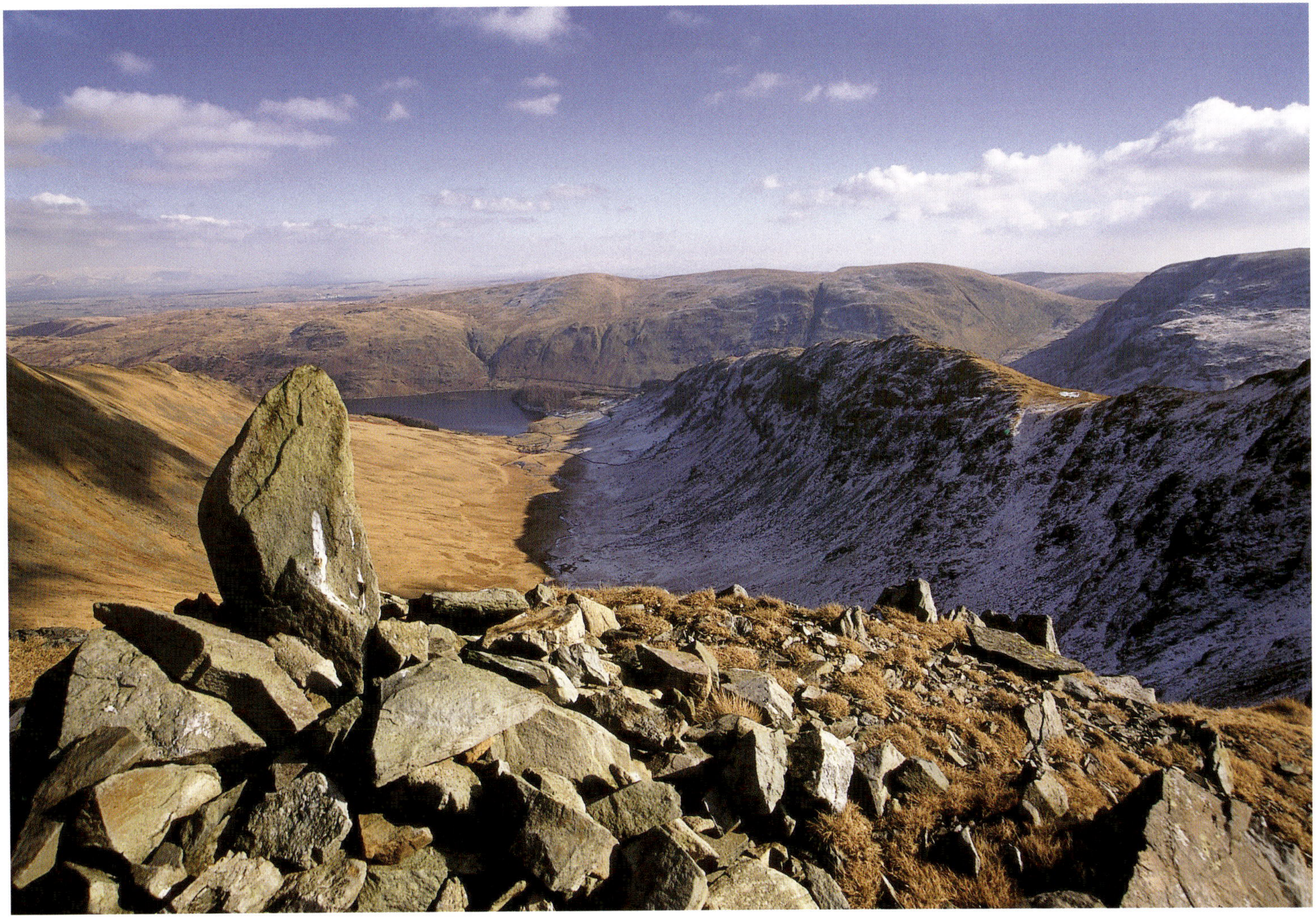

The southern reaches of Mardale viewed over Riggindale; in the background are Branstree and Selside Pike.

Where eagles fly: Haweswater and a view across into Riggindale.

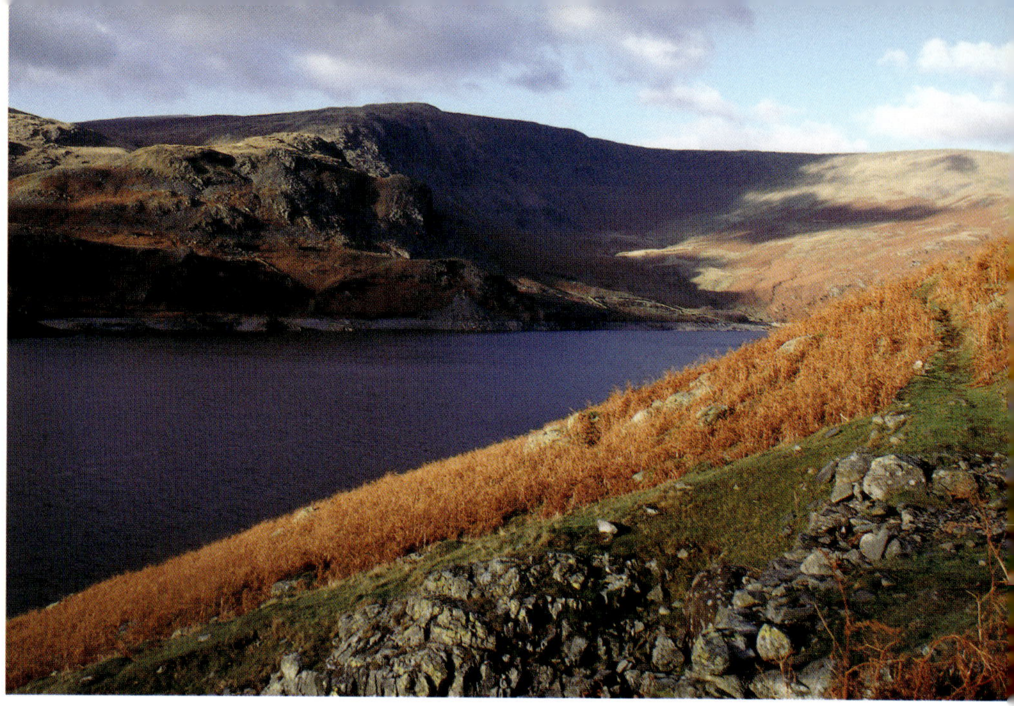

above the probing Riggindale and deer-patrolled Randale, quiet dales that squat beside the ridges of Rough Crag and Kidsty Pike.

For every thousand who pass through Patterdale's charms, maybe only one comes this way. There's time to collect your thoughts here, and the peace in which to hear them. To the west lies the long grassy ridge crossed by the Romans, starting in High Raise and culminating above Pooley Bridge in distant Barton Fell. On the way, streams combine to flow into Measand Beck and the boggy clutches of Fordingdale. From Loadpot Hill, where the sense of isolation is also great, the streams flow east in lonely Cawdale, a sparse place with a scattering of trees in wistful groups.

Like Cawdale, the virtually-unknown Heltondale spills down from the flat top of Loadpot Hill. Among these bracken-clad fells, the hardy Swaledale and Cheviot sheep roam freely. Traditionally bracken, which is a potential problem in and around Heltondale, was used as an animal winter bedding material, which was then spread on the land in spring to fertilise the fields. A rich source of humus with a wide range of trace elements ensured that the meadows and pastures got off to a good growing season.

Once free of Mardale's influence, the Lowther flows through low-lying pastoral scenery to leave the National Park north of Askham, an ancient and pleasing village built around two greens. The village, which boasts many whitewashed cottages dating from the seventeenth century, is overlooked by the towers of Lowther Castle. This pleasant ruin was built between 1806 and 1811 by Robert Smirke, who later built the British Museum, the east wing of Somerset House, the Carlton Club and the College of Physicians in Trafalgar Square, in London.

Askham is one of the most attractive villages in the former county of Westmorland. In 1280, the manor was bought by Sir Thomas de Hellbeck, and passed by marriage to the Swynburn family in 1314. The Swynburns were responsible for building the first defensive structure where the present hall now stands. In 1375, the manor was transferred once more, this time to the Sandfords. After they settled in the village, Askham Hall, set back at the foot of the village, was the home of the Sandford family. It later became, and still is, the home of the Earls of Lonsdale. The fifth Earl, Hugh Cecil Lonsdale (1857-1944) instituted the Lonsdale Belt for boxing and was the first president of the Automobile Association.

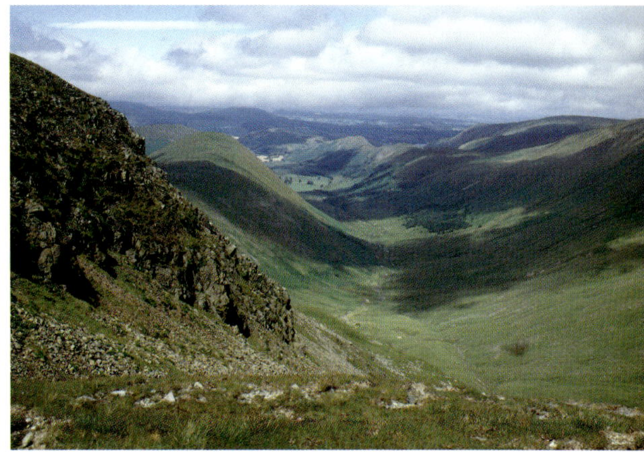

Martindale in summer green.

The area around Askham has been inhabited since the Late Stone Age, and there are prehistoric settlements, two roughly oval, embanked enclosures, on nearby Skirsgill Hill. Each contains hut circles. More prehistoric burial sites exist at nearby Moor Divock. These were opened in the nineteenth century, and found to contain cremated remains.

Eamont ways

To most visitors, the River Eamont is 'Patterdale' or 'Ullswater'. The confusion is understandable, as the river doesn't announce itself until it reaches Pooley Bridge at the northern end of the dale.

The Eamont has a huge gathering ground, reaching high into the corries of Caudale, Dovedale and Helvellyn. Surrounded by craggy fells and with a fine view across Ullswater to the distant heights of the eastern fells, the scattered hamlet of Martindale lies in one of Lakeland's most sequestered spots.

Embracing more than one dale, it lends its name to a vast sprawl of land known as Martindale Common. Here are Fusedale, Martindale itself – which takes the long, U-shaped line of Rampsgill Beck and in its upper reaches divides into Bannerdale, and, running south from Sandwick, the long finger of Boredale.

A striking view down the length of Martindale from the edge of Rampsgill Head.

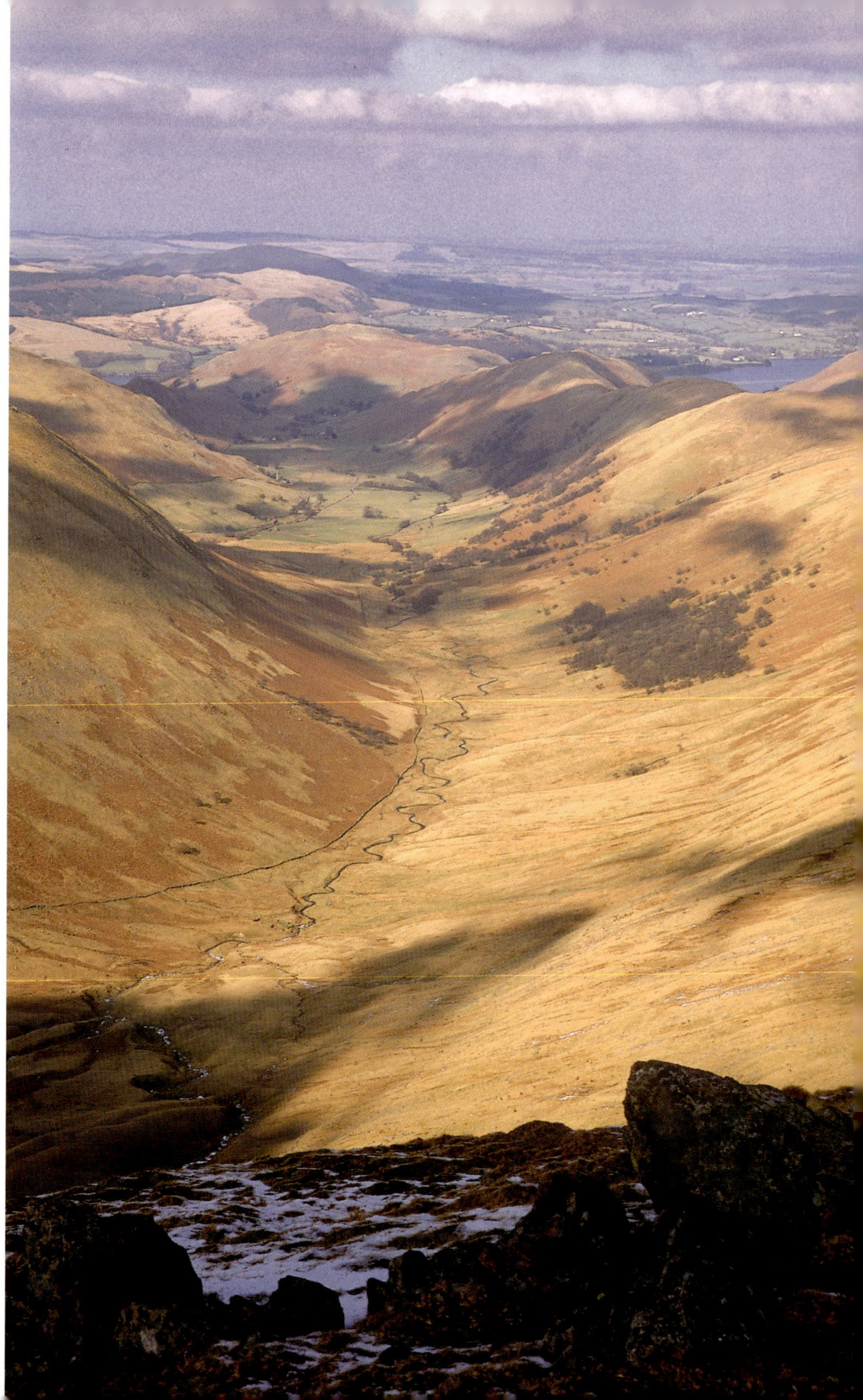

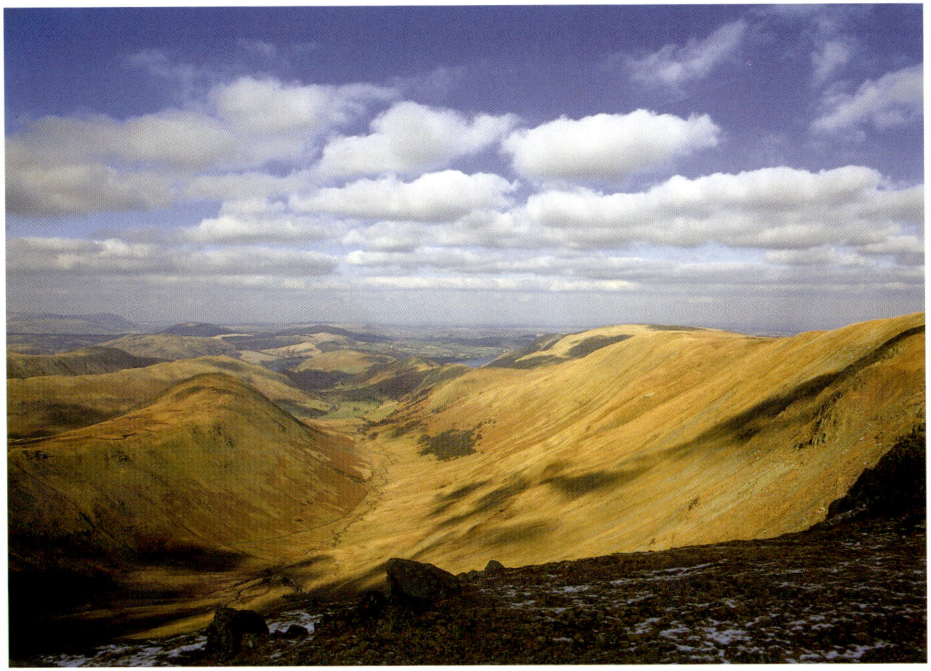

The Martindale Fells from the top of Rampsgill Head.

Fusedale provides a fine route up onto Wether Hill along which walkers are likely to be outnumbered by deer and sheep. Fine stands of relict woodland, mere remnants of a once-extensive forest that covered much of Lakeland, are a lovely feature of Martindale, as are the roe and red deer that roam the fell-sides, dotting the landscape below Rampsgill Head. The next time you're on High Street, take a walk up onto Rampsgill Head; most people pass it by. But from this eyrie there is a stunning, bird's-eye view down the length of Martindale to the scattered hamlet and its ancient chapel. And check out those boulders in the valley bottom; a lot of them may be deer!

Patterdale begins the moment you cross the Kirkstone Pass. The descent into the dale can be a hazardous route for motorists especially in winter. Thomas de Quincey had a memorable experience here in the nineteenth century, describing in *Recollections* how 'Once, in utter darkness, after midnight, and the darkness irradiated only by continual streams of lightning, I was driven down the whole descent, at a full gallop, by a young woman.' Another young woman, Celia Fiennes, crossed Kirkstone on her great journey of 1698 and described it as being: 'walled on both sides by those inaccessible high rocky barren hills which hangs over ones head in some places and appear very terrible.'

Looking down on Patterdale from the track up to Boredale Hause.

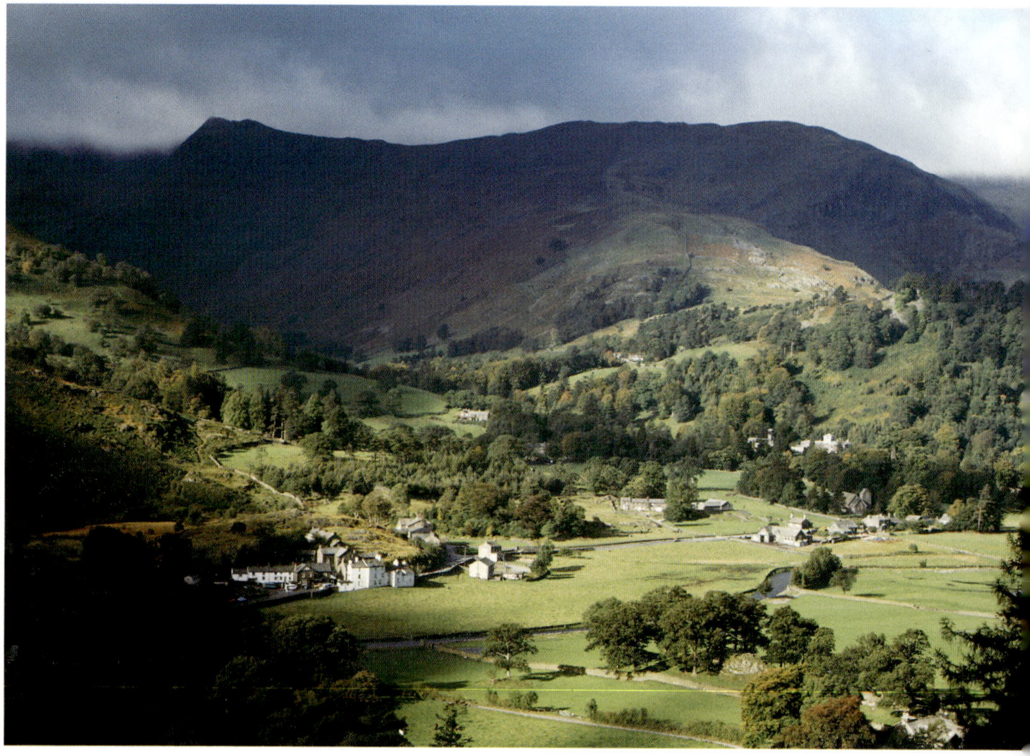

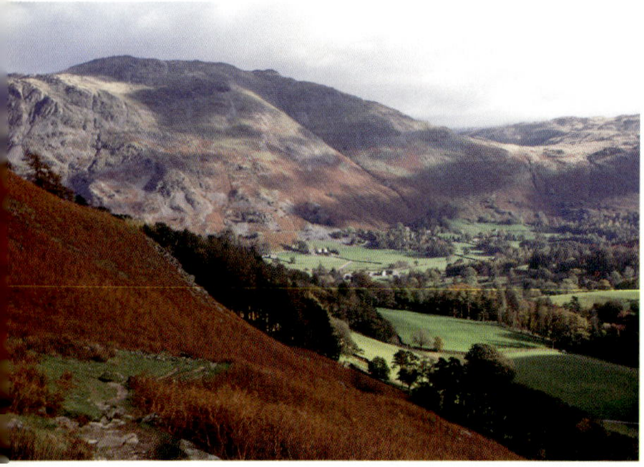

Place Fell dominates the village of Patterdale in this view from the track up to Helvellyn.

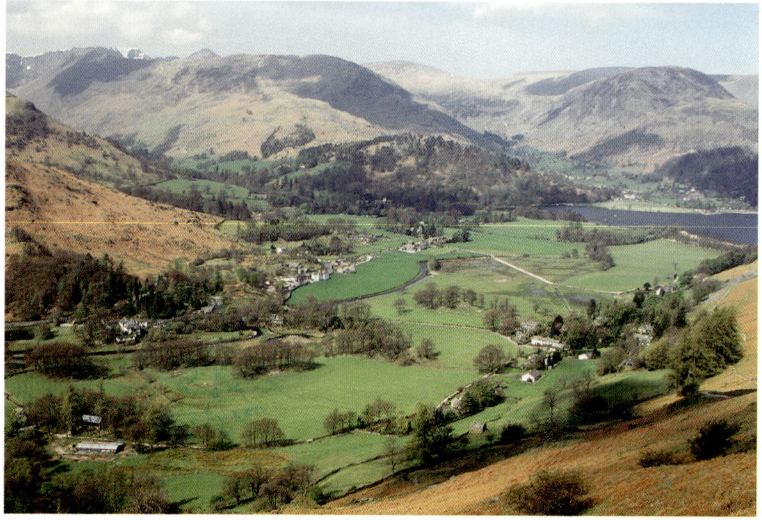

An aerial view of Patterdale from Boredale Hause.

Today, the pity is that the permissive path that branches left from the descending road to the foot of Caiston Glen doesn't do so much sooner. On the left rise the steep red-coloured screes of, predictably, Red Screes, a summit, for all its proximity to a main highway, that is rarely ascended from Kirkstone.

To the east, Stony Cove Pike squats at the head of two dales: Caudale and Pasture Bottom. The former, embraced between two arms of Caudale Moor, is bleak, steep and culminates in the craggy rim of Caudale Head. The latter is a delightful thoroughfare, a superb route onto Thornthwaite Crag and High Street, but one that is often neglected. Soft water ripples across stony beds in its lower reaches.

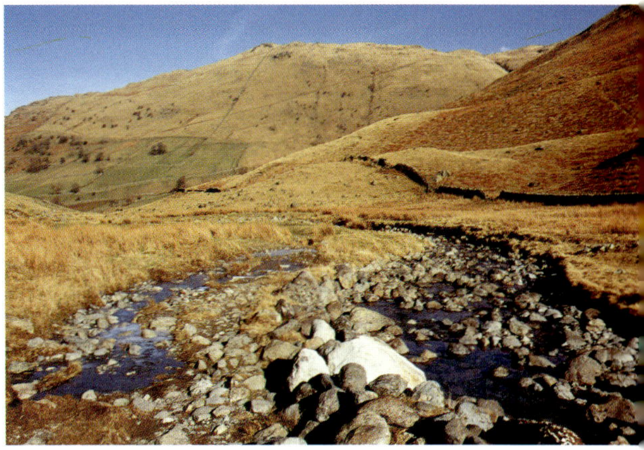

Pasture Beck takes a lazy route through the side valley of Pasture Bottom, near Hartsop.

Up in Threshthwaite Cove, stepping stones lead across boggy ground onto a rocky ascent to Threshthwaite Mouth and a superb view down the length of Trout Beck. Between Thornthwaite Crag and its northerly outlier Gray Crag

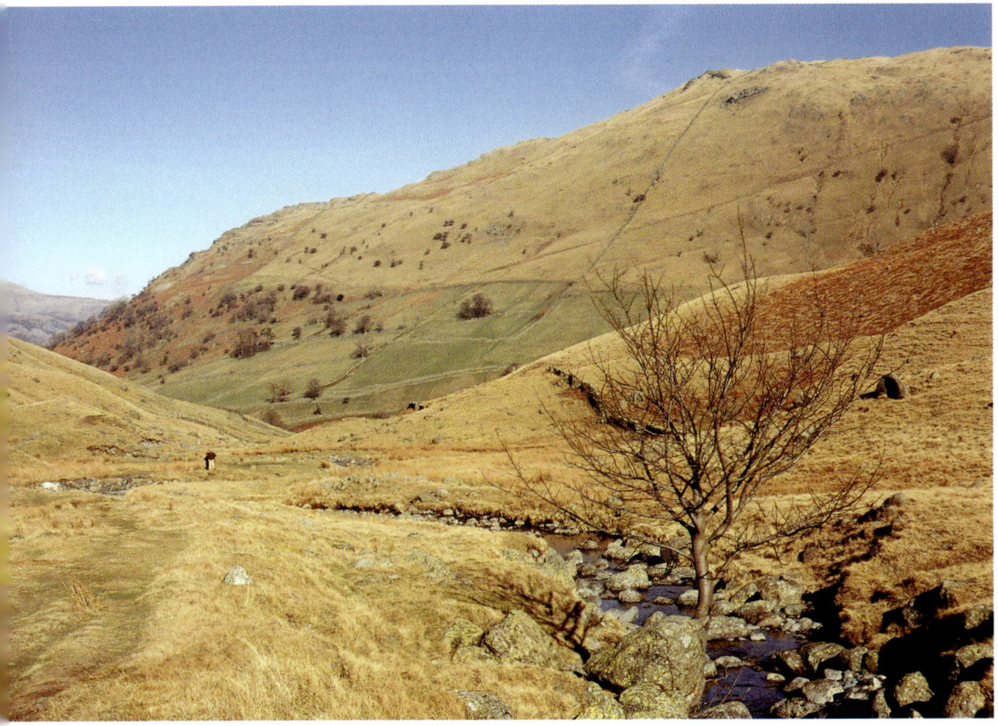

Walking through Pasture Bottom.

Hayeswater nestles in a sheltered hollow between The Knott (right) and Gray Crag.

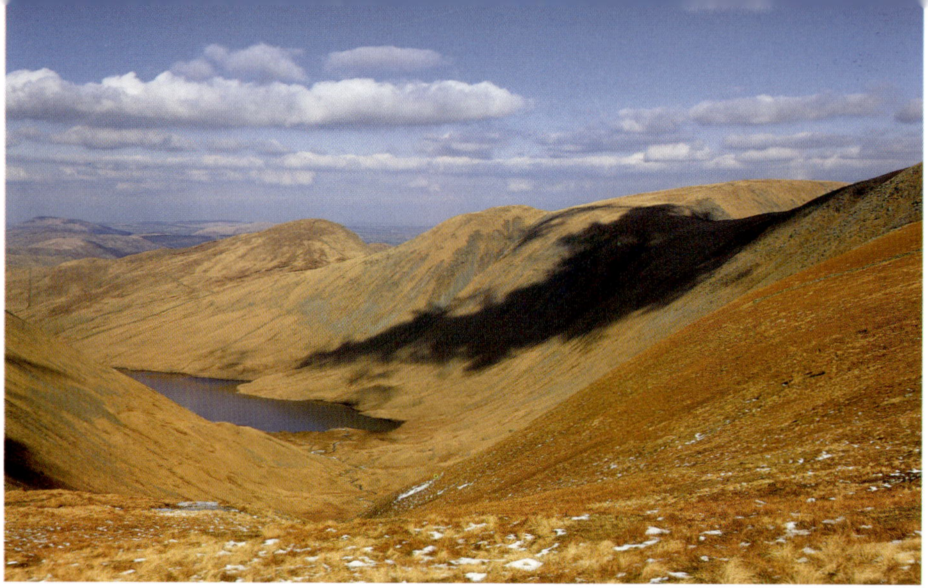

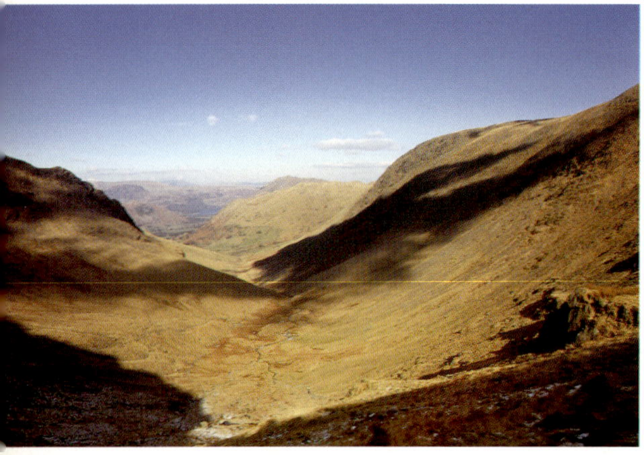

Pasture Bottom from Threshthwaite Mouth.

and the vast spread of High Street, Hayeswater occupies a dark and sombre dale, its flanks rising steeply to the fell tops, yet in summertime, its banks are greatly popular and an easy walk from the village of Hartsop. This is a perfectly formed glacial corrie, with extensive moraine deposits, and is another peaceful place among the fells.

Once renowned for wool spinning, Hartsop lies in a cul-de-sac at the southern end of Patterdale. A number of its grey-stone cottages, some of which date from the seventeenth century, still have their spinning galleries, and are typical of Lakeland fell-side villages. The village was within a vast hunting forest used for sport by ancient kings, and Hartsop's name may derive from the deer that once extensively populated the area.

On the other side of the main valley from the village stands Hartsop Hall, a National Trust property. There has been a dwelling of some kind on this site since the thirteenth century, though the present hall dates from the sixteenth, being extended in the following century by the de Lancasters family. Towards the end of the seventeenth century it passed to Sir John Lowther, the first Lord Lonsdale.

Caiston Glen is a neat way onto, or off, the fells of the Fairfield Horseshoe. Linked with Scandale, it provides an excellent linear walk from Ambleside to Patterdale, but is rarely visited in spite of its bright green walls studded with boulders, through the middle of which the beck spills in miniature waterfalls to the flat ground at Sykeside.

Opposite page: *Hayeswater and The Knott.*

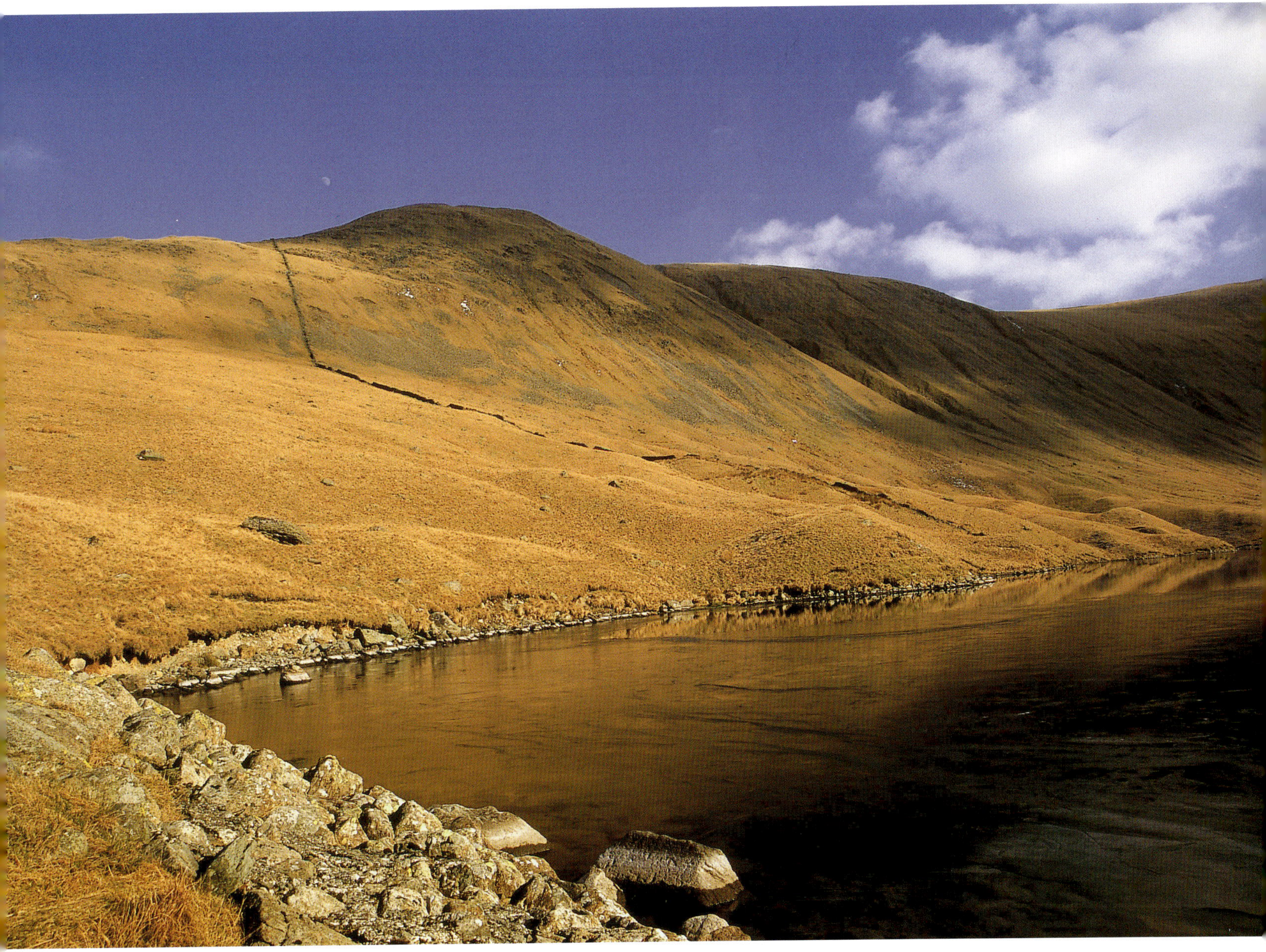

Dovedale and Dove Crag seen across Brotherswater.

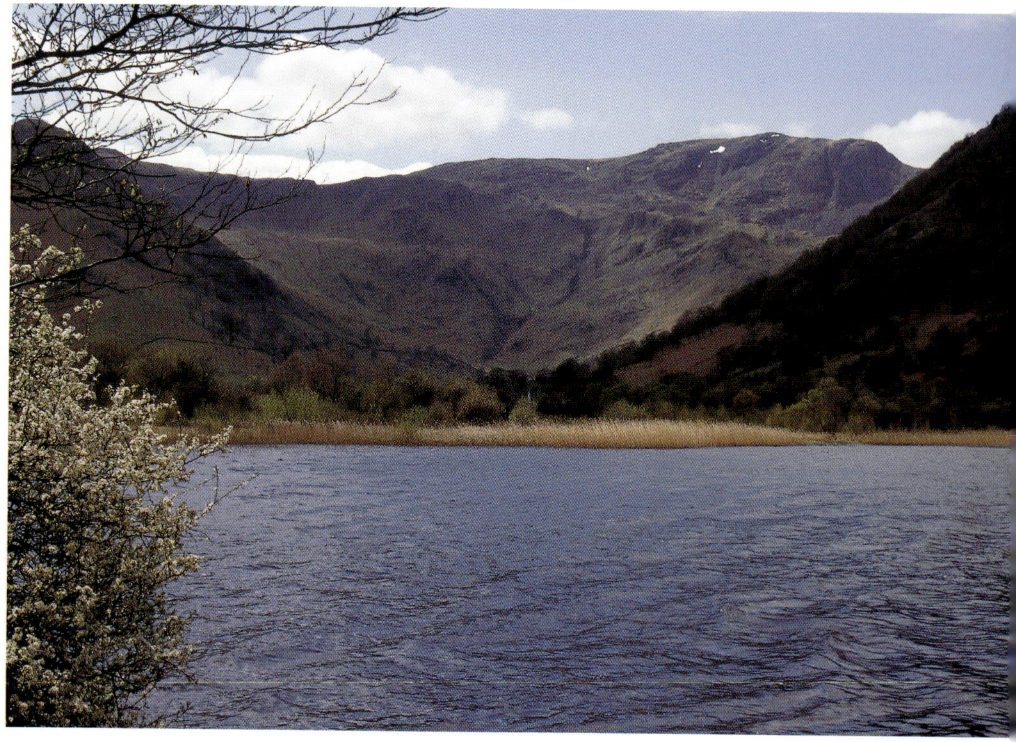

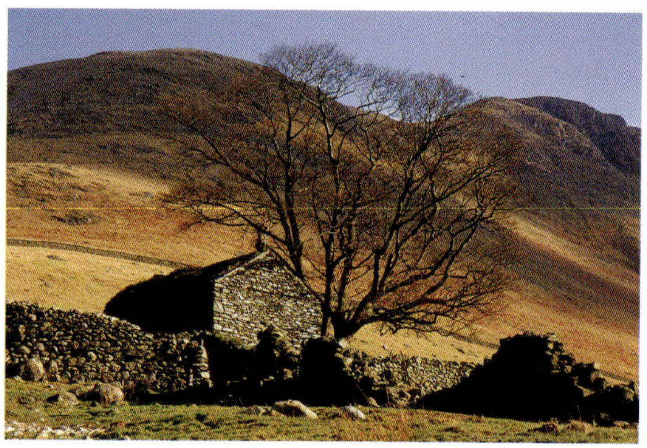

A ruined field barn below Gray Crag, Hartsop.

Likened by one eighteenth-century writer to a 'soft and delicate maiden', Dovedale is one of the most attractive dales, yet by comparison, it is yet another relatively infrequently-visited place. Wild and magnificent are words that describe it just as well. The crags that abound here are renowned among the rock climbing fraternity for their severity and quality. Before the Second World War, rock climbers tended to keep away from the crags of the eastern fells, preferring better fare elsewhere. Dovedale was the exception.

In 1910, 'Rusty' Westmorland pioneered routes on Dove Crag, though little further exploration took place until 1939, when an aptly named climb, 'Hangover', was devised up the leaning central buttress. High on the face of the crag is a cave known as Priest Hole. Unseen from below, it was probably quarried by dalesmen, and has often been used as a bivouac, intentionally and otherwise.

The entrance to the dale is marked by lovely, light woodlands, leading into '...a sweet little dale, a green cradle among crags, sprinkled with hazel woods and

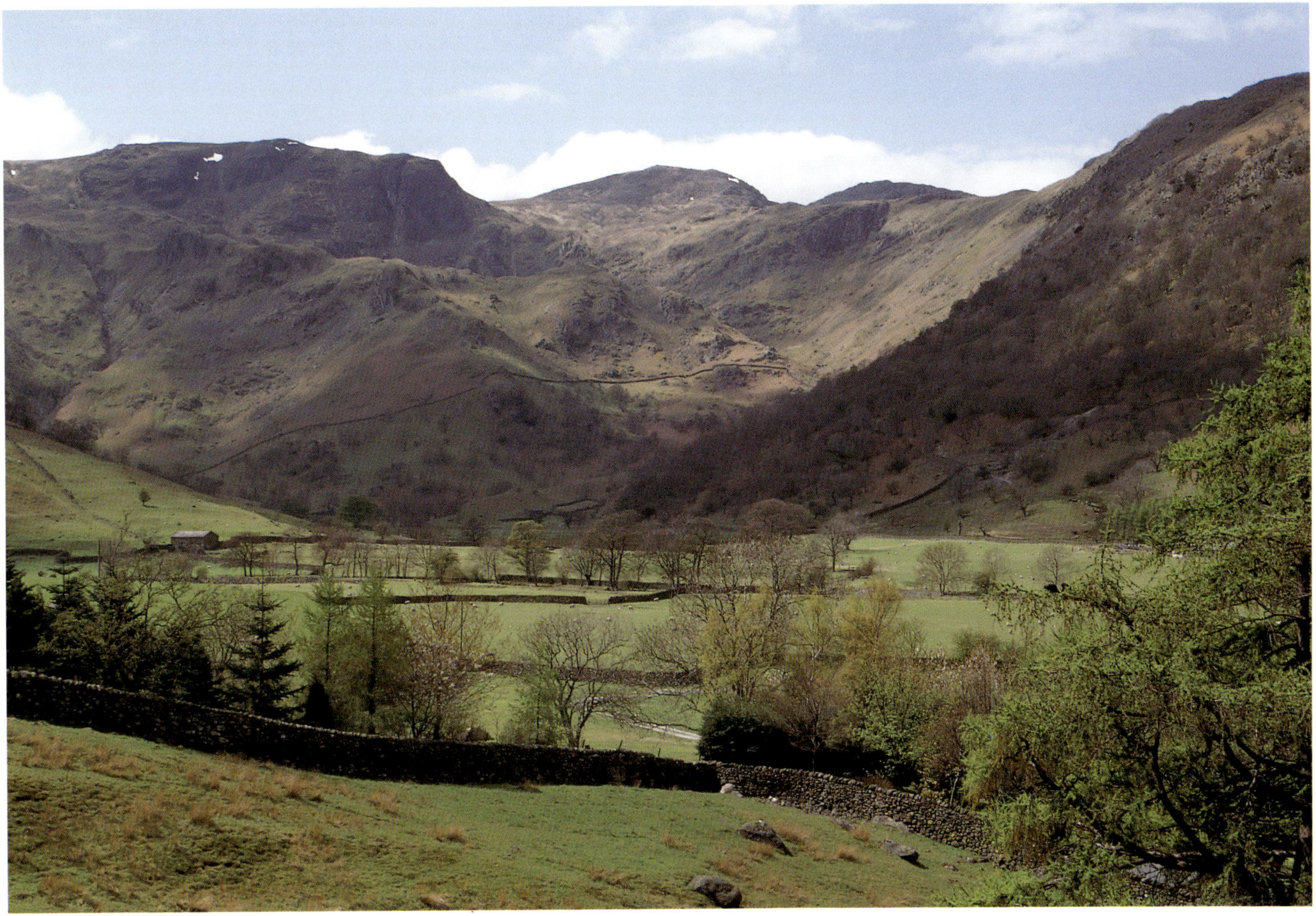

The entrance to Dovedale.

A view of the Fairfield group of fells rising above Dovedale, viewed here from Hartsop Dod.

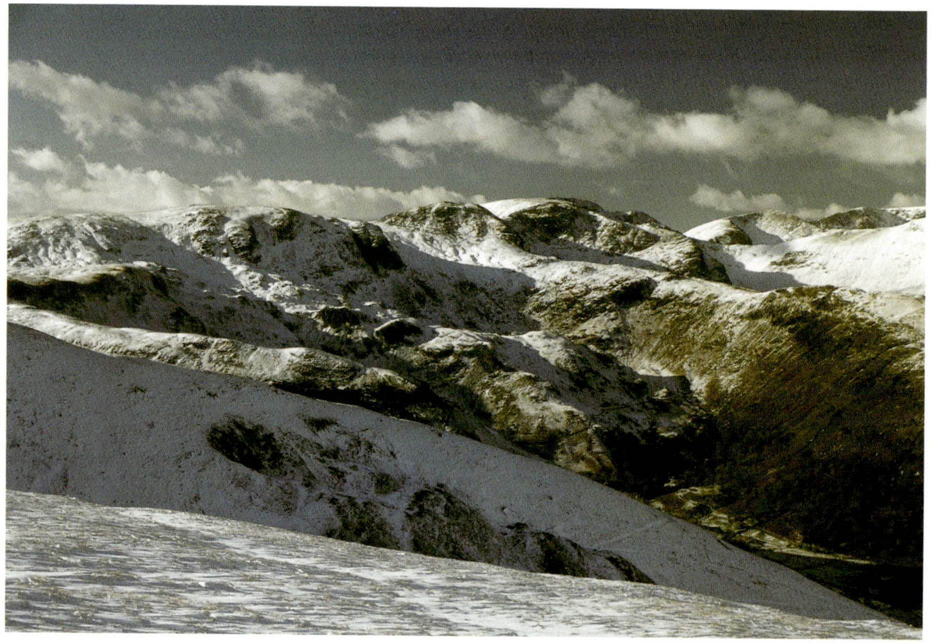

berried rowans, with the beck, crystal clear, chuckling over bright stones', as Lancashire writer Jessica Lofthouse described it in the late 1940s.

Nearby Sykeside Farm was for forty years the home of 'Old Charlie Dixon', who died there in 1936 at the age of eighty-three. Charlie never left the Lake District but became world famous for he was the original shepherd in some of the most famous pastoral photographs ever taken – 'The Shepherd and the Lost Sheep', 'A Westmorland Shepherd' – are lost to modern generations, but revered by photographers for whom the Box Brownie was a state-of-the-art device.

Once known as Broad Water, Brotherswater, an attractive spread of water that reflects the golden fells above, was renamed after an accident in which two brothers drowned in the lake.

Opposite page: *Deepdale and Hartop-above-How: Place Fell is the summit in the background (left) and the Angletarn Pikes.*

Lying beneath the eastern gaze of Fairfield, and wedged between shapely St Sunday Crag and the long and splendid ridge of Hartsop above How, Deepdale is a lush, green dale in a dramatic setting. At its entrance, Deepdale Hall is a Grade II listed seventeenth-century farmhouse situated on a working Lakeland hill farm, but it is of far grander design, being built around 1670 for the Duke

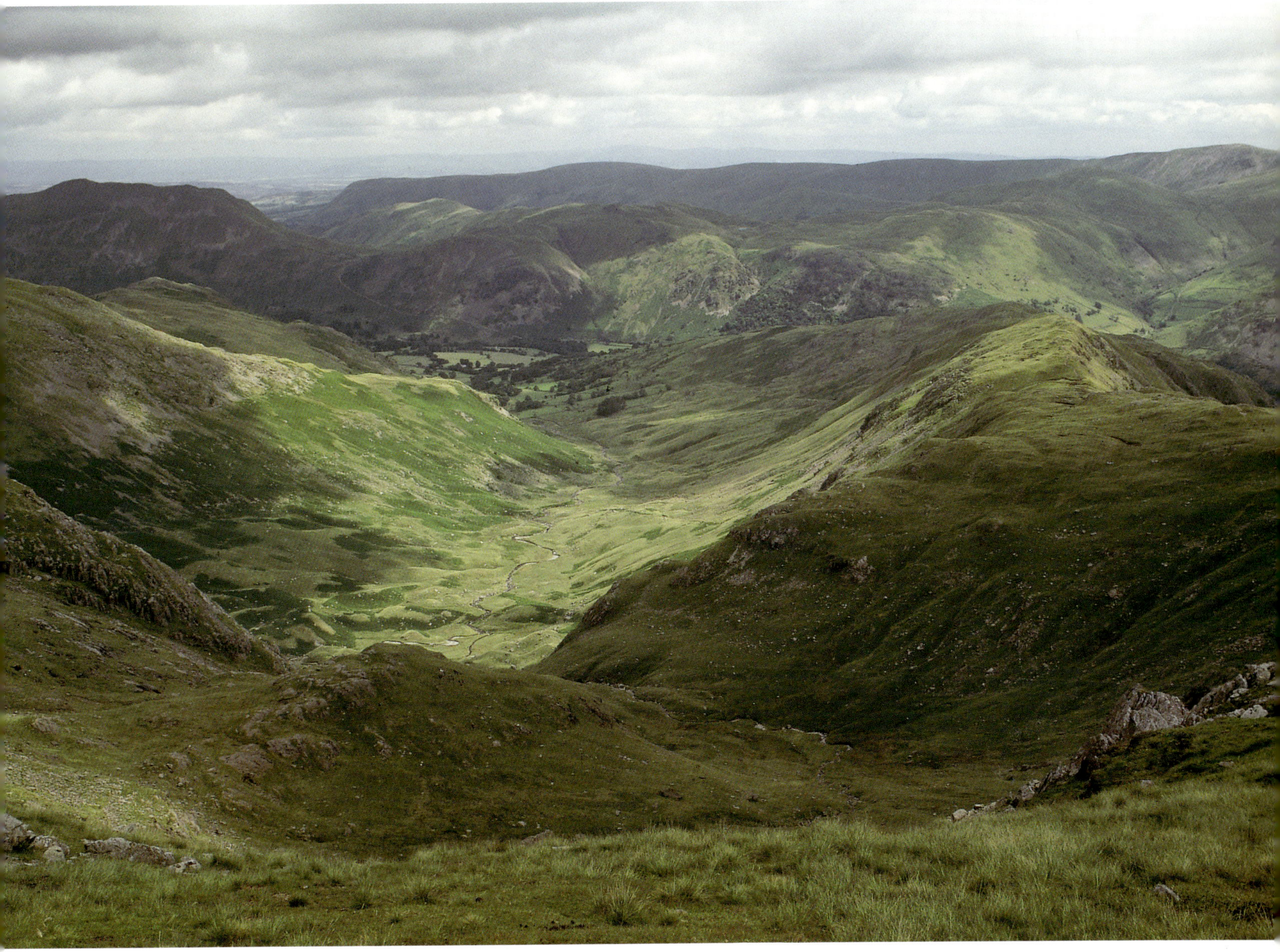

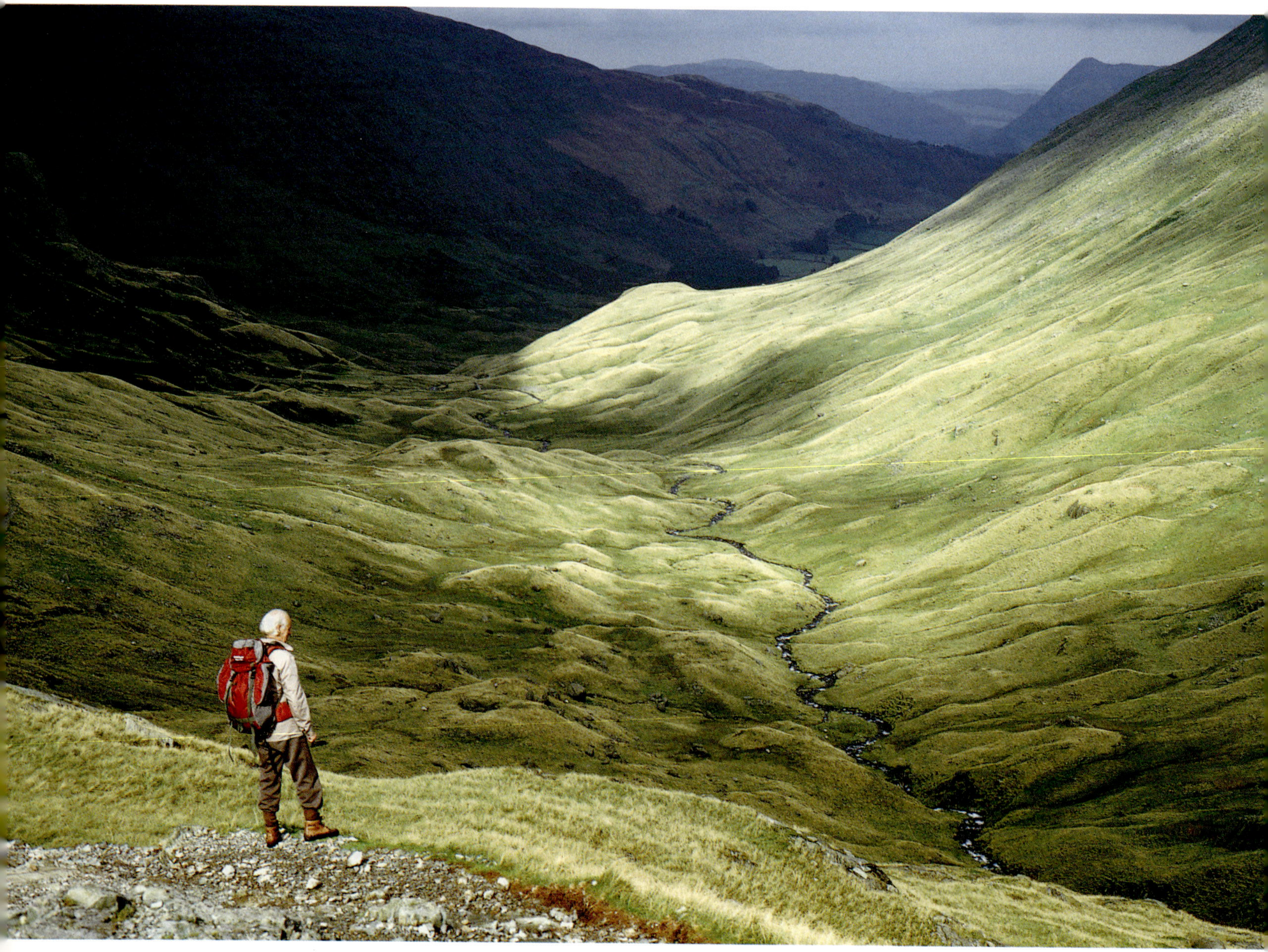

of Norfolk. There is still a manor of Deepdale and the current owner of the hall is also the lord of that manor. The lounge of Deepdale Hall was once the court of the Lord of the Manor. The Howards were, and arguably still are, one of the most important noble families in Cumberland and Westmorland, and their name still appears on documents as recent as 1883 when they carried out the traditional beating of the bounds ceremony to re-enforce the boundaries of the manor of Deepdale.

Buttressed by high fells all around, Patterdale is an elongated village at the southern tip of Ullswater, today catering largely for walkers and day trippers. The dale that today we call Patterdale is named after St Patrick, one of three famous missionaries (the others were St Ninian and St Kentigern) thought to have travelled in this region on evangelical missions during the early years of the fifth century.

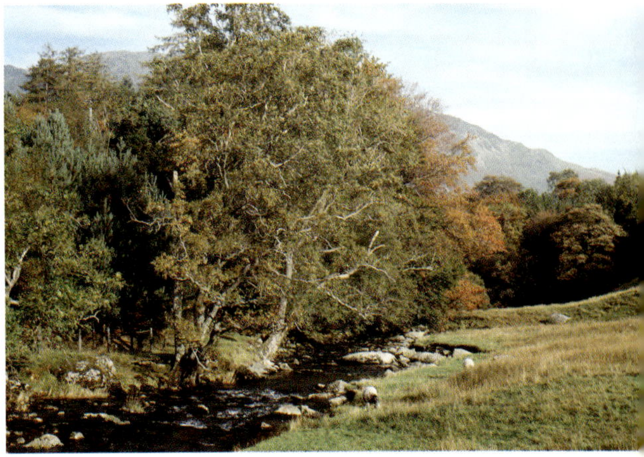

Grisedale Beck.

The modern village was described by Baddeley in his *Guide to the English Lake District* as 'one of the most charmingly situated in Britain, and in itself clean and comely'. Many of these remote villages were presided over by one dominant family. In Patterdale it was the Mounseys, who were described as the 'kings of Patterdale', and lived at Patterdale Hall, now rebuilt, but dating from around 1677.

Another local 'character' was Lancelot Pattinson, who lived a normal life in the dale until his wife died. Faced now with a family to raise, 'Lanty Patty', as he became known, moved his family into a cave near Goldrill Bridge, which later was named 'Lanty's Castle'. From this humble abode, Lanty managed to raise his family, and lived to be ninety-five himself, dying in 1865.

Grisedale is one of the finest dales in Lakeland, and a popular through-route to Grasmere, though most visitors use it as a way onto Striding Edge or as access to other fells. The dale lies along a geological fault, but was once occupied by a glacier that fed into the main Patterdale ice flow. The dale is remarkable, however, for some of its incredible drystone walling, built during the eighteenth and nineteenth centuries under the Enclosure Acts. Ruthwaite Lodge was built in 1854 as a shooting lodge, but more recently has been used as a climbing hut.

At the head of the dale – '...two or three yards below the outlet of Grisedale Tarn, on a foot road by which a horse may pass to Patterdale...' Wordsworth and his brother John parted for the last time. John was going to his ship, the *Earl of Abergavenny*, which was wrecked on 5 February 1805, off Portland Bill.

Opposite page: *Hummocky glacial moraine at the head of Grisedale.*

Grisedale Tarn, a lovely expanse of water surrounded by high fells.

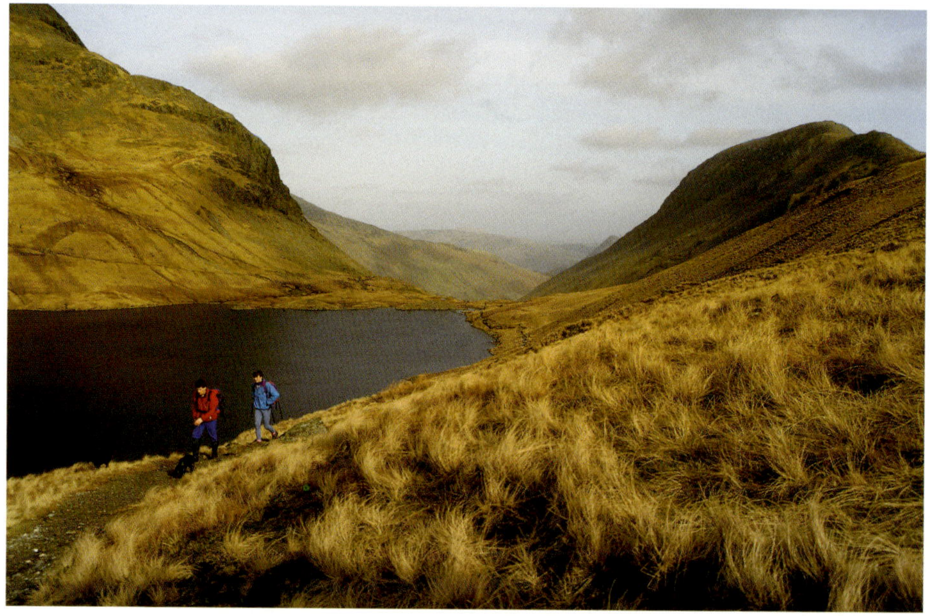

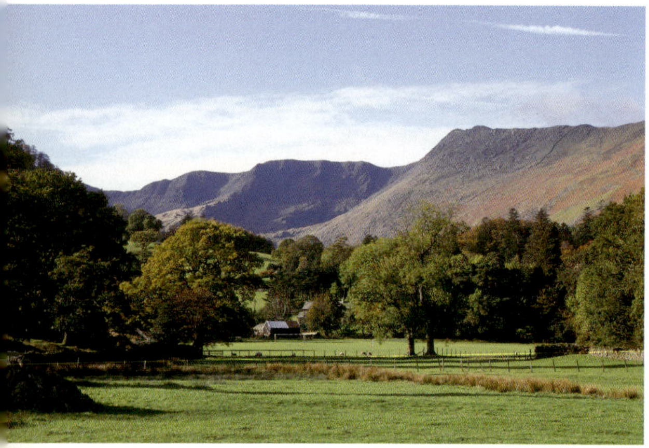

A view into the centre of Grisedale, above Patterdale.

Greatly moved by the loss of his brother, William returned to Grisedale Tarn with his wife and sister four months later, and later wrote the *Elegiac Verses* to his brother's memory. Some accounts make more of this incident, the brothers' parting, than is suggested by Dorothy Wordsworth's own *Journals*. In September 1802, Dorothy and William were in London, and there met John, who was between East Indian voyages. That was the last time they saw him, for he never came north on his return in the autumn of 1804, and perished only a few months later. The *Brothers' Parting* almost certainly refers to John's last visit to the Lake District.

Glenridding is a small, largely tourist village that grew in importance with the development of the Greenside Lead Mine. Lead ore was first discovered in the 1650s at the head of the dale of Glenridding, at what became the Greenside Lead Mine. The first levels were driven by Dutch adventurers in the 1690s and dressed ore was carried to the Stoneycroft smelter at Keswick. Production at the mine, however, did not really begin until the late eighteenth century, and the mine was not extensively worked until 1825. Power was originally provided by waterwheels, the water being supplied by the damming of nearby tarns. One of them, Keppel Cove, burst its banks in 1927, bringing disaster to the village below. Much the same happened four years later, when flood waters smashed through the concrete of High Dam.

Opposite page: *Ullswater from near Pooley Bridge.*

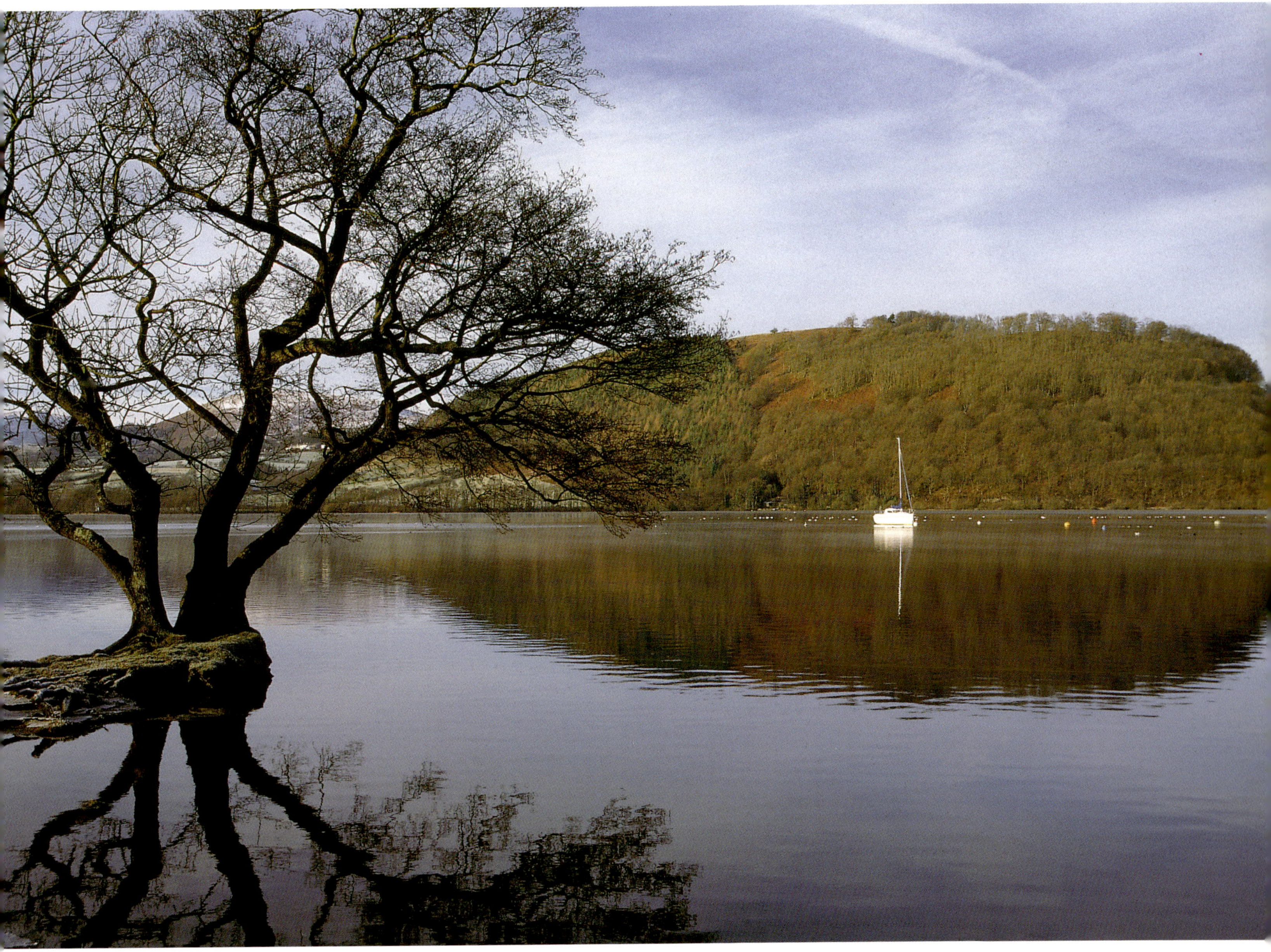

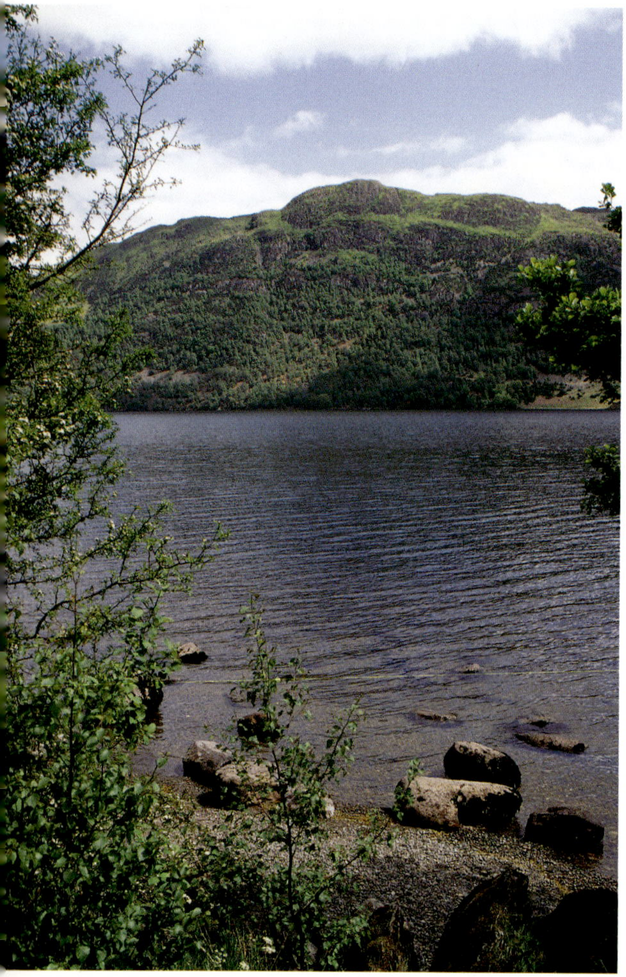

Ullswater shore and Place Fell.

By the early 1960s it had become uneconomic to continue to extract lead from the mine, and it closed. But that was not entirely the end of the story for the mine was then used to test instruments designed to detect underground nuclear explosions. Most of the mine buildings are now gone, but a few remain and see service as a youth hostel and mountain huts.

Just north of Glenridding, two small dales penetrate into the fells. One, Mossdale, is virtually unknown, a narrow, brief and wooded gully containing Mossdale Beck and little else. Glencoynedale has little more about it, being, as De Quincey recalls, a 'silent' glen, approached beautifully through the leafy embrace of Glencoyne Wood and passing a row of cottages that delight in the name Seldom Seen.

And so to Gowbarrow and Aira Force. On the 15 April 1802 William and Dorothy Wordsworth were walking around Gowbarrow Park when, as Dorothy recalls in the *Journals*:

> *...we saw a few daffodils close to the water side. We fancied that the lake had floated the seeds ashore and that the little colony had so sprung up. But as we went along there were more and yet more and at last under the boughs of the trees, we saw that there was a long belt of them along the shore, about the breadth of the country turnpike road. I never saw daffodils so beautiful...*

If folk remember few of Wordsworth's poems, most can at least recite the opening line: 'I wandered lonely as a cloud.....', and correctly attribute it. It was these near-immortal words which have made this part of the Lake District so well known.

Close by, the water of Aira Beck makes a fantastic dash into a narrow ravine from the moorland recesses of Deepdale below Great Dodd. This modest region is known as Matterdale, the wild moorland slopes of Matterdale Common providing a watershed between the Derwent catchment and ultimately that of the Eden. Small hamlets, Dockray and Matterdale End, sit beside the main road north to the A66, scatterings of farmhouses and cottages in artistic repose, set against the rounded domes of Great Mell Fell, Little Mell Fell and Gowbarrow Fell.

The River Eamont, which only appears as such at Pooley Bridge, is bound soon to leave the National Park as it heads eastwards to collect the River Lowther and press on to join the Eden.

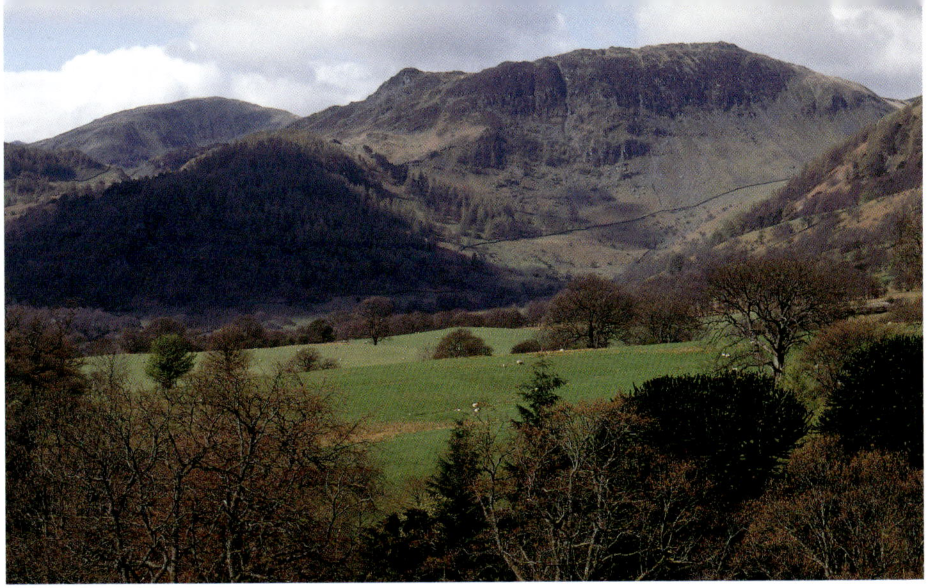

Infrequently-visited Sheffield Pike from Gowbarrow Park.

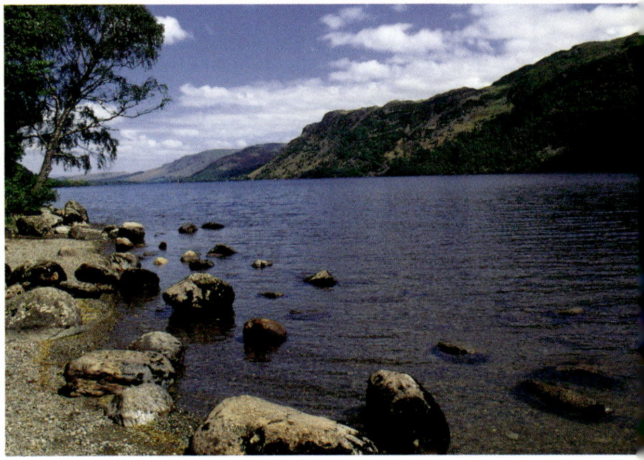

The Ullswater shoreline at Gowbarrow.

Spread out along its two main streets, both lined with charming, old, stone houses and cottages, Pooley Bridge spans the River Eamont, which used to be the boundary between Cumberland and Westmorland. Before the bridge was built in the sixteenth century, the village was simply called Pooley, a corruption of the 'pool by the hill'. The hill in this case is Dunmallet, which bears a small, but undistinguished Iron Age fort.

Today, Pooley Bridge, with its splendid views down the length of Ullswater, caters for tourists, though it has been a busy place in its own right in past times. That the village held a regular market can be seen from the widening of the village streets to accommodate the one-time market square, where, among other things, there used to be a fish market. There is no doubt, however, that Pooley Bridge was always overshadowed by Penrith, and by the middle of the nineteenth century, the only evidence of trading at Pooley Bridge was its sheep and cattle fair.

Eusemere House, near the bridge and just to the south-east of the village, was the home of Catherine Clarkson, the wife of Thomas Clarkson (1760-1846) the anti-slavery campaigner. Mrs Clarkson, referred to as such throughout her journals, was a close friend of Dorothy Wordsworth, and both Clarksons and Wordsworths spent much time together and in correspondence.

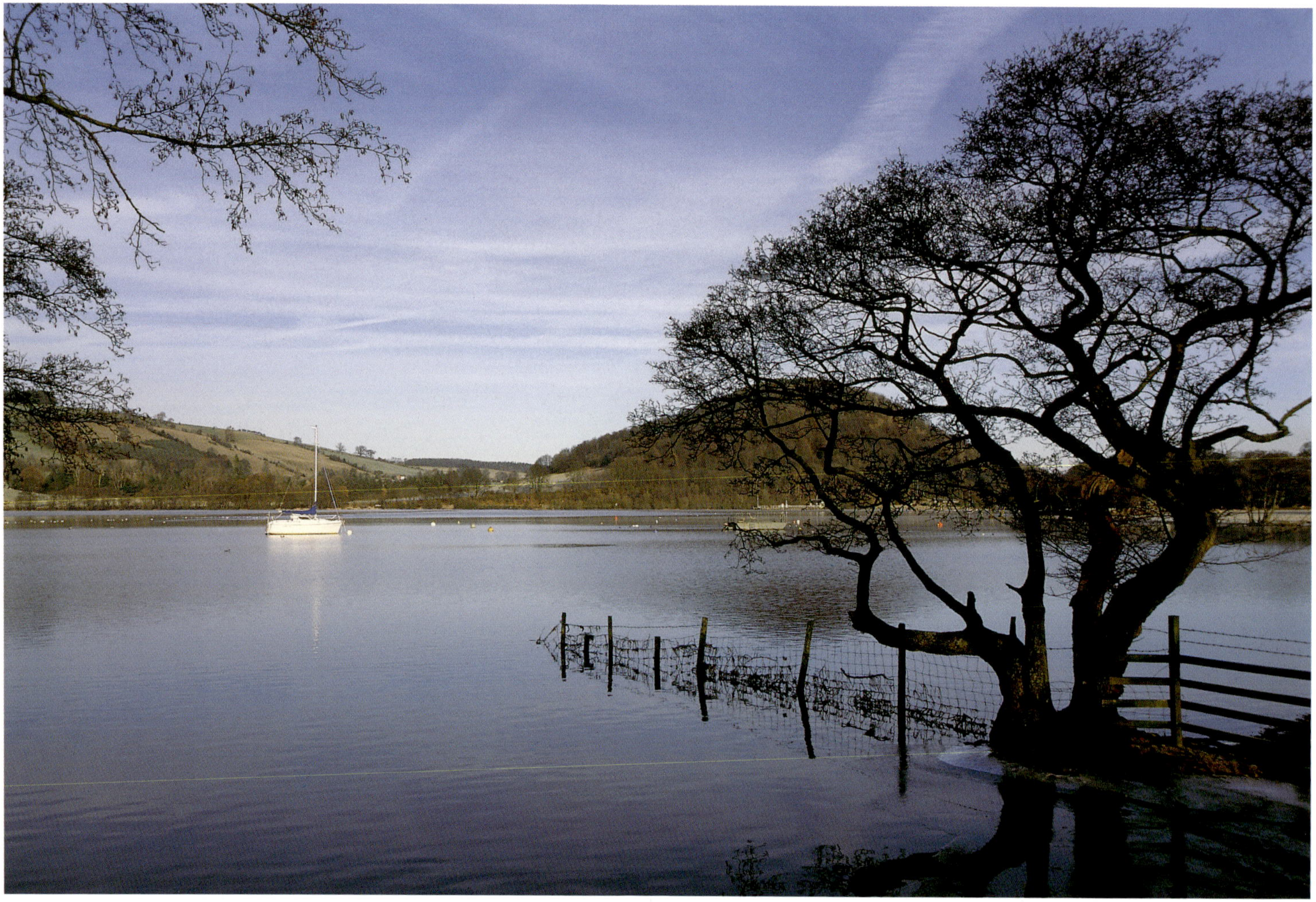

Ullswater near Pooley Bridge; the lake is very popular for boating.